ECOLOGIES OF A STORIED PLANET
IN THE ANTHROPOCENE

Salvaging the Anthropocene
Stephanie Foote, Series Editor

TITLES IN THE SERIES

Almanac for the Anthropocene: A Compendium of Solarpunk Futures
Edited by Phoebe Wagner and Brontë Christopher Wieland

Ecologies of a Storied Planet in the Anthropocene

Serpil Oppermann

WEST VIRGINIA UNIVERSITY PRESS / MORGANTOWN

Copyright © 2023 by West Virginia University Press
All rights reserved
First edition published 2023 by West Virginia University Press
Printed in the United States of America

ISBN 978-1-952271-62-5 (paperback) / 978-1-952271-73-1 (ebook)

Library of Congress Control Number: 2022948275

Cover design by Than Saffel / WVU Press

To the loving memory of my mother, Yüksel Tunç, who gave me the gift of empathy and resilience, and to the loving memory of my dear father, Basri Tunç, from whom I learned to be strong-minded.

Contents

Introduction 1

1 The Storied Planet in the Anthropocene 13
2 The Scale of the Anthropocene and New Anthroposcenarios 45
3 Migrant Ecologies of the Anthropocene 79
4 Postnatural Ecologies of the Anthropocene 106
5 The Ecology of Colors in the Anthropocene 135

Coda 161
Acknowledgments 167
Notes 171
References 179
Index 203

Introduction

Ecologies of a Storied Planet in the Anthropocene

It matters what stories make worlds, what worlds make stories.
   —Haraway (2016, 12)

The gist of this book could not be expressed in more potent terms than Donna Haraway's words above. Her words highlight in a nutshell the material ecocritical claim that the Earth is a living planet where everything that is *is* a storied subject of an ever-unfolding planetary tale shaping the world while being shaped by that very world. Stories, in other words, create the world by which they are created and configure the very reality by which they are engendered. The mutual constitution of stories and worlds are never in categorical opposition; rather, when stories and worlds fashion each other in manifold ways, a process occurs through which the world is recognized as both discursively and materially determined. In her pioneering book in feminist science studies, *Meeting the Universe Halfway: Quantum Physics and the Entanglement of Matter and Meaning* (2007), Karen Barad formulates this dialogical process as material-discursive practices in which epistemology and ontology become integral parts of each other. It means to think the social and the natural, the discursive and the material, through one another "without defining one against the other" (30) or without "collapsing important differences between them" (25). Grounded in this complementary perspective, or, as Barad would say, onto-epistemological framework, *Ecologies of a Storied Planet in the Anthropocene* presents five essays allied by their material ecocritical concerns about the Anthropocene's conceptual, existential, and physical forces, which increasingly disrupt the Earth's communities and material agencies no matter how resilient they may be in the face of existential threats. Being "semiotically active" (Haraway 2008a, 250) and "potentially expressive" (Abram 1997, 81), they communicate cautionary tales about the deteriorating conditions in the planetary ecosystems. These stories are overwhelmingly about the catastrophic effects of human activities on the planet's biogeochemical cycles that specifically foreground the increasing vulnerability of terrestrial life, if not its inevitable dissolution on a planetary scale. That is why we need to listen to their voices, pay attention to their stories, and remember that, as Michel Serres, the polymath French philosopher, so eloquently explains in his book *Biogea*:

> We aren't the only ones to write and read, to code, to decipher the codes of others, to get decoded by others, to understand, mutate, invent, communicate, exchange signals, process information, encounter one another . . . to thus win our lives. Everything in the world does it, like us: the light, the wind, the rain, chemical reactions and the reactions of living things, the yews and the sperm whales. The world resonates with a common language, no doubt formal, I don't know if it's poetic but what does it matter, the essential thing remains sharing these codings, this universal language, music and science. (2012, 172)

This vision of nonhuman storying of the Earth is at the heart of *Ecologies of a Storied Planet in the Anthropocene*, which is grounded in the material ecocritical "account of the narrative power of matter, that is, its capacity to produce its own meanings and constitute its own stories" (Oppermann 2016b, 91). Overall, the main rationale is to expand our sense of awareness about the Anthropocene agencies (organic and inorganic alike), which—to quote Derrida out of context—"so far has been left in the shadows of neglect" (1987, 27). But, in effect, by moving across the social and the natural, they all emerge within relational fields in meaningfully articulate ways as if the mind "is Earth's" (Abram 2010, 123), even if this mind is undergoing extraordinary stress in the Anthropocene today.

Material agencies include a long list of things, landscapes, substances (such as toxins, metals, food, pollutants, artifacts, bodies), and even geological forces like hurricanes, tornadoes, earthquakes, and volcanoes that can be "full-fledged actors in our collective," as French sociologist and anthropologist Bruno Latour describes them (1999, 174). As such, they are strung together in agentic assemblages (or, in Latour's terms, "collectives") in shifting and elusive relations with humans who are entangled with them often in competitive and risky ways. Agentic assemblages or collectives, however, should not be conceived as mere aggregates that produce mechanical actions. Rather, collectives are formed by their autonomous parts that bring forth synchronic action especially when the nonhuman (including all abiotic objects) is entangled with the human. At this juncture we find what Michel Serres defines as "coding-coded things." In his words,

> these things—formerly mute and said to be objective because passive like the slaves of an activity that would belong only to us—these coding-coded things, as though awakened, speak just as much and perhaps better than us, they also say, write, sing, communicate among themselves, through a kind of reciprocal encoding, a kind of common language, a kind of music, harmonic, disharmonic—I don't know yet—but whose voices I am sure to hear. (2012, 131)

Serres is right in affirming that these things can be quite expressive, or, in renowned political theorist and new materialist Jane Bennett's words, "reveal[ed] themselves to be expressive 'actants'" (2012, 239). They are also, as clarified by Jeffrey J. Cohen, another famed new materialist theorist, "inorganic compounds that act like living creatures" (2013, xxii). As such, the so-called inanimate objects (or "things") can be considered alive in a sense, as molecular biologist Lawrence E. Hunter explains in *The Processes of Life*: "Insights into the molecules of life have clearly demonstrated how fundamentally ordinary materials can be alive in so many extraordinary ways" (2009, 1). Being alive in many ways means that ordinary matter is not a static or inert entity but has a creative and expressive agentic capacity with internal experience and signifying power. We enlarge our understanding of matter by acknowledging its ability to exert creative influence on the environment and by accepting "its right to be the protagonist of its own story" (Cohen 2015, 39). Such a radical reconceptualization of matter first and foremost allows for the reassessment of the "question of what, exactly, is alive" (Hunter 2009, 4), as Hunter pertinently asks. Accordingly:

> While some materials (like DNA and proteins) are found in nearly all living things, it is not a special kind of stuff that makes something alive. The mere presence of any particular material (including DNA) doesn't make something alive. The materials of life, it turns out, are just fairly ordinary chemicals, in particular combinations. What makes something alive is not what it *is*, but what it *does*. (Hunter 2009, 2)

If *doing* is the life principle, material agency is the enactment of its ongoing materialization. Taking account of matter's performative enactments opens quite a legitimate pathway for a more ecologically enlightened understanding not only of life in general but also of gender, sexuality, and corporeality, invalidating all oppressive practices, gendered and other dualisms, anthropocentric and phallogocentric mendacities, and ecophobia, "an irrational and groundless fear and hatred of the natural world" (Estok 2011, 4). The point is that thinking of matter in terms of signifying performative agencies irreducible to human emotions and "representations" (Bryant 2011, 23) compels us to acknowledge *being* as comprised of heterogeneous partners intersecting one another, rather than as signifiers of human cultural codes or norms, ecophobic or holistic notwithstanding.[1] In this theoretical framework, whether biotic or not, everything becomes with each other "in earthly worlding and unworlding" (Haraway 2017, M45) that unfold in the mutual engagement of all agencies in the aerial, terrestrial, and aquatic domains by way of their correlative relations. In other words, to quote Hunter again: "Living things all exist in the midst of complex communities of other organisms, called ecosystems" (2009, 17). So do all material agencies, which may not fall into the category of "living things" but are nevertheless effective, generative, and creative with emergent agentic potentiality. Giving credence to matter's agentic capacity opens up new pathways for rethinking life, which, in turn, stimulates deeper understandings of matter endowed with creative becomings and dynamic expressions. This is the world of storied matter that manifests "in the form of ontologically hybrid forms of expressions, assemblages, and collectives or as narrative agencies," all of which produce, as I have previously argued, "configurations of meaningful expressions that merge with our modes of knowing and being, making us, other species, and all material forms and processes, with varying degrees of compounding relationships, ontologically inseparable in the animate earth" (Oppermann 2016b, 89).

It is through such compounding relationalities that material agencies become central players in meaning-making processes whereby matter and meaning intersect in their inextricable dynamics. In this vision, linguistic systems and living systems (i.e., biomes) are "aspects of a co-evolving and necessarily de-centered life in which the organic and the inorganic interweave," as Australian cultural theorist Claire Colebrook—quoting Cary Wolfe—also argues (2011, 4). Hence, this new materialist gesture is not a "redemptive return to matter," Colebrook clarifies, because matter "can never be retrieved as some prior originating ground, but its critical force ... has a strategic force" (2011, 3). It is an acknowledgment of what philosopher Manuel DeLanda calls in an interview ([1996] 2012) "concrete fleshy stuff that is important to consider." According to DeLanda, "theories of self-organization, matter and energy themselves without humans and even without life are capable of generating order spontaneously." This order, claims DeLanda, "can be seen in lava or in winds or in many phenomena in our planet," such as hurricanes. For him, hurricanes "are creatures which inhabit the atmosphere . . . creatures that create themselves. They don't have genes, they don't have anything that tells them what to do. They are completely spontaneous creatures." DeLanda's statement is significant in understanding the true nature of material agencies, which are to some extent incipient determinants of life. Accordingly, each facet of baryonic matter (everything that has form) enacts "a cauldron of creativity" (DeLanda 2003, 279), like fire, the element that possesses "vigor, ardor, intensity, vehemence, fervor, passion, fury, magic, inspiration, genius, brilliance" in Morgan Llywelyn's novel *The Elementals* (1993, 76). This striking image arrestingly captures the gist of the new materialist theories and material ecocriticism, stimulating our interest in what Eileen Joy (2014), director of Punctum Books, calls "creative materialism of things," and encourages "critical examinations of the aliveness and agency of animals, objects, environments, and other nonhuman forces and propensities, all enmeshed with humans." I have previously compared this enmeshment of humans, biotic forces, and material agencies to "a map of agentic expressiveness found across different spectrums and vibrancies of being" (Oppermann 2016a, 282), noting that this narrative map includes

> organisms, languages, ideas, and imagination as in symbiogenesis—a merger of two organisms from distant lineages into a more complex organism. It is not, of course, a narrative written by humans, but consists of layers of stories, meanings, and signs stored and encoded in material processes, organisms, and semiotic objects that become visible when in interaction with human imagination. This narrative resembles symbiogenesis in its fusion of human and nonhuman codes. . . . (282)

The new materialist theories that are nonanthropocentric and nonspeciesist issue forth from this understanding, challenging human exceptionalism and construing agency from nondualist perspectives. This is an undeniable "pluralistic coexistence," as feminist posthumanities scholars Cecilia Åsberg, Redi Kooback, and Ericka Johnson also confirm, that "cannot be contained within cultural, discursive, or human-centered domains of analysis" (2011, 222). Because the nonhuman constitutes our bodies and the world, the authors maintain, "we need to acknowledge their presence, not as something new-found, but as the pre-existing, 'always already' . . . of forces outside our anthropocentric imaginary" (219). Heeding this call of acknowledgment, *Ecologies of a Storied Planet in the Anthropocene* represents the crisscrossing strands of nonhuman stories with examples from scientific research as well as literary accounts to make readers more attentive to the world that is now becoming more vulnerable to human exploits. My aim here is to espouse the co-emergence of matter and meaning, or, expressed better by art historian Michael Ann Holly, *"the meeting of matter and imagination"* (Rosler et al. 2013, 15; italics in original). In *The Botany of Desire* Michael Pollan (2001) provides a classic example of this convergence, which he calls an upside-down perspective, in his stories of the apple, the tulip, cannabis, and the potato . Taking these familiar plants as "nature's greatest success stories" (xxiii), Pollan gives expression to their agentic becoming by pointing to their physical interchanges with humans: "All these plants, which I'd always regarded as the objects of my desire, were also, I realized, subjects, acting on me, getting me to do things for them they couldn't do for themselves" (xv). The picture that emerges from this conjecture shows the human in a relational category with the nonhuman, not in opposition to it, enhancing the life principle of matter within the congeries of entwined agencies. According to molecular biologist Stuart A. Kauffman, "agency is part of life and its evolution, and that evolution . . . cannot be derived from or reduced to physics" (2008, 259). But even in quantum physics we observe a rudimentary form of creative materiality (or agency) as an effect of the entanglement of the human observers and the observed particles.

The conundrums raised by physicists about the agency of elementary particles expose the complexity and the unpredictability of the properties of matter. Here, the strange performativity of subatomic particles underpins matter's expressive dynamism that eludes our control in some ineffable way. On every level, then, the world's dynamic self-articulation and performativity offer a radical perspective, one that strangely "alters the tenor of our reflections and the tonality of our dreams" as eloquently articulated by cultural ecologist and philosopher David Abram (2010, 141). This is a world in which matter—whether in mineral, vegetal, molecular, or animal form—fashions the environment and our discursive maps in profound ways, making the poetics of matter an ethical-cultural imperative. Michael Ann Holly, for example, claims that materiality "is bouncing back from a variety of directions" (Rosler et al. 2013, 15) on a complex map of embodied, distributed agency of human, nonhuman, and abiotic material forces and substances in which the human subject, being fundamentally dethroned, comes to realize its co-emerging, co-constitutive, and co-evolving interactions with the world's innumerable bodily natures and forces, which are heavily threatened by the darkening waves of the Anthropocene. This is the focus of chapter 1, "The Storied Planet in the Anthropocene," which explores matter producing trajectories of unfolding stories in bodily natures, geological processes, and ecological networks. I argue that all earthly beings and things are involved in ongoing processes of communication with everything else around them. As indicated by the title, the world itself expresses its mind in terms of narratives often shaped by an intelligence beyond the human. The world, then, is a site of narrativity populated with narrative agencies that transmit stories of ecological and existential relationships through signs, colors, and gestures. Ongoing for about four and a half billion years, the Earth has housed many forms of creativity and expressiveness that pervade nature at large. In this astonishing dance of evolution, narrative agency is our collaborative partner in the shaping of things on this living planet of communicative, vibrant material agencies, and narrativity is their essential capacity.

Narrative agencies invalidate our habit of worlding as if we are the only storied beings. They urge us to attune to the more-than-human stories of survival and resistance and offer eloquent pathways into the multilayered ecologies of our storied planet, making us realize that we are afflicted by a reciprocal deception in the dark ontology of the Anthropocene. Narrative agencies can also provide a viable answer to the question of who we really want to be on the verge of ecological collapse. Fundamentally, being attentive to the articulate world and its stories can move us into more Earth-friendly modes of thinking so that we can refashion our objectifying attitude to the world.

Ecologies of a Storied Planet in the Anthropocene is thus committed to modes of thinking beyond anthropocentricity, arguing that the message our storied planet conveys about the ongoing disruption of its rhythms and biocycles, species, materials, and ecosystemic processes is crucial. After all, the Earth itself is a "living system made up of the indivisible community of all life systems and living beings, interrelated, interdependent, and complementary, which shares a common destiny" (Heise 2016, 116). They also share a common trait, which material ecocriticism studies as the expressive dimension of nature's constituents at every scale of being in their mutual entanglements and enduring connections that are interpreted as stories. Embodied in material formations, these stories compel us to envision the physical world as *storied matter* teeming with countless narrative agencies that make the world intelligible and expressive; for the story to exist it must always be framed by some sort of articulation, performance, or intelligibility. Finding expressive creativity encoded in every form of agentic matter brings about a perceptual change, which entails a critical self-reflection on our part as humans and our moral accountability. It also enables us to be part of the Earth's physical systems so that we cannot perpetuate forms of injustice, both ecological and social. Hence, *thinking with nature*, with all species, elements, minerals, bodies, physical environments, and all agentic matter ensures respect and protection for all life-forms and their right to survival. They all have a natural right to exist and express their sense of being in the world. Most importantly, as Donna Haraway reminds us, "we think, act, narrate, metabolize and come into and out of existence through each other" (2015b, vii).

Espousing the idea of human–nonhuman and biotic–abiotic co-emergence, exchanges, and communications in the Anthropocene, *Ecologies of a Storied Planet in the Anthropocene* engages in the conceptual and the existential conundrums of the Anthropocene, which has arguably ended the Holocene—the present interglacial epoch that began at the end of the last Ice Age, approximately 11,500 years ago. Let us recall that geologists split the 4.5-billion-year-old Earth history into large units of time called eons, which are further subdivided into eras. Those in turn are made up of smaller units called periods, and the little divisions *within* a period are known as epochs. So right now, we are living in the Quaternary period of the Cenozoic era, which is part of the Phanerozoic eon, covering 541 million years to the present. The Quaternary period is divided into two epochs: the Pleistocene (2.588 million years ago to 11,700 years ago) and the Holocene (11,700 years ago to today). The dividing lines between epochs correspond with important moments in Earth's history, such as abrupt climatic changes. The question of the current epoch was discussed in 2016 by the Anthropocene Working Group of the International Union of Geologic Sciences (IUGS), who voted to recommend the Anthropocene as a formal geologic epoch. The Geological Society Stratigraphy Commission, formed to study the scientific validity of the term, has accepted the Anthropocene as a useful concept for describing the profound "chemical and biological effects of global human activity" (Zalasiewicz et al. 2010, 2229).

Since the anthropogenic changes in the Earth's climate, land, oceans, and air are evident, the Anthropocene indicates humanity's epoch-making signature on the planet's geosphere, atmosphere, hydrosphere, and biosphere. This is why in its emergent discursive stages the Anthropocene privileged the idea of the Anthropos as a self-distancing and epoch-making human entity. It is true that we cannot find any sense of comforting detachment from the enormous scale of human impacts on the planet's biogeochemical cycles when we consider the multiple threads of effects produced by massive environmental transformations. Indeed, they prevent any denial of the planet's metabolic disorder instigated by "anthropic ignorance" (Ruiz III 2008, 26), but it is wrong to adhere to a category mistake in accepting a generic human figure manifesting itself as an epoch-making geological force, operating across multispecies habitats in messy ways, as I argue in chapter 2, "The Scale of the Anthropocene and New Anthroposcenarios." This chapter is a critique of the mainstream discourse of the Anthropocene embedded in the *global scale* vision of geobiochemical human activities having an unprecedented planetary impact. Since the global scale does not adequately address the complexities and the intersecting stories of the Anthropocene agencies, I offer a material ecocritical vision as an alternative. This chapter also criticizes the Anthropos figure as "a category mistake in the conceptualization of the Anthropocene, and a recipe for political paralysis," as Australian geographer Lesley Head claims (2014, 116). But if we reformulate the Anthropos figure as an earthbound being ultimately inseparable from other species and the environment, we can better understand and care for all multispecies relations to prevent an unlivable future. It is because the Anthropocene mirrors the worldly entanglements of many species in overlapping trajectories of social, ecological, and geological forces, and thus opens a path to the possibility of new Anthroposcenarios. We need to find ways to attune to the more-than-human stories of survivals and resistance on a wounded planet. To exemplify, I conclude with Turkish psychiatrist and artist Rahşan Düren's art installation *E-Motions* (2015), which confronts the Anthropocene by bringing our emotions and motions together and makes us rethink the Anthropocene in terms of affective empathy for our planet.

Be that as it may, we still do not have a grounded epistemological sense of how the forces of the Anthropocene gathered in human volition increasingly disrupt the Earth's communities no matter how resilient they may be. We are not fully cognizant of what it means for nonhuman communities to live and die in the Anthropocene and how poignant their stories are. Even worse, in famed entomologist Edward O. Wilson's words, "we really don't know what we're doing" (2017, 162). This epistemological quandary is the order and the consequence of the Anthropocene's diverse range of effects in human communities as well, which is discussed in chapter 3, "Migrant Ecologies of the Anthropocene." The negative impacts of the Anthropocene can indeed result in planetary-scale human migrations and cause "geologically unprecedented transglobal species invasions and changes associated with farming and fishing, permanently reconfiguring Earth's biological trajectory" (Waters et al. 2016, 137). When human groups, living species, and pathogens, germs, microbes, and viruses are migrating, we encounter tragic stories of not only human groups but also nonhuman animals caught in the Anthropocene's conundrums. Some human groups are driven by political reasons and economic deprivation, some others by changing climates; but many of them are on the move because of sectarian conflicts, regional wars, and, above all, environmental catastrophes. The saddest stories of climate change, however, are about nonhuman migrations as the threats from changing climates with diminishing food sources affect the chances of survival in great measure. Enmeshed in ecological, political, and sociocultural dilemmas, environmental and social crises, cultural and ethical concerns, all these stories also signal the imminent threat of a postnatural world.

The multilayered ecologies of our storied planet, which is afflicted by a reciprocal deception in the dark ontology of the Anthropocene, has indeed produced postnatural ecologies, which is the focus of chapter 4, "Postnatural Ecologies of the Anthropocene." This chapter explores how the effects of the Anthropocene produce postnatures marked by humanity's stratigraphic signatures in sediments and ice. Many geologists indicate "technofossils" (Zalasiewicz et al. 2014) as the most recent anthropogenic signatures detected in concrete, microplastics, radionuclides, and inorganic carbonaceous particles. These technofossils not only transform the planet into a postnatural home but also percolate through human biology and nonhuman organisms. They are reconfiguring the atmosphere, geosphere, hydrosphere, and biosphere as waste spheres. Environmental historian Marco Armiero and political economist Massimo De Angelis (2017) have therefore proposed "Wasteocene" as a more proper name for the Anthropocene epoch, which this chapter also discusses. Despite this gloomy scenario, however, not all is lost, because the narrative agencies of the Anthropocene can help us fashion new forms of knowledge and resistance to counter this phenomenon, which might trigger a deep change in our mindset.

One way to initiate a deep change in human collective intelligence while facing the consequences of the Anthropocene can be through the acknowledgment of prismatic ecologies of the Anthropocene, which is the focus of chapter 5, "The Ecology of Colors in the Anthropocene." This chapter suggests that even if the Anthropocene is muddying nature's polychromatic richness, the ecology of colors can help reclaim the entangled colors of life and enable us to rethink our relationship to life on Earth in terms of our intimate connections to the prismatic living world of which we are part. Transformation is possible if we can reconnect with our storied world and with life as an expressive force. It is possible to reimagine the prism through which this existential challenge is framed, and the ecology of colors can *affectively* reconnect us to our storied planet and with life itself in less harmful ways.

In pursuing these lines of argument, I suggest that the Anthropocene and its multiscalar, multigenerational, multistory effects can be scrutinized (and rectified) from the perspective of material ecocriticism. Following geological, biological, and literary stories that are embedded in the Anthropocene's epochal swirls, *Ecologies of a Storied Planet in the Anthropocene* claims that being attentive to the articulate world and its stories and embedded meanings can help us find sustainable solutions to the planet's current predicament. It is now time to terminate the "act of writing ourselves into rock record" (Heringman

2015, 58), close the "narratives of worldly obliteration" (Cohen 2017a, 246), and open those of interdependence, relation making, and collaborations quietly told by everything that is more-than-human. This is the vision that propelled me to write *Ecologies of a Storied Planet in the Anthropocene*, which is intended to inspire new hopes for sustainable biotic existence and for sustaining multispecies interconnections amid the pressing forces of dark ecologies made even darker with the arrival of the new coronavirus in 2020.

We have been learning the art of coping with this deadly virus in the midst of global environmental challenges, which seem to have made a clarion call for a new understanding of environmental responsibility within the context of interdisciplinary knowledge practices. We are also learning the "arts of living on a damaged planet" by experiencing the direct effects of global climate instabilities.[2] This alone shows that we have long been complicit in harming the Earth's ecosystems as agents of destruction in the planet's natural cycles, which led us to the current reality of pandemics and ecological decline. Reconnecting with the storied planet and its numerous narrative agencies may be one of the paths to redemption, which begins with redirecting attention to planetary ecosystems from which we have been disconnected and reimagining human–nonhuman relationalities on our wounded planet to ensure a livable future. It is possible to rewrite our earthly tale furnished with nonanthropocentric meanings, which can materialize with new forms of resistance, new narratives, and new imaginative vocabularies that heed the unheard voices of disrupted nonhuman entities as well as human communities. Although dire ecological conditions will not suddenly dissolve, nor will deadly viruses unexpectedly vanish, we can continue to listen to the voices of the Earth and learn to decipher the stories of all beings that suffer the consequences of environmental transformations. If we bear in mind that "we are interconnected as a biosphere and a civilization," as science-fiction writer Kim Stanley Robinson (2020) reminds us, we can communicate a message of revaluing all earthly agencies facing threats of extinction.

This point is related to the hope that the book will generate the creativity to imagine better ethical responses to our storied planet, taking into account the voices of everything that is more-than-human, the diverse communities of flora and fauna that make our planet livable, and all the material agencies that struggle to unburden themselves of escalating toxicity. We may experience ecological uncertainties, sometimes despair, and may even succumb to pessimism in these critical times, but the solutions lie with us. For as long as we continue to press for ethically sustainable and socially adaptable ecological visions and solutions in the face of global challenges, there will be hope.

To respond to the objections that might be voiced against this note of hope in the face of alarming ecological decline, let me underline the fact that although humanity's enduring desires for economic profits born of technoscientific and biochemical practices are insatiable, not all humans are responsible for the systematic destruction of biotic communities. The major actors behind the ongoing degradation of ecosystemic processes are "those who hold the reins of world governance in their hands" (Marchesini 2021, 3) while the majority of people across the world are all tangled in many forms of ecological disruptions and social turbulences. Moreover, the hope I advocate does not lie in "the same masculinist and human centered solutions that have created the problem in the first place" (Grusin 2017, ix), such as geoengineering. Seeking solutions in such capitalist projects accentuates more worries about the future of life. To prevent the urge to venture into a further discussion of what so obviously ripples through the interconnected social systems, we can learn to pay more attention to the narrative agencies of the endangered planet and to the intertwined stories of humans and nonhumans that shape planetary health, justice, ecology, and politics. Taking narrative agencies as our collaborative partners in shaping intersecting stories of our planet's living things, we center on working through their practical implications as a new ground for action and resolution of environmental problems. After all, narrative agencies in the Anthropocene send us many warning signals about our ruinous destiny, calling out to protect our world so we can relearn to honor it and understand its fragility before it is too late. Eminent physicists David Bohm and F. David Peat once said, "The challenge that faces humanity is unique . . . a new kind of creative surge is needed to meet it" (1989, 207). The chapters that follow address this need with the material ecocritical concepts of *storied matter* and *narrative agencies* and demonstrate that there is no ontological divide between the human and nonhuman realms. We cannot remain separate from the biosphere and its communities of which we are part. That is why we must "have pity on this small blue planet searching through time and space" (Winterson 1997, 5).

Chapter 1

The Storied Planet in the Anthropocene

What if we envision our world as a storied planet where all earthly entities (including the inorganic ones) produce meaning-filled encounters with everything else in ongoing processes of communication? Are humans the only beings with the ability to "spin yarns and to make history" (Oppermann 2016b, 89)? What if matter itself is eloquent and can build meaningful connections across a wide spectrum of materialities? In light of these questions, this chapter challenges the traditional humanist idea that more-than-human entities know neither memory nor history to be expressive and that storytelling is all-too-human. This is the material ecocritical vision that goes beyond the regulatory cultural frameworks.

Material ecocriticism is the study of the narrative dimension of the material world, a critical exploration of stories embodied in nature's constituents, or material agencies, as volatile subjects that are "semiotically active" (Haraway 2008a, 250) and "potentially expressive" (Abram 1997, 81). Material ecocriticism claims that the world expresses its mind in terms of narratives often shaped by emergent intelligibility beyond the human. It aims to bring about a shift in our ways of thinking about narrative, storytelling, creativity, and how intelligibility infuses the world's "semiotic materiality" (Haraway 2008a, 163). Karen Barad's definition of intelligibility as "an ontological performance of the world in its ongoing articulation" (2007, 149) offers a compelling example of the insights involved in discussing narrative as an *instance* of the material-semiotic world at large. Challenging the traditional understanding of narrative as a specific human capacity, or a form of human imposition of meaning and coherence on the world, material ecocriticism provides a more encompassing definition of narrative as the ability to produce meaningful expressions through which all signifying agencies (biological organisms and abiotic flows, forces, and substances) represent their relations to the world. In this account, matter's agentic expressions, inherent creativity, and innate meanings are deeply interlaced with human mindscapes, reflexivity, and imagination via our literary traditions. Far from being an exclusively human universal, then, narrative, if we recall Roland Barthes's remark, "is simply there, like life itself" (1977, 79). We are surrounded by nonhuman narratives, stories embedded in places, things, and beings, which pervade and mediate our understanding of the world, producing "symbolic interactionism" and making "our everyday practical accounts . . . not only reflexive and self-referring, but also constitutive of the situations to which they refer" (Parsons 2009). Storied matter, in this regard, is the ground where the imaginary and the actual intersect to engender conditions of creativity for the nonhuman narratives to be visible to the human interlocutor.

When the human and the nonhuman interact in actual and imaginative contexts, surprising potentialities emerge for subverting the anthropocentric paradigm, which not only shaped social systems for hundreds of years but also produced a planetary crisis of geological scale, manifesting in the reality of the Anthropocene whereby human actions, to borrow one of the foremost theorists of posthumanism N. Katherine Hayles's words, "are unleashing forces far beyond our ability to control them" (2017, 196). In this approach, matter in all its forms, from subatomic particles to stellar formations, is storied matter composed of narrative agencies actively producing configurations of meaningful expressions that merge with our modes of knowing and being, making us, all other species, and material forms and processes ontologically inseparable. Hence, reflecting on the stories of matter is reflecting on our own coexistence and coevolution in the story of the Earth itself. The narrative agencies of this encompassing story are all amenable to "the lively relationalities of becoming of which we are a part" (Barad 2007, 393). Matter's narrative creativity is an emergent possibility of becoming in material processes, producing trajectories of unfolding stories in bodily natures, geological processes, and ecological networks. Matter's creativity also intersects with human creativity in the sense that narrative agencies invite us to read the world differently, which obviously "requires arts of imagination" (Swanson, Tsing, and Bubandt 2017, M8) as well as arts of attentiveness to be able to recognize the agentic capacities and expressive potentials of everything that is of this world.

Being attentive to the nonhuman storying of the world and thinking matter in terms of its creative expressions "irreducible to representations and freed from any constant reference to the human" (Bryant 2011, 23) also liberates us from our "modes of narrative self-enclosure" (Colebrook 2014, 63). Such an approach would actually "draw us into deeper and more demanding accountabilities for nonhuman others" (van Dooren and Rose 2012, 2). Narrative creativity, to use Thom van Dooren and Deborah Bird Rose's words, can be defined as "the capacity to experience places as meaningful and significant . . . shared well beyond the human species" (2012, 5). This is meant to emphasize the point that there is a better alternative to the inherited paradigm of anthropocentricism, which considers experience, expressivity, and creativity only in human terms. Pointing the way forward, material ecocriticism reaffirms the new interpretive option by enlarging our understanding of creative experience embodied in and expressed by everything that is more-than-human.

Pursuing this line of argument, this chapter elaborates on matter's expressive creativity in general, and thus sheds light on the conviction that exploring the meanings of material intimacies in a storied planet "that is, by itself, fully articulated and active" (Latour 2014, 13) is important and worthy of study. I argue that being attentive to the astonishingly articulate world and its stories and meanings can generate ecologically credible modes of thinking and ways of solving the planet's current predicament. I also contend that the narrative agencies can transform our mindset and provide a viable answer to the question of who we really want to be on the verge of ecological collapse. Accordingly, the material ecocritical theorization of storied matter is quite useful for refashioning our objectifying attitude to the world. It is now time to open ourselves to interdependence, relation making, and collaborations with nonhuman entities, especially when there is reliable empirical evidence (including the atomic and molecular levels) that creative and expressive becoming really exists in material agencies, living and nonliving notwithstanding (see Hassan et al. 2018, 1101; Mayburov 2011, 260–65).

This chapter will proceed in two sections. The first introduces material ecocriticism and its conceptual tools—storied matter and narrative agency—while the second traces their origins to the concepts developed by the process philosopher Charles Hartshorne (1897–2000), who claimed that all material entities are "compound individuals" entangled in processes of creative becoming (Hartshorne 1936). The discussion of compound individuals sheds light on how narrative agencies exercise various degrees of creative experience based on their level of appropriating data in their surroundings to produce meaningful articulations. I consider Hartshorne as one of the most significant precursors of the new materialist paradigm from which material ecocriticism derives its fundamental arguments about expressive materiality. The second section is therefore a theoretical revisiting of Hartshorne's relational ontology, which is also at the root of the new materialist theorizing of matter's agentic capacities.

The Material Ecocritical Interpretation of the World

Intrinsic to material ecocriticism is the idea that "the world's material phenomena are knots in a vast network of agencies, which can be 'read' and interpreted as forming narratives, stories" (Iovino and Oppermann 2014, 1). Ingrained in this vast network are modes of "worlding" marked by exploits of material expressions that demand to be imagined in-depth and interpreted with new knowledge practices so that matter's stories can come to life in ways that we can "feel the world's word" (Dillard 1988, 72). Seen in this light, "'worlding' is theorizing and storytelling that is rooted in the historical materialities of meeting between humans and nonhumans" (Tsing et al. 2017, M23). Material ecocriticism develops this vision further, suggesting that narrative agencies invalidate our habit of worlding as if we are the only storied beings and moves us toward an awareness of the stories all material entities embody through which the Earth, as the only life-generating planet in the solar system, gets shaped and reshaped by the semiotic creativity of its agentic segments.

Material ecocriticism proposes that matter's stories emerge through the interplay of natural and cultural forces, through their trajectories and flows, forming constellations of matter and meanings. Atoms, elements, genes, cells, stones, water, landscapes, and machines, among innumerable others, are embodied narratives, repositories of storied matter. Inhabiting not only the material but also the discursive spaces spawned by human agency, these variously agentic material formations as narrative agencies become consequent upon social and economic processes, making material practices and their discursive formulations mutually constitutive. This is a "tangled world," Stacy Alaimo affirms in her article "States of Suspension: Trans-Corporeality at Sea." In such a world, she writes, "science, politics, ethics, and the mundane but consequential practices of ordinary humans, swirl together" (2012, 489).[1] Discourse in this perspective is not a linguistic construction exterior to materiality; it does not refer to signifying systems, representations, or utterances of a unified subject. Rather, as Karen Barad compellingly argues, the "relationship between the material and the discursive is one of mutual entailment" (2007, 152). Hence Barad offers the term "material-discursive" to explain "the causal relationship between discursive practices and the material phenomena" (34). In this sense, matter with its "intensely alien activeness" as Jeffrey J. Cohen concurs, "is never *merely* constructed (not abstract, not a social or discursive fabrication, not passive)" (2015, 42; italics in original). Matter is part of the material-discursive composition, an integral domain of being and knowledge.

What this material-discursive co-emergence signals is the dissolution of anthropocentrism and thus its binary logic deeply enmeshed within the social and cultural practices of othering the more-than-human-world. In Barad's cogent account, the compound term "material-discursive" registers a sense of an integral understanding of social and natural phenomena and removes matter and discourse from "one balkanized enclave or the other" (2007, 25). Considering the material and the discursive together, however, does not mean "collapsing important differences between them" but "allowing any integral aspects to emerge" (Barad 2007, 25). This is diffractive thinking—thinking concepts and matter through one another—that material ecocriticism holds crucial in bridging the divide between matter and its social constructions, and in positing the co-emergence and coevolution of humans and nonhumans in their narrative creativity.

Inspired by Barad's definition of matter as "a dynamic expression/articulation of the world in its intra-active becoming" (2007, 392), material ecocriticism insists that with their dynamic expressions nature's constituents offer eloquent pathways into the multilayered ecologies of our storied planet. Despite struggling within the Anthropocene's epochal swirls today, the world we inhabit is filled with beings and things whose patterns of interconnections produce meanings and stories, thus generating an astonishingly rich expressive dimension. Everything that connects us to the planet—biological rhythms, multispecies entanglements, ecological relations, geological processes, elemental forces, and climatic patterns—partakes in this dimension, transmitting stories of ecological and existential relationships through "codes, signs, shapes, colors, sounds, gestures, and signals" (Oppermann 2016b, 89). The human stories—whether they are literary, scientific, historical, ecological, technological, sociopolitical, medical, economic, or personal—flourish together with nonhuman stories that compel us to think beyond ourselves, which we would never have imagined until recently. But today, as anthropologist Anna Lowenhaupt Tsing eloquently notes, "the time has come for new ways of telling true stories beyond civilizational first principles. Without Man and Nature, all creatures can come back to life" (2015, vii–viii). And when they do, the result is, in Donna Haraway's words, a "stunning narrative . . . of structural-functional complexity" (2008b, 163). This narrative dimension is always vital to becoming, to world-making; in this realm of semiotic materiality, stories come to presence under the signifying forces of multiple relatings in the complex webs of naturecultures.[2]

Principally, as the new materialists have long insisted, the composite reality of the world that we share with all nonhuman beings and material agencies can best be defined as "naturalcultural." Haraway (2003) uses this compound term in *The Companion Species Manifesto* to breach the categorical schism between nature and culture, promoting the term as a mode of thought that helps us to envision naturecultures as sedimented together in the Earth's rhythms, cycles, climate, and metabolic processes that are inseparable today from technological, socioeconomic, medical, and cultural ecologies. If we consider how earthquakes, floods, volcanoes, and climate crises have regulated civilizations since time immemorial, and that the human microbiome is not wholly human, we can understand why the Earth's phenomenal geostory (in Latour's terms) of ecological balances and evolutionary relations is a naturalcultural one. Haraway explains that "90 percent of the cells are filled with the genomes of bacteria, fungi, protists, and such, some of which play in a symphony necessary to my being alive," then clearly "diverse bodies and meanings co-shape one another" (2008a, 3–4). Indeed, from the moment we are born, as environmental author Anthony Doerr also writes in his perceptive article "The New You" (2014), "we are colonized, seized, and occupied by other entities," and "to even write that you are 'you' and the microbes are 'them' is, perhaps, a failure of pronouns." The microbial entities inhabiting our bodies, like the parasitic helminth worms in our immune system and bacteria colonies in our elbows Jane Bennet mentions as examples in her pioneering book *Vibrant Matter* (2010, 120), bespeak an intriguing map of "interconnections between various bodily natures," which Stacy Alaimo defines as transcorporeality (2010, 2). In fact, the human is always enmeshed within and coexists with other beings and things because, as Bennett reminds us, the "human agency is always an assemblage of microbes, animals, plants, metals, chemicals, word-sounds, and the like" (2010, 120–21). The body is indeed a hybrid zone where nature truly converges with culture, making so-imagined zip-logged boundaries between them manifestly porous. Consider for a moment novelist Margaret Atwood's incisive explanation (2012) that "the inside of your body is connected to the world around you, and your body too has its ecology, and what goes into it—whether eaten or breathed or drunk or absorbed through your skin—has a profound impact on you."

All these arguments perceptively show that it is nearly impossible to maintain any kind of ontological separation between natures and cultures. In this regard, Bennett is right in designating the world as "an interstitial field of nonpersonal, ahuman forces, flows, tendencies, and trajectories" (2010, 61), which extend into the corporeal and social dimensions of human reality. These ahuman forces and flows are now coming into public attention with the increasing media exposure of global pollution, toxicity, and the humanly made substances like plastic passing through our bodies and the bodies of birds, fish, and other species in so many discrete ways. Therefore, recognizing interconnectedness is key to understanding this process of corporeal entanglement with the uncanny agencies that populate the living spaces alongside the Earth's native vegetal, mineral, and animal entities. Just as it is important to conceptualize how we can feel "the tangible textures, sounds, and shapes of the biosphere"[3] and to know that "our bodies are always intertwined with the broad flesh of the Earth" (Abram 2010, 63, 127), it is also important to consider how the deviant toxic agents have now become part of this expanding cartography of transcorporeality. Like Alaimo's model of transcorporeality, Andrew Pickering's (1995) metaphor of the mangle and Barad's (2007) notion of intra-action also provide a useful index of overlapping models and concepts in articulating this vision of interconnectivity and emergent materiality. These conceptual tools are helpful in theorizing the codependency between ecosystems, landscapes, climate, species, and the social and cultural textures of human habitats, all of which intersect in the ceaseless rhythms of life and death.

In this ongoing process, human agency is so reciprocally connected and constitutively intertwined with nonhuman agencies that they all become "mangled in practice" (Pickering 1995, 23). Arguing thus, Pickering notes the "degrees of symmetry between human and material agency" (17), which emergently define and sustain each other. Drawing attention to a mangle of practice in science studies, Pickering observes that we are "constitutively engaged with the world of material agency" (20). He illustrates his contention by referring to particle physicist Donald Glaser's experiments with elementary particles in bubble chambers and explains how Glaser's detectors "*did* things . . . and that these doings were importantly separate from Glaser" (51). Glaser had taken a passive role when the bubble chambers produced "tracks and photographs in a way that is not substantively attributable to any human agent" (52). The detectors in the laboratory showed a definite agentic capacity, quite independent of the human observer. Pickering explains this "as a particular combination of material elements that *acts* in a particular way" (52) and claims that "material agency is irreducible to human agency" (53), but he also stresses the significance of the "emergence of material agency" as "bound up with that of human agency" (53). This means that the emergence of material agency is entangled "with human agency without, in any sense, reducing the former to the latter" (54). In other words, humans are *part* of the ontology of the material world *not* by way of control, nor even observation and reflection, but rather, as Barad (2007) explains, by way of "intra-action"—the mutual constitution of entangled agencies—of the observers and the observed. In this constitution, the scientist does not interact with the material agency as a controlling agent but remains part of the experiment through intra-action. Barad argues that the usual interaction "presumes the prior existence of independent entities or relata" (139), but "the notion of intra-action recognizes that distinct agencies do not precede, but rather emerge through, their intra-action" (33). In other words, there is no agential separability in the phenomena constituted by ontological relations "without preexisting relata" (139). Consequently, our discourses and technologies, philosophies and sciences, and ethics and aesthetics become inseparable from the very material world within which they intra-act. It is in this onto-epistemological framework that we can begin to talk about material agency that is bursting with life, "vital materiality" (Bennett 2010, 55), and surprising narratives.

Matter's Agentic Powers

In the material ecocritical perspective, agency exists beyond the biological world, emerging even in the so-called synthetic matter, which exhibits "itself in matter's overlapping biotic and abiotic components transmitted through technoscientific practices that seek to graft the technological onto the biological" (Oppermann 2016a, 274). Duke University professor of literature Luciana Parisi describes this as "inorganic nanodesigning of biophysical systems (2008, 294). A research project at the University of Glasgow provides a concrete example of the creative experiences of carbon-free, inorganic chemicals. Attempting to create life from inorganic chemical compounds, in 2011 the scientists built inorganic chemical cells they named iCHELLs, which were fabricated "at the liquid-liquid interface between aqueous solutions of simple polyoxometalate clusters (POMs) and organic/coordination-complex cations" (Cooper et al. 2011, 10373). Just like carbon-based cells, the inorganic chemical compounds were capable of self-replicating and evolving.[4] In their article "Modular Redox-Active Inorganic Chemical Cells: iCHELLs," Cooper and co-authors write that they

> can controllably produce robust, spontaneously repairing membranous iCHELLs with diameters that range from 50 µm to cell-like compartments of several millimeters. The membranous pouches display intrinsic physical properties that reflect their molecular building blocks, such as redox activity or chiral structure, while also being able to partition chemical components within a system. As such, the inorganic "cells" can be manufactured in bulk or can be "nested" within one another to produce clearly separated domains within a single structure. (Cooper et al. 2011, 10373)

These presumably posthuman agencies expressly point to "a 'biologization' of inorganic matter, refiguring our foundational notions of agency, matter, and life" (Oppermann 2016a, 286). Their story, in this sense, can be read as "the story of matter as a dynamic becoming, because iCHELLS are queer constructions, hybrids of life and nonlife, with a capacity to evolve" (285). In the concluding paragraph, the authors declare that their aim is

> to construct complex chemical cells with life-like properties because the development of non-biotic inorganic chemical cells could be one route to probe how life emerged from the "inorganic world" around 4.3 billion years ago and how new synthetic or inorganic biology . . . could be achieved in the laboratory today. (Cooper et al. 2011, 10376)

In fact, this aim had already been achieved a year earlier, proving that iCHELLs were not the "world's first synthetic life form" (Sample 2010). On July 2, 2010, famed geneticist Craig Venter and his twenty-three colleagues published a landmark report in *Science*, titled "Creation of a Bacterial Cell Controlled by a Chemically Synthesized Genome" (Gibson et al. 2010), announcing "the creation of an artificial bacterium genome (copied from DNA sequences of *Mycoplasma mycoides*) which was transferred into a closely related microbe which began to successfully reproduce, making over a billion copies of itself" (Ussery 2010).[5] Venter has claimed that this single-celled organism "heralds the dawn of a new era in which new life is made to benefit humanity, starting with bacteria that churn out biofuels, soak up carbon dioxide from the atmosphere and even manufacture vaccines." Venter also announced that this new species is "a living species now, part of our planet's inventory of life" (quoted in Sample 2010; see also Callaway 2016). This is true because in the report "Creation of a Bacterial Cell Controlled by a Chemically Synthesized Genome," Gibson et al. conclude that "the cells with only the synthetic genome are self-replicating and capable of logarithmic growth" (2010, 55). In their response article, "Craig Venter's Synthetic Bacteria: The Dawn of a New Era?," biologists Manuel Porcar and Andrés Moya (2010) concur that it was "a landmark heralding the dawn of a new era: depicted by Venter as the first time a living organism on Earth has a computer for a parent."

It must be clear by now that matter, even in its synthetic forms, is equipped with a capacity of self-organization, intrinsic vitality, effectivity, and productive agency and has its own "emergent generative powers (or agentic capacities)" (Coole and Frost 2010, 9), always disclosing a process of dynamic becoming. In today's posthuman reality, it is also projecting interesting and often alien life patterns that issue from the traffic of nonliving and living entities. These intersubjective fields of collective activity may relish an uncanny sense of an enfolding coexistence in the planetary narratives of creativity, but the point here is that being "differentially distributed across of wider range of ontological types" (Bennett 2010, 9), matter has the power to instigate long-standing effects, like the *E. coli* virus outbreak in Europe in 2011 that afflicted the entire agricultural economy of Spain and the more recent coronavirus pandemic that has shattered world economies since its appearance in 2020. Or consider the effects of the oceanic plastic literally changing the water's ecology and the plants that transform cultures.[6] Michael Pollan, for example, convincingly argues that the potato "altered the course of European history" (2001, xviii), which instantiates quite visibly the fact that "the linguistic, social, political and biological are inseparable" (Hekman 2010, 25). Taking plants as nature's alchemists, Pollan claims that plants are "experts in transforming water, soil, and sunlight into an array of precious substances, many of them beyond the ability of human beings to conceive, much less manufacture" (2001, xix). These are agentic activities overflowing with such vitality and meaning that they often elude technological, social, or cultural control. In light of these views, we understand that matter is not only conceptually more important today but also ontologically more meaningful than previously thought. As "an emergent property created through dynamic interactions between physical characteristics and signifying strategies" (Hayles 2005, 3), matter is no longer viewed as a passive substance but an effective player in an "ontologically heterogeneous field" (Bennett 2010, 23). In this sense, reality can be redefined as a site of various layers of creative and expressive materiality, cognition, meaning, and also as "matter-energy" as suggested by Manuel DeLanda ([1997] 2005, 21), In his words: "Rocks and winds, germs and words, are all different manifestations of this dynamic material reality, or, in other words, they all represent the different ways in which this single matter-energy *expresses itself*" (21; italics in original). The multiple constellations of these forms, whether they are geological, biological, organic, inorganic, social, or linguistic, map our material-discursive reality.

In such a radical rethinking of the environment as a dynamic comingling of human and nonhuman agencies, discrete and conjoined forces, pliable elements, and co-emerging meanings and matter, the world comes to be seen as a terrain of complex interchanges between innumerable generative forces. These "mutually interconnected webs of relationships," in Haraway's apt definition (2008a, 388), reveal a dance of creative becoming involving multiple agentic forces and entities. Regardless of whether they are "carbon, silicon, or something else" (250), all material agencies participate in meaning-making activities in the undivided field of concrete reality. This field is thick with stories projected by material agencies with undeniable signifying forces, interacting within material-discursive networks. The close study of these networks has precipitated in the new materialist "break-through of the schism between sign/culture/language and referent/nature/matter" (van der Tuin 2011, 288), which also has deep material ecocritical resonances. Put another way, the conceptual horizons of the new materialisms I have been sketching so far provide an onto-epistemological frame for ecocritical investigations of the nonanthropocentric alliances, compositions, and performances of nonhuman natures and bodies, and more materially grounded appropriations of human–nonhuman relations through which many stories persistently emerge. Indicated by this framework, we come to realize that we dwell in a world crisscrossed by nonhuman agencies, which combine and collide with the agentic field of our species.

These encounters, however, are not a new discovery. Bennett observes that "humanity and nonhumanity have always performed an intricate dance with each other. There was never a time when the human agency was anything other than an interfolding network of humanity and nonhumanity. Today this mingling has become harder to ignore" (2010, 31). The reasons for this last statement are evident. Pollution, poverty, environmental and social injustices, species extinction, depletion of local ecosystems, global warming, and disseminated toxic matter are all facets of a global ecological crisis in the Anthropocene. These environmental crises are fostered through what quantum physicist David Bohm calls "fragmentary thought" ([1980] 1995, 7) to explain "the habit of seeing reality and acting toward it as if it were constituted of separately existing fragments" (8). One strategy to contest this mode of thought, suggested by the new materialist conjecture, is to shift our focus and acknowledge that everything in the living world has creative agency, which should not be exclusively associated with human intentionality but be seen as part of the material generative dynamism that signals the necessity to change our anthropocentric values and destructive practices. Material ecocriticism sees this dynamism as composed of narrative agencies that "have the ability to communicate something of themselves to other beings" (Abram 2010, 172). The concept of narrative agency not only undoes the stubborn dichotomies of anthropocentric thought as animate/inanimate, alive/dead, organic/inorganic, and observer/observed but also draws attention to meaningful signs issued by many life-forms and nonliving things. Meaning here should be seen as "an ongoing performance of the world in its differential intelligibility" (Barad 2007, 335). Although overlooked by the human part, intelligibility emerges when "part of the world becomes differentially intelligible to another part of the world" (342). This realization (becoming aware of lively, creative, intelligible nonhuman agency) alone is enough to dissolve the anthropocentric cataract in the human vision.

Thus understood, agency manifests in many ways and is distributed across humans, other biological organisms, nonbiological players, and synthetic biologies, as in the case of iCHELLs. Even in garbage there is vibrant materiality, as journalist and author Robert Sullivan (2006) insists in *The Meadowlands:*

Wilderness Adventures on the Edge of New York City. Bringing attention to the alien agency of waste in New York City, Sullivan argues that the "garbage hills are alive" and quivering with "billions of microscopic organisms thriving underground in the dark, oxygen-free communities" (96). Whether detrimental to ecological health or not, in its ongoing materialization every agency enacts what David Abram calls "expressive magic in its own manner" (2010, 171). But, unlike the relentless agency of the pollutants and toxic chemicals that circulate in and out of bodies, in food, air, and water, Abram's examples reveal a more lyrical picture of narrative agencies that are part of the collective network of agentic forces and entities: the whispered hush of the uncut grasses at dawn, the laughter of birch leaves, tumbling waterfalls, gusts of wind, compost piles, rusting automobiles, feathers, grains of sand, dormant volcanoes, snowdrifts, diamonds (2010, 172). They are—though not all of them deemed alive—eloquent, and thus "participate in the mystery of language" (172). This is the foundational premise of material ecocriticism, which espouses Barad's definition of matter as "a dynamic expression/articulation of the world in its intra-active becoming" (2007, 392). Understood in this context, narrative agencies become specific enactments of creativity and vitality found across the nonhuman world. By venturing into the realm of storied matter and theorizing it as a site of narrativity through which matter's eloquence is engineered, material ecocriticism also makes a strong point about how understanding the meanings storied matter convey unveils the intertwined narrative of our own interdependence. That is why reading the Earth in its narrative dynamics is important, as it elicits a recognition that this world "is a creative community of beings that reorganizes itself age after age so that it can perpetuate and even deepen its vibrant existence" (Swimme and Tucker 2011, 56).

Meanings disseminated by the "creative community of beings" across this storied world form a web of entangled relations with human reality. This fusion of horizons has a liberating effect of moving the human vision from the language of otherness to that of differential co-emergence. It thus helps to overcome the habitual mode of thought "guided by a fragmentary self-world view" (Bohm 1980, 2). Moreover, such recognition not only urges us to act responsibly as part of the world but also underlines the importance of the ethical subject as "an embodied sensibility," the embodied self whose "ethical relations extend to the other-than-human" (Barad 2007, 391–92). Emphasizing this radical rethinking of human and nonhuman relations is the attempt to dehierarchize our conceptual categories that structure dualisms, which in turn determine our oppressive social, cultural, and political practices. Therefore, destabilizing such artificially naturalized systems of meaning is a precondition to resolve many complex issues, such as climate change, and to update our logocentric and anthropocentric discourses. In this journey, material ecocriticism can orient us toward "a new integrating story" (Swimme and Tucker 2011, 3).

The main thread of this trajectory entails "relational ontology"[7] premised on the causal correlations and co-constitutive relationships among all entities and meaning-making processes. The key to relational ontology is understanding reality and being in terms of dynamic relationalities and "communion as the modality of all existence" (LaCugna 1991, 250). Indeed, endorsing relational ontology, as ethologist Roberto Marchesini concurs in consensus view, "life is primarily a relational system" (2016, 151), and human beings are not outside this horizon of relationality; rather, humans "evolved from nonhuman relations" (152). Listing a number of our abilities and skills, such as affection, competence, tendency to collect, arts of mimicry and creativity, communicative disposition, and use of signs in representation, Marchesini affirms that "these are all things that were left to us by nonhuman creatures in their diachronic path of relation with the world" (152). This relational existence is more succinctly and memorably expressed by process philosopher Charles Hartshorne: "To be is to be in relation" (1970, 114). This is the key formula in understanding relational ontology, and the actual world itself. Though not acknowledged in the new materialist discussions, Hartshorne's account of the "relations of existential or dynamic connectedness" (205) and his insistence on the "creative freedom" found among nature's constituents are implicit in the new materialist ontologies, and they also form the basis of material ecocritical conceptualization of storied matter—a vehicle of signifying forces in a multitude of interconnected agencies, systems, and processes—and its narrative agencies. The following section acknowledges material ecocriticism's theoretical debt to Hartshorne's conceptualization of material agencies as compound individuals and creative becoming.

Nature's Creative Entities as Experiencing Individuals

According to Charles Hartshorne, "all concrete reality is in principle creative.... Reality is always in part self-created, causa sui, creativity being, in this philosophy, the supreme transcendental. All creatures have creativity above zero, all are creators" ([1967] 1989, 82). Hartshorne's words from *A Natural Theology for Our Time* highlight the fundamental principle of the actual world: an agentic reality characterized by inherent creativity, which he further explains in *Creative Synthesis and Philosophic Method* as "creative freedom that is found on this planet" (1970, 190). Deeply inspired by Alfred

North Whitehead's "organic realism,"[8] Hartshorne's vision contrives a creative ontology, allowing him to "imagine the universe as a vast system of experiencing individuals on innumerable levels. Each individual is in some measure free; for experiencing is a partly free act. Thus creativity . . . is universal" (1970, 6). Among the experiencing individuals, which Hartshorne calls "compound individuals" (in consonance with Whitehead's actual entities), "the human experience is only one form" (1970, 6) among many others, including atoms, molecules, and cells. Similar in some ways to Whitehead's process-relational philosophy, what Hartshorne called "creative experience" suggests a fusion of diverse elements from an entity's past/memory/happenings, which are synthesized into an ongoing process of relation making. In Whitehead's account, "creativity" is synonymous with "being," "entity," and "thing," and creativity "lies in the nature of things" ([1929] 1978, 21), which means that whether organic or inorganic, everything that is earthly is agentic, dynamic, generative, and transformative. In his magnum opus *Process and Reality: An Essay in Cosmology*, Whitehead argued that "*how* an actual entity becomes constitutes what that actual entity is. . . . Its 'being' is constituted by its 'becoming'" ([1929] 1978, 23); that is, although "there are gradations of importance, and diversities of function," actual entities "are on the same level"; they are all "drops of experience, complex, and interdependent" (18). That is to say, all entities are interrelated in processes of creative becoming, and each process of creative becoming is the continual result of entangled relations among entities, beings, and things. In this relational ontology, one can say, quoting Haraway, "the world is a knot in motion" (2003, 6) in which nothing can persist merely in a static way of being.

It is in this philosophical horizon that Hartshorne affirms the principle of creativity in life, arguing that all individuals (human and nonhuman) possess some degree of creative experience. More importantly, "creative" for Hartshorne means "unpredictable, incompletely determined in advance by causal conditions and laws. Accordingly, it means *additions to the definiteness of reality*" (1970, 3; italics in original). Creativity, then, is a causal enactment of the process of becoming enfolded into experiencing individuals that form and emerge "within relational fields" (Coole and Frost 2010, 10). Being entangled in lively relationalities produce what Diana Coole and Samantha Frost call "choreographies of becoming" (2010, 10), which constitute the way material reality is: a flux of interconnected entities, forces, and processes that are ontologically inseparable despite their "gradations of importance" (Whitehead [1929] 1978, 18). Hartshorne anticipated this vision and compellingly argued that "creative becoming is a reality, at least in human experiences, and that it is not obviously impossible that it should be universally real, present in all things from atoms to deity, and constitutive of reality as such" (1970, 13). More precisely, creative becoming is a transformative process of complex interactions of material agencies that can never be conclusive. Stated another way, creative becoming is the overall character of all compound individuals—species assemblages, inorganic actors, elements, and planetary forces—all entwined in "unfinished configurations of places, times, matters, meanings" (Haraway 2016, 1). We can think of this process in terms of dynamic Earth cycles as well, just like in the example of limestone nature writer Robert Macfarlane (2019) provides in *Underland: A Deep Time Journey*. Limestone is formed, writes Macfarlane, "of the compressed bodies of marine organisms . . . that died in waters of ancient seas" (32), and they built themselves by metabolizing the mineral content of the water. Limestone's creative becoming is part of the process of animal becoming mineral becoming rock.

To sum up, creative becoming is encoded in the entangled processes of world-making and will be ever-present in the futures to come for as long as compound individuals exist, which is crucial in Hartshorne's account. To explain in more detail, I now turn to Hartshorne's vision of compound individuals, as his claims about nature's constituents and the workings of the material world open a potential bridge to contemporary environmental theories about agency, life, matter, and nature. Hartshorne's view of the composite world of experiencing entities instantiates the significance of taking into consideration, philosophically and culturally, agentic materiality composed of relational modes of existence. Evidently, Hartshorne's account of compound individuals anticipates the new materialist understanding of material agencies that possess internal experiences and are involved in a meaningful process of interpreting their environment and making an effect on surrounding entities, processes, and flows of materialities. The concept of the compound individual has striking parallelisms with the new materialist conception of effective, creative, responsive, and distributive agency observable across a wide spectrum of living and nonliving matter. Hartshorne's account is thus deeply relevant to the new materialist theories of nonhuman entities. His concept of compound individuals is even more significant for material ecocriticism as it enables a new approach to the way expressive becoming is understood in material ecocriticism.

Compound Individuals

In Charles Hartshorne's philosophy, the material world is comprised of compound individuals, or material entities "comprising even the most elementary levels of nature" (Griffin 1998, 161) compounded of each other's experience and responses. Hartshorne developed the concept of the compound individual with varying degrees of compounding relationships embedded in the interactive processes of animal, vegetal, and mineral forms. A compound individual can be high-grade, such as humans and animals with central nervous systems, or low-grade, such as plants, molecules, cells, and bacteria. All compound individuals, however, enact and epitomize creativity and possess some degree of imagination, intelligence, and experience. More complex life-forms have a higher degree of cohering experience, which enables them to express a unity of feeling or purpose, but less complex life-forms also respond to their environment in a creative way. Bacteria, for example, as low-grade compound individuals, are the most prolific life-forms that literally designed the planet, determining the evolutionary processes on Earth, and they continue to orchestrate survivals and extinctions. Bacteria's creative experiences are enmeshed in evolutionary relations, ecological balances, and the precarious entanglements of human and nonhuman life. Being composite and distributed, bacteria make all species and material agencies with varying degrees of compounding relationships ontologically inseparable, thus urging us to review our coevolution in Earth's phenomenal geostory. In fact, coexisting with every life-form and biogeochemical forces on this planet, bacteria characteristically illustrate how creative experience has governed symbiotic relations in the microbial context, creating alliances and negotiations between and across species for about three billion years of life on the planet. The history of our planet is, therefore, the history of bacteria whose tales span unimaginable geological times and are intermingled with the stories of all living organisms and with all things that are, by definition, representations of past and present life. Molecular microbiologist Trudy M. Wassen writes that "approximately 1100 million years after" our planet formed, "bacteria already existed. We know this from fossil stromatolites," which "are 3.6 million years old and can only have been formed with the help of bacteria that lived in those early times" (2012, 2). As single-cell organisms, or prokaryotic cells that constitute the origin of all life, bacteria contain coded DNA.

For billions of years, then, bacteria were the only architects of life on the planet, driving planetary cycles of carbon, nitrogen, sulfur, and phosphorus, harnessing solar energy and releasing oxygen, and thus preparing the atmosphere for more complex cells to emerge, such as eukaryotic cells that comprise our bodies. Ingesting bacteria but not totally destroying them, the eukaryotic cells were the first living things to embody coexistence, which biologist Lynn Margulis (1999) defines in *Symbiotic Planet: A New Look at Evolution* as symbiotic assemblages—different species living in intimate relationship together. More specifically, this coexistence is called *endosymbiosis*, in which bacteria figure as symbionts. Because bacteria have been omnipresent since their emergence, we can call them the most ancient terrestrial artists of elemental creativity. Enmeshed in the rise and fall of civilizations, regulating processes of extinctions and survivals, and being expert ecosystem engineers, these common ancestors of all biological organisms on Earth are the perennial scribes of terrestrial and aquatic stories and the undeniable authors of all the processes of life. They are everywhere, including extreme environments: in Antarctic ice, in hydrothermal vents, in acidic waters, in volcanic rocks, and in every conceivable body that exists. Since they never cease to communicate with one another, bacteria never cease to be the active narrators of our planet's common geostory.

Using chemical signaling molecules to communicate with one another, bacteria are thus the prime example of creative and expressive becoming. Bacterial behaviors, as molecular biologists Stephan Schauder and Bonnie L. Bassler note, "are regulated by quorum sensing, including symbiosis, virulence, antibiotic production, and biofilm formation. Recent studies show that highly specific as well as universal quorum sensing languages exist which enable bacteria to communicate within and between species" (2001, 1468). Bacterium is a complex cell to perform creative expressions and belongs to the minimal physical systems. Stuart A. Kauffman, a prominent molecular biologist, calls this system "a molecular autonomous agent" (2008, 74) that is able to modify its immediate environment: "I mean that the agent can act on its own behalf in an environment, like the bacterium swimming up the glucose gradient or me going to the hardware store" (78). Like cells, molecular agents, according to Kauffman, are emergent, can self-reproduce, store energy, and "carry out at least one thermodynamic work cycle" (79). They can act and "evolve by heritable variation and natural selection that assembles the molecular systems in the cell that allow response to food or poison, typically by doing work" (79). That is why bacteria can be considered as one of the most distinctive low-grade compound individuals. Their distinctiveness comes from their successful way of "unsettl[ing] the human's place in the great chain of being and allow[ing] the agentic capability of nonhuman actors to be noted and appreciated" (Fishel 2017, 5). If a bacterium can be so effective as to unsettle human exceptionalism, then it is worth looking further into the agentic capabilities of other so-called low-grade compound individuals that Hartshorne thought enacted phases of creative becoming.

These low-grade individuals that creatively experience their becoming mentioned by Hartshorne are plants and stones. In his celebrated essay "The Compound Individual," Hartshorne argues that "plants and, to a lesser extent, metazoa without brains are of the latter or non-personal class. They are individuals only in a slight degree" (1936, 215). Although he prefers to call them "composite" instead of compound individuals, they are individual entities compounded of subordinate individual entities. A stone "as a colony of swirls of atoms (crystals)" (215), Hartshorne claims, is a composite individual of active electrons rather than inert, lifeless matter as it is believed to be. A stone is a low-grade individual in the sense of the "rhythmic repetition, and perpetual process" (216) of its electrons that comprise the stone. Hartshorne further contends that "the inner natures of electrons, atoms, or molecules are different from elsewhere; for their individualities have been in some degree suppressed or modified by the more powerful individuality to which they belong" (214). Therefore, he uses the terms high- or low-grade individuals to explain how creative freedom and experience arise at various levels of individuality.

In Hartshorne's conceptualization, regardless of being high- or low-grade, each compound individual has memory, even if utterly minimal, of a definite past, and anticipation, though it may be short range, of a partly open future. "The future, for all life," he writes in *Creative Synthesis and Philosophic Method*, "is what the past implies *plus* step by step decisions, none of which is concretely given until it has actually been taken. This is an example of the sanity inherent in life as such" (1970, 94; italics in original). In Hartshorne's vision, all compound individuals display a response-ability, and, regardless of their size, all make an effect on the surrounding entities, processes, and forces in their immediate environments. Compound individuals emerge from diverse patterns of creative processes that yield various agential possibilities (low or high grades) as emergent capacities to experience "creative becoming," which the new materialists interpret as "agentic properties inherent in nature itself" (Coole and Frost 2010, 20). Hence, agentic experience is an enactment of the causal dynamics of creative becoming through which the poetics of mutual life-making emerges.

Consisting of infinitesimal connections, effects, differences, and carrying layers of information on many levels, life is undeniably about coexistence. The coevolution of bees and flowers, microbes and immune systems, bodies and bacteria represents this postulation as viable instances that reflect deep patterns of coexistence. This is an ongoing process, the nature of which is shaped by immense creativity and experience exercised by compound individuals that exhibit self-organizing dynamics and internal relations. Creative experience is a capacity, which Hartshorne calls "spontaneous activity" discernible in the dynamic interactions of compound individuals' experiences in responding to their environment. In this "relational structure" (1936, 121), Hartshorne also observes that even "atoms, molecules, and still more nerve cells, seem to exhibit signs of spontaneous activity," claiming that "we can set no limits to the pervasiveness either of spontaneity or of feeling in nature.... This gives us a tremendous new speculative possibility, a great alternative to the Newtonian 'world-machine,' and to the dualism free mind and blindly obedient matter" (Hartshorne 1970, 8).

Against the objections raised to his claim that atoms also possess creative experience and some degree of feeling, Hartshorne states, "If atoms respond to stimuli (and they do), how else could they show that they sense and feel? And if you say, they have no sense organs, the reply is: neither do one-celled animals, yet they seem to perceive their environments" (1970, 6). Acknowledging the subjective experiences of compound individuals, Hartshorne concludes that "we have no conceivable ground for limiting feeling to our kind of individual, say the vertebrates, or even to animals" (144). The idea that the low-grade individuals may have some degree of experience is supported by contemporary science: "physiology has revealed that paramecia" (unicellular organisms) with neither motor nerves nor muscle cells "can swim," and "protozoa" (a diverse group of unicellular organisms) "can digest without a stomach and can oxygenate without lungs" (Griffin 1989, 11). If experience goes all the way down to subatomic particles too (protons, neutrons, electrons), then Hartshorne's claim gains legitimate ground. On this account, Hartshorne elaborates on the key ideas of Alfred North Whitehead's process philosophy. Whitehead had claimed that subatomic particles construct physical relationships with their environment, explaining atomic experience as having "a vector character"—energy transmissions that drive them:

> The experience has a vector character, a common measure of intensity, and specific forms of feelings that convey that intensity. If we substitute the term "energy" for the conception of a quantitative emotional intensity, and the term "form of energy" for the concept of "specific form of feeling," and remember that in physics "vector" means definite transmissions from elsewhere, we see that this metaphysical description of the simplest elements in the constitution of actual entities agrees absolutely with the general principles according to which the notions of modern physics are framed. ([1929] 1978, 116)

Electrons are packages of energy without definite locations. They are attracted to positively charged protons in the atomic center, move between energy levels, and exhibit both wave and particle properties. Thus, in Whitehead and Hartshorne's interpretations, they can form causal relationships in spacetime. An electron, in this perspective, can be said to *experience* (without any consciousness of course) its physical relations with other packages of energy in causal relationships. This happens in the atomic world, and space around it regulated by an inherent law of interconnectedness is explained in quantum physics as "a strong nonlocal connection of distant particles and a strong dependence of the particle on its general environmental context" (Bohm and Hiley 1993, 177). As such, experience and communication also characterize the quantum world. Process philosopher Robert C. Mesle provides a deeply compelling argument in *Process-Relational Philosophy: An Introduction to Alfred North Whitehead*, where he states that "the idea that experience goes all the way down—is present throughout the natural world" (2008, 38–39). And this should not be too surprising because if experience, Mesle observes,

> does not go all the way down, how can it arise in a world whose basic constituents are totally devoid of experience? If it does go all the way down, it seems unsurprising that, as these elementary drops of feeling are organized into successively more complex forms, like molecules and cells and animal bodies, central nervous systems and brains, the complexity of those feelings will increase until it crosses a crucial threshold into conscious self-awareness such as you are having right now. (37)

Mesle's reasoning is quite convincing, but for those in search of supportive scientific evidence about experience going all the way down to the realm of subatomic particles, let us briefly review a thought experiment that has been tested to prove the interconnections internal to "vibrant" essence of matter, or what Whitehead would call "occasions" of experience. When quantum physicist John A. Wheeler (1978) proposed a *Gedankenexperiment* known as a "delayed choice experiment," claiming that a photon in the double-slit experiment would know in advance whether an observation was going to be made, change its behavior to that of a wave or particle accordingly, and respond to the experimenter's delayed-choice instantly, physicists began to search for experiential evidence. It was not easy, but on February 16, 2007, French physicists from the École Normale Supérieure de Cachan successfully tested Wheeler's thought experiment and demonstrated that photons infer the presence of an observer before they are emitted.

> Our realization of Wheeler's delayed choice Gedanken Experiment demonstrates beyond any doubt that the behavior of the photon in the interferometer depends on the choice of the observable, which is measured, even when that choice is made at a position and a time such that it is separated from the entrance of the photon in the interferometer by a space-like interval. (Jacques et al. 2007, 968)

A similar experiment took place in 2009 in the Canary Islands, where "the successful transmission of one photon of an entangled pair was recently achieved" between La Palma and Tenerife (Fedrizzi et al. 2009, 389). If such interconnectedness exists in the subatomic realm from which higher orders of experience emerge, then in much the same way high-grade individuals are intimately connected in the reciprocal way each experiences the world. The significance of this knowledge for environmental thought is that, quoting Mesle again, "we could finally leave behind the last vestiges of Cartesian dualism, finally leave behind a supernatural view of the human mind, and finally see ourselves as 100 percent natural instances of the larger world around us" (2008, 37).

For his part, Hartshorne's interpretation of compound individuals demonstrates similarly that all life-forms, and even "lifeless" entities like electrons, have a certain degree of cohering experience and creativity. Compared to atoms, molecules, macromolecules, and cells, more complex life-forms like multicellular animals have a higher degree of cohering experience, which enables them to express a unity of feeling or purpose. Human beings are the most complex kind of compound individuals, though not ontologically different from the low-grade ones. The difference in question lies in the complexity of being compounded of other bodies, and thus appropriating highly complex data, and the evolution of the mind. This is what David Ray Griffin, another prominent process philosopher, proclaims. Following Hartshorne's explication of less complex low-grade individuals, like the "quantum and vibratory phenomena" that have "a briefer memory span" (Hartshorne 1936, 213), Griffin contends that "low-grade individuals, such as protons, appear to remain virtually the same for millions or even billions of years, whereas human minds obviously change their characters over time, incorporating novel elements into their relatively enduring characters" (1998, 193–94). In comparison, electrons "can appropriate only very little data," while molecules driving data from their subatomic constituents "can appropriate a little more" (193). In this line of reasoning, as Griffin concludes, "greater increases in richness of experience and in self-determining capacity would occur in macromolecules, then viruses, then bacteria and organelles" (1998, 193). Interestingly, however, both high- and low-grade individuals are "characterized by increasingly significant hybrid physical prehensions" (195).[9] Principally, this premise leads to the conclusion that, like the mind that depends on the prehensions of "the billions of living occasions in the brain cells" (Griffin 1998, 197) to function, the human body is composed of countless entities that coordinate the experiences of any part of the body, and to do so they must have rudimentary forms of self-determination, memory, and thus some form of sentience. In Hartshorne's account, if there are "degrees of immanence, degrees of memory, and of originative power, the entire known structure of the world may be interpreted, from space-time as the most general pattern of immanence to the specific characters of photons, molecules, plants, and animals" (1936, 213). Hartshorne offers a vivid sense of the human body as "a vast nexus or interlocked colony of relatively low-grade individuals" (212), such as nerve cells. Everything that comprises the body is "mutually dependent on each other, although certain cells (nerve cells) have greatest influence" (213). Rather than acting mindlessly or without any sense of self-determination, nerve cells exhibit some degree of sentience subtended by internal relations (internally related to other cells). In Hartshorne's words,

> the cells of one's body are . . . constantly furnishing their little experiences or feelings which, being pooled in our more comprehensive experience, constitute what we call our sensations. And the cells, in their fashion, respond to or experience our experiences, as is shown by the influence which our thoughts and feelings have upon our bodily changes. (1970, 7)

The point here is that nerve cells possess agency constitutive of their internally related activities and experiences. This takes us to the idea that no entity exists independently of its environment, and all entities have a degree of self-determination in their coevolutionary process, even if self-determination may be minimal, for instance at the atomic level. This is not only a philosophical suggestion: biologists have provided evidence that supports this view that all entities have internal relations. According to the findings of empirical investigations, as molecular biologist Charles Birch suggests, "an internal relation determines the nature of the entity, indeed even its very existence" (1988, 70). Birch affirms that what makes matter more than mere matter "is the degree of self-determination exercised by natural entities in response to possibilities of their future" (75). This is what the biologists today confirm. Considering the new evidence, plants, for example, exhibit signs of associative learning, determining what dangers to avoid and what interactions to form with other organisms. These are "ecologically meaningful signals involved in different interactions of plants with biotic and abiotic agents" (Pinto et al. 2019, 708). Biologists H. M. Appel and R. B. Cocroft (2014) demonstrated that plants are able to detect the chewing sounds of herbivores and respond rapidly to possible threats. They report that "*Arabidopsis thaliana* plants exposed to chewing vibrations produced greater amounts of chemical defenses in response to subsequent herbivory, and that the plants distinguished chewing vibrations from other environmental vibrations" (2014, 1258). Referring to the same study, evolutionary ecologist Monica Gagliano also notes that such scientific studies prove the existence of "vegetal subjectivity and awareness" among plants (2017a, e1288333-3). The fact that plants have internal relations is evinced by their "ability to learn through the formation of associations," which Gagliano observes,

> involves the ability to detect, discriminate and categorize cues according to a *dynamic internal value system*. This is a subjective system of feelings and experiences, motivated by the overall sensory state of the individual in the present and its extension via internal representations of the world experienced in the past; representations that, as mentioned earlier, play a fundamental role in the decision-making process by providing a reference for the kind of expectations that the individual projects in the future. (e1288333-2-3)

These studies offer new critical pathways for understanding how the nonhuman (plants in this case) regulates its ways of becoming, connections with other species, and being in the world to ensure "conditions of livability and collective survival" (Gan 2017, 88). The plant's networks of relations, its capacity for self-determination, and its decision-making in battles for survival verify Hartshorne's conviction that "to live is indeed to decide, and decide anew each moment," and also "to foresee, to deal with the future" (1970, 6). Inviting us to reimagine the world, these new developments in scientific fields, as anticipated by Hartshorne, have important consequences for "the overall quality of relationships . . . between human beings and the rest of nature" (Bohm 1988, 59). In other words, the evident agentic capacity observed in agentic entities changes our understanding of the more-than-human world from the Cartesian view of life based on the mechanistic models of nature to an ecological model that acknowledges the living world in its complex networks of relations. In essence, this model amounts to a change in our understanding of agency, consequently giving rise, as David Bohm had hoped, "to a new order, in the consciousness of both the individual and society" (1988, 59).

We have seen that when we take the notion of agency into account in terms of the internal relations of both high- and low-grade individuals, agency in the physical phenomena stretches not only across species and abiotic matter on macroscopic but also microscopic scales of existence. This is, then, in the words of process theologian John B. Cobb Jr., a "dynamic world of interrelated activities" (1988, 109) that constitute more-than-human environments, and among them are the cellular activities in the human body out of which human experience grows. The human body is "made of cells, which are made of molecules, which are made of electrons, protons, and neutrons, which are bundles of energy/experience bound together in spatial-temporal fields of causal relationships" (Mesle 2008, 37). Considering these bundles of energy as "elementary drops of feeling" that are "organized into successively more complex forms, like molecules and cells and animal bodies, central nervous systems and brains," Mesle notes that "the complexity of those feelings will increase until it crosses a crucial threshold into conscious self-awareness such as you are having right now" (37). If agency functions this way, it must be composed of multiple interacting entities, including the most elementary units of matter that experience the world in various degrees of creative becoming. From the subatomic to the higher levels of evolution, as Hartshorne's philosophy of "shared creative experience" (1970, 1) suggested, internal relations mark the agentic capacities of both the most elementary particles and the most advanced forms of matter. Seen as such, agency is not restricted to human intentionality and action; it is an enactment of creative response distributed over multiple material forms experiencing "creative becoming" (Hartshorne 1970, 13). This is how Hartshorne had conceived reality, compelling us to "imagine the universe as a vast system of experiencing individuals on innumerable levels. Each such individual is in some measure free; for experiencing is a partly free act. Thus creativity, emergent novelty, is universal" (6). It follows that the same claim is in the new materialist paradigm, albeit in different terminology that nevertheless maintains the same orientation toward the universality of creativity. Hence, what Hartshorne called the compound individual resurfaces as "agentic matter" in the new materialist theory and as "narrative agency" in material ecocriticism.

The Compound Individual as Material Agency

In the new materialist perspective, Diana Coole and Samantha Frost explain in their memorable introduction to *New Materialisms: Ontology, Agency, and Politics* (2010), compound individuals are material agencies with "active, self-creative, productive, unpredictable" (9) and "immanently self-organizing properties subtended by an intricate filigree of relationships" (13). The defining feature of the new materialist paradigm is the claim that matter exerts agency and possesses creative power as part of its generative dynamism, seen as "a swarm of vibrant materials entering and leaving agentic assemblages" (Bennett 2010, 117). Material ecocriticism expands this vision, claiming that all vibrant materials are storied with different capacities of expressive creativity while surging through and shaping the material-semiotic world in which we are also corporeally and viscerally immersed.

If reality is conceived as "creative disclosure" (2010, 113), as Diana Coole suggests, echoing Hartshorne's notion of creative becoming, then ultimately life turns out to be consciousness "in a more or less dormant or active state," as the material-feminist theorist Elizabeth Grosz (2010, 148) expounds, also curiously echoing Hartshorne's vision. For Grosz, consciousness is "the projection onto materiality of the possibility of a choice, a decision whose outcome is not given in advance" (149). Her concession that even the most elementary lifeforms, "from the protozoa upward, exhibit a kind of incipient freedom in some of their most significant actions" (149), is like a postscript to Hartshorne's conjecture, a reframed endorsing of his central idea of compound individuals that possess innate modes of self-transformation and various degrees of internal relations. Since Grosz's views are presumably at the crux of the new materialist discourse, Hartshorne's account of the agential dynamics of matter gains a specific significance. It is in this context that the new materialist discourse intersects with Hartshorne's description of compound individuals. His emphasis on creativity and experience resurfaces in the accounts of the key new materialist theorists: for instance, with the wider onto-epistemology of Karen Barad's agential realism, which explains the world's dynamism as agency, defined as "*'doing' or 'being' in its intra-activity*" (2007, 178; italics in original); with Jane Bennett's theory of vibrant materialism that recasts matter as onto-story where "everything is, in a sense, alive" (2007, 117); with Donna Haraway's vision of "multidirectional relationships, in which always more than one responsive entity is in the process of becoming" (2008a, 71); with Bruno Latour's actants, entities that "seriously modif[y] other actors through a series of trials" (2004, 75); with Andrew Pickering's mangle, a shorthand for "the emergently intertwined" human and nonhuman agencies (1995, 21); and with the views of Manuel DeLanda, Rosi Braidotti, David Abram, Jeffrey J. Cohen, Vicki Kirby, among many others. Yielding a view of nature as a realm of creative experiences, Hartshorne's conception of the compound individual is undeniably a significant source for the new materialist theorizing of matter's agential propensities.

In an interview with Adam Kleinman for the Italian magazine *Mousse*, Barad also complements Hartshorne's concept with her notion of agential intra-actions by proposing a similar theory of "individuals" that "only exist within phenomena (particular materialized/materializing relations) in their ongoing iteratively intra-active reconfiguring" (2012a, 77). Intra-action is a viable mode of interpreting the complexity and differences of compound individuals within the phenomena constituted by "the entanglement—the ontological inseparability—of intra-acting agencies," and through which "the boundaries and properties of 'individuals' . . . become determinate and particular material articulations of the world become meaningful" (77). The phenomena can be seen as relational fields within which compound individuals move with "differential responsiveness" and "differential articulations" (Barad 2007, 335), thus revealing emergent patterns of intelligibility. This is central to understanding the new materialist vision that "life . . . is not an inherent property of separate individual entities but rather an entangled agential performance of the world" (Barad 2008, 174). In this sense, Hartshorne's concept is congruent with Barad's conception of matter, and thus consonant with the fundamental parameters of the new materialist paradigm.

Since Hartshorne's insights also inform material ecocriticism's conceptual frames, the compound individual must be acknowledged in tracing the genealogy of narrative agency. The concept of the compound individual not only invites a more relational vision of reality but also provides compelling reasons for exploring the expressive dimension of vibrant materiality in terms of its embodied narratives. Material ecocriticism reworks Hartshorne's concept of the compound individual as a narrative agency instantiated in all entities that possess expressive creativity, intelligibility, and effectivity. One of the main achievements of material ecocriticism, then, is to have restored awareness of creative expression as a built-in constituent of matter.

The Compound Individual as Narrative Agency

Based on the premise that if matter is agentic, it must also be capable of expressing itself, and if it can express itself, then it is storied matter capable of producing narratives, material ecocriticism claims that the world is an ancient site of narrativity whereby material agencies communicate intelligibly with other entities and produce meaning-filled encounters with everything else around them. Signifying a nonlinguistic performance inherent in every material formation, narrative agency is the building block of storied matter "in its ongoing articulation" (Barad 2007, 149). Storied matter is "the defining property of all matter beyond and including the biological world" (Oppermann 2018, 412). Perceiving all material agencies as "storied subjects of an ever-unfolding onto-tale," material ecocriticism claims that matter has a signifying agency with "ongoing configurations of signs and meanings that we interpret as stories" (Oppermann 2018, 412). Accordingly, matter is never semiotically inert and inseparable from the general field of signification in which narrative agencies produce a stream of creative expressions, but as Hartshorne would say, in "different degrees of compounding . . . relationships(s)" (1936, 212). Let's consider stones again, which just stay where they are unless moved by an external force and show no sign of having feelings, desires, and purposes or any power of self-motion. Is an ordinary stone, then, an expressive, creative compound individual? Is stone a narrative agency? According to Hartshorne, stones may not have dominating experience, but the highest centers of feeling and self-determination are the atoms and molecules that comprise the stone. Refuting the understanding that the "stone and its molecules are presumed to be absolutely dead" while "the animal body and its cells are alive" (1936, 215), Hartshorne reminds us of the stone's active electrons that are not revealed to the senses but make the stone quite alive as a low-grade individual. In *Stone: An Ecology of the Inhuman*, Jeffrey J. Cohen similarly contends that stone is neither dead matter nor a static entity; rather stone has innate vitality and its stories become apparent when humans form alliances with it. "Stones bring story into being" (2015, 4) says Cohen, and they are our partners with which, he argues, we "build the epistemological structures that may topple upon us. They are ancient allies in knowledge making" (4). Stones, then, are narrative agencies, and like every other narrative agency, stones also "enhance receptivity to the impersonal life that surrounds and infuses us" (Bennett 2010, 4), and they pull the allegedly separate human back into the collective life story.

David Abram also argues that matter's "expressive, telluric power" (2010, 171) makes it a meaning-producing embodiment of the world in its creative becoming. This implies that "the creativity we find in ourselves has its correlations in the surrounding cosmos" (Abram 2010, 71). As if restating Hartshorne's postulation of creative becoming, Abram's pertinent vision is that "each sensible thing is steadily bodying forth its own active creativity and sentience" (170). In Hartshorne's view, although compound individuals such as cells, molecules, or animals are composed of one another, they are not mere aggregates of one another (for example, cells are not aggregates of subatomic particles); rather, they are internally related to each other by virtue of their experiences. They are not "ontologically different in kind, only different in degree," as in the example Griffin provides of the cells and their constituting parts composing the brain, which is "the *regnant* or *dominant* member" (Griffin 2001, 147; italics in original). This means that as high-grade individuals, our experience "is a series of discrete drops of experience" (157) arising out of the low-grade individuals' experiences. But all constituent parts of our body exercise "a degree of self-determination" (135). As Griffin further explains:

> In a compound individual, the more complex experience enjoyed by the regnant member includes a greater capacity for self-determination. Because the human being is not simply an aggregational society, but a compound individual, the spontaneity existing at the level of subatomic

particles is, far from being canceled out by the law of large numbers, greatly amplified. (147)

The only, perhaps minimal, difference between Hartshorne's conception of the compound individual and narrative agency is that, in the latter, matter's expressive capacity is not *wholly* subject-centered (even though it carries nuances of individual entities) but unfolds in manifold relations in agentic assemblages extending to collectives of nonhuman beings, microorganisms, subatomic particles, inorganic macro-matter, and geological forces. Expressed differently, agency is "diffused across multiple entities and achieves its capacity within assemblages" (Carranza 2018). Hence, narrative agency is "spread across a wide spectrum of [matter's] organic and inorganic forms" (Oppermann 2018, 412), representing the storied world in which "we—along with the other animals, plants, and landforms—are all characters" (Abram 2010, 270). In this world, human beings are, in Roberto Marchesini's poetic rendering, "a Gordian knot of relational stories, insoluble and inextricable, intertwining time in a dialectical assimilation" (2016, 146). So are animals, plants, glaciers, stones, genes, cells, atoms, and the list goes on, whose narratives of biogeological evolution surface time and again not as "incompossible storylines," to borrow Ridvan Askin's term (2016, 22), but as interwoven threads of storied matter. Human or nonhuman, everything is in fact "in this strange ontogenesis, stratified—like a novel—into constitutively different chapters" (Marchesini 2016, 146).

In such a stratified novel, the multiscalar, multigenerational chapters of narrative agencies unveil the multilayered ecologies of our storied planet that are always in dialogue with its storied parts in "a long thread of relations, where every adaptation, competition, confrontation, or symbiosis is inscribed in [its] body, like moraines drawn by glaciers" (Marchesini 2016, 146). What Marchesini says about phylogenesis also holds true for our planet at large: "simultaneously a book to read, a storyteller, and a diary recording a billion-year-old journey" (2016, 146). As cosmologist Brian Swimme similarly intimates, the planet and all its life-forms tell stories: "Rocks, soils, waves, stars . . . tell their story in 10,000 languages throughout the planet, they bind us to them in our emotions, our spirits, our minds, and our bodies. The Earth and the universe speak in all this" (1988, 56). Moreover, moving with its own rhythms, Swimme claims, "the universe at its most basic level, is story" (48). The late biosemiotician Wendy Wheeler also affirms that "life is made of stories" (2014, 77).

If life is a manifestation of creative expressions, then everything in and around us must be an extension of matter's creative experience. This is the diagnostic character of an evolving self-articulate universe and our storied planet itself, conveying, as astrophysicist Eric Chaisson concurs, "a rich and abiding story of our origins that is nothing less than an epic of creation as understood by modern science" (2005, xiii). Likewise, physical chemist and Nobel laureate Ilya Prigogine declares, "Everywhere we see narrative stages" (2003, 8). Moreover, narrative agencies "enter the world of communication and meaning," as Gregory Bateson would argue, "by reports of their internal and external relations and interactions" (1979, 61). The material ecocritical interpretations of this pervasive narrativity entail a relational understanding of "nature" as a realm of intra-acting agencies connected through multiple relations and communicative acts to realize their creative becoming.

If narrative agency is framed by a communicative process, then narratives are specific enactments of creative becoming found across the nonhuman world, making language "a property of animate earth itself" (Abram 2010, 171). Whether perceived or interpreted by the human mind, every organism, every geological formation, every object carries copious stories, which "shape trajectories that have a formative, enactive power" (Iovino and Oppermann 2014, 7).

It is important to note here that the narrative agencies of storied matter emerge "through humans but not entirely because of them" (Bennett 2010, 17). Jeffrey J. Cohen agrees with Bennett's view that the stories of matter emerge through humans, but at the same time, he claims, "humans themselves emerge through 'material agencies' that leave their traces in lives as well as stories, so that narratives are always animated by multifarious vectors and heterogeneous possibilities not reducible to mere anthropomorphism" (2015, 36). In his view, storied matter "is thick with surprising narratives," some are "vivid," some barely legible or easily identifiable, and "others impossible to discern or translate" (275). Be that as it may, narrative agencies slide through human "expressways" often unnoticed but always exerting their influence in conceptual and material habitats, like Jane Bennett's trash items in the gutter in Baltimore: "one large black work glove, one dense mat of oak pollen, one unblemished dead rat, one white plastic bottle cap, one smooth stick of wood" (2012, 238), which she says, "revealed themselves to be expressive 'actants'" (239). The signifying function of these items, Bennett notices, may be interpreted as emergent narrative agencies of storied matter calling for exploration. Bennett realizes that this "call" should be taken seriously, "taken, that is, as more than a figure of speech, more than a projection of voice onto some inanimate stuff" (239). As this example shows, in a very real sense, the Earth with all its constituent parts is a storied world with a rich narrative efficacy and creative agency, insofar as it is "characterized by myriad and complex processes of materialization" (Haynes 2014, 134).

Impressed in all forces, energies, processes, elements, and organisms, narrative agencies unfold from these human–nonhuman interactions in which the human is intimately entangled with the nonhuman in complex encounters, confrontations, and negotiations. In other words, the genealogies of humans and nonhumans overlap, creating a "meshwork of alliances" (Cohen 2015, 33) in the storied world. Such an alliance is realized when we notice that we share a world with other beings, which, as Tim Ingold notes, "continually *unfolds* in relation to the beings that make a living there" (2011, 30; italics in original). Resembling the Apollo–Dionysus pair in ecospheres, microscopic realms, eruptive climates, as well as in cultural and literary spaces, human and nonhuman agents produce narratives that may be compellingly affirmative (the songs of whales, the whisper of the wind) or unexpectedly disruptive (plastics in the oceans, deadly viruses, toxic substances). Hartshorne saw a "creative synthesis" (1970, 18) in this world of wondrous as well as disruptive vitality, and forty years later Bruno Latour would coin the term *compositionist* to describe it: "this common world has to be built from utterly heterogeneous parts that will never make a whole, but at best a fragile, revisable, and diverse composite material" (2010, 474). It is in this composite materiality that narrative agencies convey their stories, connecting genetic, metabolic, ecological, and social realms. They are the implicit authors of the planet's "epic of evolution" (Swimme 1998, 2–5). In Eric Chaisson's memorable elucidation:

> Together, genes and fossils chronicle an amazing story of life on Earth. Biochemists who amass digital genomes are now pooling their talents with paleontologists who scour fossilized bones. The results provide increasingly robust details of that story, regularly revealing torn and tattered pages here, occasionally uncovering whole new chapters there. (2005, 299)

This unfolding story principally confirms the timeless existence of storied matter abundant with meaningfully articulate forms of creative becoming. Storied matter only dissolves our conceited worldview and disturbs our conventional sense of storytelling, but it also helps us notice how trees, for example, "make meaning as well as oxygen" (Macfarlane 2019, 110). Although not every narrative agency of storied matter is metabolically alive, their stories of life "take us beyond the modern individual" (Swanson, Tsing, and Bubandt 2017, M9). Understanding storied matter, then, is synonymous with understanding the implicit textuality in the creative becoming of material formations that carry stories of evolution, survivals, extinctions, dissolutions, and relationalities, intra-acting with human wit and imagination. With this position, we have the basis for sympathizing, in Hartshorne words, "with the universal 'life of things,' the 'ocean of feelings,' which is reality in its concrete character" (1970, 144).

At the close of this chapter, I want to specifically underline the point that narrative agencies do not spill out of some vicarious poetic fancy or literary imagination, nor is storied matter a mere conceptualization or a cultural construction to grant the nonhuman meaningful existence. On the contrary, narrative agency represents a new ecology for understanding the ultimate ontology of a meaningfully articulate planet in which compound individuals "lure us toward the possibilities of engaging the force of imagination in its materiality ... in its ongoing thought experiments with being/becoming" (Barad 2012b, 216). But, more than a thought experiment, narrative agencies are real agentic entities that can modify our understanding of nonhuman natures. Emphasizing a wide spectrum of vibrant ontology, they incorporate the self-organizing structure of living matter in its creative becoming, as Hartshorne had suggested.

Moreover, storied matter not only makes us aware that the world we inhabit is, in various senses, alive with signs, sounds, colors, and stories but also issues serious warnings from the flows of Earth changes that reflect a global ecological crisis. We need to understand that the stories narrative agencies convey today are profoundly troubling, like the traumatic tales of countless plastic objects that compose the infamous Great Pacific Garbage Patch. These objects are narrative agencies that veered off course to demonstrate the dire consequences of the social and the natural interpenetrating each other in the slow death of so many marine species. The stories of plastic-choked Laysan albatross on Midway Island in the North Pacific Ocean also epitomize how plastic as storied matter can produce profoundly distressing trajectories. If we consider this oceanic plastic interacting with human lives via the food chain, we can clearly see that storied matter is full of cautionary tales about our mutual existence and destiny. This is a catastrophic creativity, an unfolding story of disrupted ecologies that propels us to act toward change for healthier environments.

The communicative network of intelligence encoded in nature evoked an "ocean of feelings" for Hartshorne, but today it is an "ocean of grief" when we reflect on the health of the planet's increasingly deteriorating biospheres and ecosystems.[10] Therefore, heeding the stories of matter can help us better understand fragile ecosystems, polluted landscapes, carbon-filled atmosphere, acidifying oceans, changing climate, species extinctions, and social crises. Through these stories we learn to listen to the voices of the Earth, which have become quite disenchanted with catastrophic human practices. Hence, thinking about matter's expressive dynamics, its creative experience in the overly disenchanted world, also means thinking seriously about how our invasive social and economic practices produce planetary cycles of pollution, how our political decisions and cultural meanings are enmeshed in their production, and how they all enfold into one indissoluble process. Reading the world as storied materiality that binds all beings, forces, and substances with interconnected stories can help impart new ideas and insights about our experiences and perceptions of the planet. This is what material ecocriticism especially espouses: recognizing the creative expressions in the storied world, engaging in nonanthropocentric conversations with the nonhuman realities, and developing critical self-reflection on our part as humans. Then new Anthroposcenarios can emerge, reclaiming our storied planet as a site of interdependent human and nonhuman meanings and value. If such visions infuse our thinking and acting in both private and public terms, the destructive impulse of anthropocentrism can be eliminated.

Chapter 2

The Scale of the Anthropocene and New Anthroposcenarios

A lonely sphere in the surrounding cosmic vastness, our blue planet in our solar system is the only world known so far to harbor multilevels of life. However, with about 200 plants, insects, birds, and mammal species becoming extinct every day (Vidal 2011), the Earth will likely face the sixth mass extinction. There is no sign that help will come from another world to save us from the folly of our own conceits, as astrophysicist Carl Sagan once said (1994, 13, 36), and nowhere else, at least in the near future, to which we could migrate, let alone settle. In his foreword to Thomas E. Lovejoy and Lee Hannah's edited collection *Biodiversity and Climate Change: Transforming the Biosphere,* the influential biologist and entomologist Edward O. Wilson notes that the estimates of such unprecedented disappearance "range between one hundred and one thousand times the rate that existed before humanity spread around the world. And it is accelerating" (2019, xii). This is a seismic rupture in "the continuous flow of life" and in the "fundamental processes that nurture that flow" (Leakey and Lewin 1996, 6). As noted by many scientists, intellectuals, activists, and concerned citizens across the globe, life that took millions of years to evolve is now being dismantled on many levels, and it is no longer possible to ignore the planet's distress signals, which force every one of us to renounce our self-deceptive dreams of mastery that only cause worsening ecological crises. Already in 2019, the chorus of cries from the burning Arctic peat, the Amazon and Australian wildfires, and dying glaciers joined other previously unheard voices of the Earth, tangibly warning us that what is to come will be extremely inimical to species survival in the long term. Recognized as a pandemic by the World Health Organization on March 11, 2020, the COVID-19 virus that emerged in Wuhan, China, in December 2019 and had a tsunami effect all over the world in the following months and years is a clear indication of this predicament. Climate change no doubt exacerbates this problem, and viruses benefit from it as they adapt to changes in a climate more rapidly than any other micro- or macroorganism. Science reporter Sarah Kaplan (2020) writes that "by altering the environment at a faster rate than any other moment in geologic history, scientists say, humans have created a wealth of chances for viruses to evolve." The coronavirus can be read as a signal of distress emerging from what Steven Hartman and I have explicitly called "the Earth's interlinked systems," which the world's nations have "failed overwhelmingly to heed" (2020, 4). In "Seeds of Transformative Change," we argued that

> these same societies have failed to act collectively on the momentous knowledge brought to their attention by the international scientific community on the global scale required if we are to avert consequences in the foreseeable future that could well be catastrophic. As organized at national and international levels, human societies seem unprepared to act upon the seriousness of the threats identified in ways that decisively ameliorate the risks they bear. Not even when more routine scientific assessments (such as the reports published at regular intervals by the IPCC for the past 30 years) give way to extraordinary warnings from the scientific community. (Hartman and Oppermann 2020, 4–5)

The future, in this respect, seems to hold the worst possibilities for humans because the coronavirus is "oblivious to human intentions, desires, and motives," as N. Katherine Hayles perceptively notes (2020). It is so because "the agency of a single gene sequence," as Simon C. Estok, famed for his work on ecophobia, proclaims, has already brought "the airline industry to its knees, cost the world trillions of dollars in losses, infect[ed] and kill[ed] millions of people, . . . and yet somehow, we seem to have collectively forgotten that pandemics are environmental events" (2021, 181). The same deadly virus, however, has offered transformative opportunities to the more-than-human world during the human lockdown all over the planet. "Since the outbreak of Covid-19, carbon emissions have plummeted," writes nature writer and activist Rebecca Solnit in an April 2020 article for *The Guardian*. The coronavirus is not only an echo chamber of the ongoing transformations in capitalist "war against the Earth," as Solnit puts it, but also a clear warning to humanity that the dynamics of this war will have devastating consequences for humanity. In essence, reveling in unsustainable economic practices that continue to trigger environmental changes might turn a distressing future scenario into present-day reality.

Many signs of change observed and documented in the oceans—for example, "in the distribution of ice, and in the salinity, levels, and temperatures of the oceans" (Glick 2019)— point to such a storyline. The Special Report on the Ocean and Cryosphere in a Changing Climate, *Global Warming of 1.5°C* (IPCC

2019)—the third in a series of reports produced in the Intergovernmental Panel on Climate Change (IPCC)'s Sixth Assessment Cycle—lists

> impacts and cascading risks of climate driven changes (e.g., sea level rise, ocean circulation, extreme events), interacting with other drivers, on habitability, infrastructure, communities, livelihoods, loss of lives and assets and territories, infrastructure, ecosystems, coral reefs, access to resources, and on institutional, social, economic, and cultural aspects.[1]

This is the interlocking reality of the Anthropocene epoch we are currently living in, calling for urgent action "to develop a credible and just plan for rapid total decarbonization of the economy," as stated in the declaration of Australian academics, "We Declare Our Support for Extinction Rebellion: An Open letter from Australia's Academics," which was published in the international edition of *The Guardian* on September 19, 2019. The same urgency has also been underlined in "World Scientists' Warning to Humanity: A Second Notice," published in *BioScience* in December 2017. As one of the signatories, I would like to reiterate that "we have unleashed a mass extinction event, the sixth in roughly 540 million years, wherein many current life-forms could be annihilated or at least committed to extinction by the end of this century" (Ripple et al. 2017, 1026). The anthropogenic climate crises and environmental changes in the Anthropocene have unquestionably accelerated, impacting every life-form on Earth, including humans who act upon the global climate with unsustainable economic practices without much ethical concern. The following "Viewpoint" article, "World Scientists' Warning of a Climate Emergency" by William Ripple et al., which I also signed (and anyone reading this should do so, too, to support this initiative), proclaims that "the climate crisis is more severe than anticipated, threatening natural ecosystems and the fate of humanity" (2020, 9) and lists disturbing signs of this reality:

> Three abundant atmospheric GHGs (CO_2, methane, and nitrous oxide) continue to increase . . . (ominous 2019 spike in CO_2), as does global surface temperature . . . Climate change is predicted to greatly impact marine, freshwater, and terrestrial life, from plankton and corals to fishes and forests (IPCC 2018, 2019). These issues highlight the urgent need for action. (8)[2]

In this article, scientists suggest six critical and interrelated steps concerning "Energy," "Short-lived pollutants," "Nature," "Food," "Economy," and "Population" (Ripple et al. 2020, 10, 11) required to lessen the dreadful effects of climate change caused by the exponential increase in the use of fossil fuel energy. They call for a qualitative social transformation to maintain the Earth in a manageable interglacial state and thus to prevent the collapse of civilizations: "Mitigating and adapting to climate change while honoring the diversity of humans entails major transformations in the ways our global society functions and interacts with natural ecosystems" (11). This discourse, however, "does not give us any hints as to how the kind of deep change in human collective intelligence that is necessary can be brought about to meet the irreversible, catastrophic and systemic consequences of the Anthropocene" (Degeorges and Oppermann 2019). But, in the face of all the indisputable evidence that the planet has been warming rapidly due to the accumulating greenhouse gases in the atmosphere, and spreading and mutating viruses making matters worse, we cannot remain neutral and disengaged from the problem. Thus, rather than embracing despair, we need "to re-imagine the prism through which this existential challenge is framed" (Degeorges and Oppermann 2019). Material ecocriticism, in this regard, can provide some valuable guidance as to how we might reimagine this and offer a way out of our apathetic responses to our planet's emergency sirens.

This chapter is, therefore, a rethinking of the Anthropocene through the lens of material ecocriticism, which helps ground the Anthropocene discourse in ethics of responsibility and poetics of care and attentiveness for the remaining more-than-human beings all swirling dangerously within the human-induced environmental crises. My main argument is that the material ecocritical vision can successfully navigate the issues, complexities, and intersecting stories of the Anthropocene agencies and human beings while still demanding that humans take responsibility for their ecosystem/climate/environment-changing actions. Material ecocriticism, in essence, opens a path to the possibility of generating new Anthroposcenarios, in which the Anthropos, a generic human figure manifesting as a geological force, will no longer be discussed as "a category mistake in the conceptualization of the Anthropocene, and a recipe for political paralysis" (Head 2014, 116). This means that, in the new Anthroposcenario, this figure will lose its status as an epoch-making subject operating across multispecies habitats in messy ways but will appear in the plural as earthbound beings ultimately inseparable from other species, substances, elements, and geobiochemical forces, or from the environment in the wider sense. The prevailing Anthroposcenarios generate a characteristic "grand explanatory species story" (Nixon 2014), or what Jeffrey J. Cohen underlines as "narratives of worldly obliteration" (2017a, 246) about humanity's geological powers fatefully entangled with fossil records, stratigraphic evidence, and living species. The standard Anthroposcenarios define the Anthropocene "as an act of writing ourselves into the rock record," implying "a kind of textual materiality in geological events" (Heringman 2015, 58). Haunted by ecological doom and disaster scenarios, such narratives yield an anxiety-driven globalist perspective on the prospects of multispecies extinctions and possible survivals. In the new Anthroposcenario, however, the stories of earthly agencies can be told in what Donna Haraway calls "multispecies storytelling" practice (2016, 10), which can be expanded to the narrative potential embedded in all forms of matter, so that humans are not understood to be the only beings capable of telling stories. Then, everything that is more-than-human will reveal the intertwined narratives of interdependence, relation making, and coexistence.

To complement this theoretical approach invested in bringing about the deep change in human collective intelligence, I also explore the power of creative arts in contributing to mindset change on emotive levels. Looking attentively at the question of whether the "storyworlds"[3] (Herman 2018) that emerge from creative engagements with the Anthropocene can emotionally and mentally help change our ways of being in the world, the last section of this chapter presents a temporary, site-specific form of art. To help reimagine the Anthropocene in terms of affective empathy for our planet, I thus discuss the example of *E-Motions* (2015), an installation by Turkish psychiatrist and artist Rahşan Düren, who confronts the Anthropocene by bringing our emotions and motions together. Placed in this context, the Anthropocene mirrors the worldly entanglements of many species in overlapping trajectories of social, cultural, ecological, and geological forces in present time, whereas the disorienting scale of geological time inadvertently obfuscates the ethics of human and nonhuman relations "in the discussion on global environmental change" (Greiner and Sakdapolrak 2013, 380). Evoked in its mainstream discourse, the global scale vision of the Anthropocene works to "numb the human mind," diminishes our "motivation to care about and act on behalf of the environment" (Slovic and Slovic 2004/2005, 18), and thus necessitates the production of new Anthroposcenarios constituted through new storytelling practices.

Contesting the Anthropocene's Global Scale Visions

When atmospheric chemist Paul J. Crutzen and biologist Eugene Stoermer coined the term "Anthropocene" in 2000, they set the stage for the ensuing debate about humanity's epoch-making signature on the planet's geomorphological processes. Since then, the extensive damage of human activities to the chemistry of the Earth's geosphere, atmosphere, hydrosphere, and biosphere has prompted Earth-system scientists to claim that the present interglacial era should be called the Anthropocene. In their parlance, the Anthropocene refers to "human-driven alterations of i) the biological fabric of the Earth; ii) the stocks and flows of major elements in the planetary machinery such as nitrogen, carbon, phosphorus, and silicon; and iii) the energy balance at the Earth's surface" (Steffen, Crutzen, and McNeill 2007, 614). The Earth has transitioned from the present interglacial Holocene—the epoch that began at the end of the last Ice Age, approximately 11,500 years ago—to a new geological epoch, the Anthropocene. In 2016 the Anthropocene Working Group (AWG) of the International Union of Geologic Sciences voted to recommend the Anthropocene as a formal geologic epoch at the 35th International Geological Congress. On May 21, 2019, the AWG voted again, this time to designate the Anthropocene as a new geologic epoch.[4] The AWG submits formal proposals to the International Commission on Stratigraphy, which oversees the official geologic time chart (Subramanian 2019).[5] But the Geological Society Stratigraphy Commission, formed to study the scientific validity of the term, has noted that although "Anthropocene" has still not gained full approval among geologists, it is a useful concept for describing the profound "chemical and biological effects of global human activity" (Zalasiewicz et al. 2010, 2229).

The Anthropos (the so-called "mankind") of the Anthropocene is so overpowering in affecting these processes that, even after its extinction, scientists proclaim, its signature will be operative through unthinkable geological time spans. Crutzen and Stoermer, for example, make it quite clear that "mankind will remain a major geological force for many millennia, maybe millions of years, to come" (2000,18). Although thinking the human impact in million-year spans is difficult to comprehend, extending on broad latitudes, the Anthropocene has come to signify a discourse embedded in the *global scale* vision of the sedimentary traces of the Anthropos even as an absent presence in the geologic. If the Anthropos gathers millennia, the term Anthropocene gets inevitably enlisted in expansive geological timescales, instituting the human in the catastrophic knots of immutability. Nothing compares, writes environmental journalist Gaia Wince, "to the scale and speed of our planetary impact," as "we've become a phenomenal global force and there is no sign of a slowdown" (2014, 3). This recurrent rhetoric makes the Anthropocene a story of scale that stretches from the deepest lithic recesses of the Earth to its unsheltered atmospheric expanses, revealing a poignant account of a crumbling home frequently exposed to hurricanes and tornadoes, landslides and floods, longer-lasting heat waves and droughts, and accumulating toxic waste as a result of a dramatic combination of many factors: deforestation, ocean acidification, soil degradation, the accumulation of carbon dioxide in the atmosphere, the extraction of coal, oil, and gas, species extinction, population growth, and biodiversity heritage loss. Crutzen and Stoermer further explain:

> Considering these and many other major and still growing impacts of human activities on earth and atmosphere, and at all, including global, scales, it seems to us more than appropriate to emphasize the central role of mankind in geology and ecology by proposing to use the term "anthropocene" for the current geological epoch. The impacts of current human activities will continue over long periods. According to a study by Berger and Loutre (14), because of the anthropogenic emissions of CO_2, climate may depart significantly from natural behaviour over the next 50,000 years. (2000, 17)

Unremittingly perpetrating such global transformations and determining the fate of the planet, the "human" here emerges as a unilateral figure of self-appointed authority who inserts themselves into geohistory by rewriting its evolutionary dynamics in highly disconcerting ways. Featuring rifts and fissures, fractures and distress in the Earth's material anatomy, this process of rewriting is a frightening one and raises concerns about the Earth's future. In *The Earth After Us*, Jan Zalasiewicz (chair of the Anthropocene Working Group of the International Commission on Stratigraphy) observes that

> if we make enough of a mess of the world, we might compete with the Yucatan meteorite, or with the mysterious forces that, almost exactly a quarter of a billion years ago, suffocated most of the Earth's oceans and killed off an estimated 95 percent of the world's species, bringing the Palaeozoic Era to a dead halt. (2008, 156–57)

Zalasiewicz wonders if this is science fiction, since the way the Anthropocene story is formulated creates such an impression, depicting the human species in terms of what Claire Colebrook calls *"ultra-humanisms"* (2014, 162; italics in original) and Eileen Crist "a Promethean self-portrait" (2013, 131). Environmental journalist Andrew Revkin criticizes this formulation as "a hubristic overstatement of human powers" (2011), and Stacy Alaimo calls it "a veneer of species pride" (2016, 144). Based on the cumulative impact of the human species represented by the Anthropos figure as a geological force permanently shaping the Earth, this definition of the Anthropocene is rather problematic. Expressed in such a monolithic perspective, the Anthropocene fuels narcissism, propagates anthropocentric arrogance, and occasions quite a dysfunctional relationship to planetary ecosystems. According to Bruno

Latour, however, it is "our common *geostory*," but, he asks, "how do we tell such a story" about what Earth has become? (2014, 3; italics in original). It is, in fact, not that baffling; as cultural studies professor Ben Dibley explains, it is a story of "the folding of the human into the air, the sea, the soil and DNA" (2012, 139). The Anthropocene is also the story of environmental uncertainties, geopolitical struggles, and social dilemmas, which create a paradoxical sense of worldly involvement in and estrangement from this tempestuous site where the human along with every other being is intimately caught within a maelstrom of erosion and disintegration. The Earth, in other words, entangles every life-form, always disallowing fence-sitting, regardless of the geological epochality of a single species pretending to occupy a position outside Earth systems.

Responses to this situation, again as specified by Dibley, are premised upon averting the calamity by either leaving the "nonhumans alone" to be safe or by appealing "'for the 'wise application of knowledge . . . to guide mankind toward global sustainable, environmental management' (Crutzen and Stoermer)" (2012, 143). While scientific discussions as such focus on the strategies of sustainable environmental management, mitigation, and adaptation through technological fixes like geoengineering the planet's physical systems and/or designing more resilient forms of life through genetic modification, ecocritical accounts engage in alternative modes of thinking and acting in the face of increasingly risky geocorporeal intimacies.[6] The Anthropocene demands that we reflect critically on the entangled tales of embodied beings intra-acting with geobiochemical forces rather than exclusively focusing on the quandaries of deep timescales and generic humanity. In that regard, intra-action must be seen as "emphasizing a shared worldedness" (Cohen 2015, 50), which undermines the habit of seeing the human as external to this reality and renders human narcissism rather senseless. To put it another way, the often-messy intra-actions of the Anthropocene's nonhuman agencies, in which human beings are also entangled, controvert the idea of universalizing humans as "hylomorphic" Earth transformers (Woods 2014). Interdisciplinary scholar Derek Woods concedes that the Earth-system scientists "narrate universal humanity—'the species'—as hylomorphic terraformer of a passive Earth" (2014, 137). And contesting this idea begins with full recognition of what Haraway proclaims: "No species, not even our own arrogant one pretending to be good individuals in so-called modern Western scripts, acts alone; assemblages of organic species and abiotic actors make history, the evolutionary kind, and the other kinds too" (2015a, 159). Haraway's call to be cognizant of the intimate entanglements of biotic and abiotic actors is necessitated by the reality of climate change and the ongoing biocide in a warming world. To fully understand why no species can act alone, or remain untouched by the unabating environmental emergency, I recapitulate the anthropogenic Earth transformations and scale issues as important determinants of the current Anthropocene debates.

The Tip of the Iceberg: Climate Change and Bioturbation

Among many anthropogenic transformations, climate change is always at the top of the rankings as the most cataclysmic fingerprint of the Anthropocene. US Secretary of State John Kerry, for example, labeled climate change "perhaps the world's most fearsome weapon of mass destruction" during a visit to Indonesia in February 2014. Similarly, in her renowned article "Enter the Anthropocene—Age of Man," environmental journalist Elizabeth Kolbert announced that carbon dioxide emissions "could easily push global temperatures to levels that have not been seen for millions of years" (2011). For Nigel Clark, professor of human geography, there is "still a more inconvenient truth than the facts of anthropogenic global heating," and that is "the realization that climate is responsive to our nudges only because it is far more precarious than we ever dared imagine" (2010, 32). According to a Goldman Sachs report (Khan 2019) presenting the impact of climate change on cities across the world, the potential outcomes of this inconvenient truth include more intense and longer-lasting heat waves, more-destructive weather events (storms, floods, fires), and pressure on the availability and quality of water for drinking and agriculture, as well as changing disease patterns caused by warmer temperatures. As Canadian poet Adam Dickinson truthfully observes, "We confront this on scales as massive as carbon cycles and as miniscule as hormones" (2015, 21).

Despite the evidence, however, that the planet is "warming over land greater than 1.5°C" (Huntingford and Mercado 2016, 5), there is not enough global political determination to unseat the main driver of climate change, the fossil fuel economy, or at least to enkindle global agreement in decarbonization policies. The reason for this apathy lies in the controversial data about temperatures that seem to be lower than estimates by most climate models (below 2°C). As ecologists Chris Huntingford and Lina M. Mercado explain, "oceans currently provide a significant thermal inertia of many decades" (2016, 1), meaning that the oceans absorb the surplus of carbon dioxide in the atmosphere, keeping it for several decades before releasing it back into the air. This interval creates the illusion that "all's well," making politicians readily ignore the inundating effects of human carbonization protocols (Oppermann 2019a, 2019b). Although some people—either brainwashed by or willfully immersed in capitalist-consumerist-colonialist ideologies—disregard the scientists' warnings, we are heading "to a very different state of the Earth System, one that is likely to be much less hospitable to the development of human societies" (Steffen et al. 2015, 737).[7]

Earth-system scientists claim, however, that "climate change is only the tip of the iceberg" (Steffen et al. 2011, 843). At the very bottom of this iceberg is something that rings more alarm bells than others: "human bioturbation," a term coined by Jan Zalasiewicz, Colin N. Waters, and Mark Williams (2014), that is modeled on what geologists have named bioturbation "to describe how living organisms affect the substratum in (or on) which they live" (Kristensen et al. 2012, 285).

Although *bioturbation* was first used in 1952, the term appeared in geomorphic literature in the early 1980s and became central to the soil biomantle concept, formulated in 1990, which is the upper part of the soil produced dominantly by bioturbation. Broadly speaking, bioturbation is the rearrangement of soil morphology and disturbance of sediments by burrowing animals, such as ants, earthworms, beavers, rodents, and plants with root movements that push away soil. Looking for food or shelter, or to create passageways for air and water, burrowing animals and plants with their roots that break up bedrock modify the fabric of the soil, change the texture of sediments, and thus play "an important role in both sediment transport and soil production" (Gabet, Reichman, and Seabloom 2003, 250). For instance, animals that mound soil produce biomantle topsoil, and tree roots that break up bedrock transport soil downslope. Due to their large impact on their environment and because they structure subsurface ecosystems, considerably modifying their contours, they are called "ecosystem engineers" and also "scenic designers, which not only set the stage, but also decide on the play to be performed, and select the potential players that enter the stage" (Meysman, Middelburg, and Heip 2006, 692). According to ecologists Filip J. R. Meysman, Jack J. Middelburg, and Carlo H. R. Heip,

> The concept of "ecosystem engineering" refers to a modification of the physical environment that strongly affects other organisms. All organisms affect their immediate abiotic environment in some way, but true ecosystem engineers reveal themselves when their presence or absence has a disproportionately large impact on the ecosystem. (692)

Today, however, these true ecosystem engineers cannot prevent the entrance of another player on their stage, the so-called Anthropos who is altering the foundational script itself by adding intolerable stress to the subsurface ecosystems with considerable biogeochemical effects, which include "the modification of the sediment texture, the bio-irrigational transport of solutes and the dispersal of solid particles" (Meysman, Middelburg, and Heip 2006, 693). Meysman, Middelburg, and Heip further clarify how this change is occurring:

> Soils and sediments are presently under pressure from various human-induced stresses, which have an impact on resident invertebrate communities. In particular, the removal of keystone bioturbators could induce large changes in the structure of the habitat as a result of reduced ecosystem engineering, with cascading impacts on local biodiversity, and soil and sediment ecosystem functioning.... In marine sediments, pressures on bio-turbating macrofauna result from bottom-trawl fishing, pollution and eutrophication-induced anoxia.... In soils, resident earthworm populations have been affected by overgrazing, fertiliser application and the invasion of exotic competitors or novel predators. (693)

This is human bioturbation or anthroturbation with "a magnitude greater in scale than any preceding non-human type of bioturbation," as Zalasiewicz, Waters, and Williams (2014, 3) put it. Since this "form of anthropogenic modification," they argue, affects the "rock structure, and therefore the Earth's geology, it is a component of the Anthropocene concept" (7). Anthroturbation inflicts permanent injuries on underground rock structures and is tremendously destructive to the sediment of the Earth itself. According to the authors, "no other species has penetrated to such depths in the crust, or made such extensive deep subterranean changes" (7). Nothing so negatively effective seems to have cumulated below the surface of the Earth during the last 12,000 years. Zalasiewicz, Waters, and Williams claim that "significant subterranean human impact" is detected "up to several kilometres below the planetary surface" (4), which, they maintain, transfers carbon from the underground to the atmosphere. Since deep subsurface changes "are permanent on any kind of human timescale, and of long duration even geologically" (4), the authors draw attention to the fact that "in imprinting signals on to the geological record, they are significant as regards the human impact on the geology of the Earth, and therefore as regards the stratigraphic characterization of the Anthropocene" (4). Even though subsurface systems, such as "sewerage, electricity and gas systems, underground metro systems, subways and tunnels" (4), which the authors call "shallow bioturbation," considerably damage the underground lithic chemistry, it is "deep bioturbation" that creates much more serious geological disturbance in the subsurface environment because it includes deep mining for coal and minerals, fracking for hydrocarbons, underground waste repositories, and nuclear tests. All these subterranean activities have the potential to precipitate planetary-scale transformations of land surface and ocean floor, leading to more frequent volcanic activity, erosion, and earthquakes. The authors also warn that the anthropogenic modification of underground rock structure, or "inert rock," as they call it, "has the highest long term preservation potential of anything made by humans, often approaching100% (until the trace eventually reaches the surface). In affecting rock structure and therefore the Earth's geology, it is a component of the Anthropocene concept" (13).

Underlying global change, anthroturbation is the worst of all human-induced alterations of Earth's fabric, leading geoscientists to reiterate that humankind has become a massive geological force rivaling "some of the great forces of Nature in its impact on the functioning of the Earth system" (Steffen et al. 2011, 843). As the lithic index of the Anthropocene, anthroturbation "intermingles humanity and geology" (Alaimo 2016, 145) and significantly destabilizes geomorphic forces. The term *geomorphic* here denotes Earth's surface configurations but also refers to the dramatic metamorphoses of the planet's materiality traceable to subsurface human activities. The accelerating interactions between humans and geological processes constitute the very cartographies of geomorphism, which encompasses many cataclysmic forces from underground and the resulting Earth changes aboveground. More importantly, geomorphic forces shape the Earth's climatic and biological features, showing how "life extends far deeper into the Earth's subsurface," as geomicrobiologist Frank Reith affirms, and the subsurface "comprises a large proportion of the biomass on Earth" (2011, 287). Hence, all disturbances in the stratified subsurface ecosystems dismally affect the deep subsurface biomass (the deep biosphere) and disturb the conditions of microbial communities which use hydrogen produced from minerals as their primary energy source (Nealson, Inagaki, and Takai 2005). So, when disrupted, all geobiochemical entities that normally sustain the Earth's feedback systems begin exhibiting catastrophic dynamics and hazardous relations. Jan Zalasiewicz, Mark Williams, Will Steffen, and Paul Crutzen argue that "when natural forces and human forces became intertwined . . . the fate of one determines the fate of the other" (2010, 2231). All these forces and the geomorphological processes transcend their geological reality and affect us culturally and existentially.[8] According to Elizabeth Ellsworth and Jamie Kruse, "these are forces to be reckoned with existentially, creatively, conceptually, and pragmatically as humans work to meet the fact that not only is our species increasingly vulnerable to the geologic, we also have become agents of planetary geologic change" (2013, 8). In this sense, the Anthropocene's underground forces, from volcanic magma to the rock bands, from rhizomes to graves, from nuclear tests to animal nests, invite not only "alternative figurations for thinking the Anthropocene subject in immersive onto-epistemologies" (Alaimo 2016, 144) but also disanthropocentric formulations of the Anthropocene beyond its global scale mapping and Anthropos-based scenarios.

Scale Critique and the Anthropos

Since the effects of detrimental human activities, exploitative economic practices, and the mindless consumption of vital resources are to some extent calculable, the concept of the Anthropocene is frequently discussed in terms of its "measurable" characteristics at the planetary level. Thus, "scale" becomes a convenient conceptual device for the global scope of geobiochemical human activities dramatically altering the functioning of the Earth systems that sustain all life. But when we zoom into the sociocultural, political, and ethical ramifications of these changes within a more perceptible temporal and spatial range than an exceptionally expansive geological one, global scale mapping becomes rather problematic, compromising our ability to formulate an ethics of scale necessary to address both the social and the material contexts of the Anthropocene "worlding."[9] Timothy Clark, a specialist in the environmental humanities, points out that large-scale in such contexts becomes "mockingly useless" or "a less than helpful scale. For, paradoxically, it is simpler to predict futures for the planet as a whole, a closed system, than to make forecasts for specific areas" (2015, 71). Calling the Anthropocene an "emergent scale effect" (72), Clark maintains that considerations of scale effects globally tend to undermine questions of politics, ethics, history, culture, and literature concerning environmental issues. Quoting Clark, Joanna Zylinska, professor of media philosophy and digital humanities, also observes that environmentalists and scholars in the humanities "suffer from this kind of scalar derangement" (2014, 27). Claiming that "the concept itself is flawed to the core," Simon C. Estok similarly notes that its scale "trivializes the matter by presenting the growing environmental crises as apocalyptic entertainment" (2018, 83). Even postcolonial historian Dipesh Chakrabarty's (2012) account of the Anthropocene inadvertently features the human species as a geophysical force in this controversial globalist vision. Addressing the question of "how human agency stretches across the spatial and temporal scales of Earth" (Woods 2014, 133), Chakrabarty proposes to "think human agency over multiple and incommensurable scales at once" (2012, 1). This human agency, however, is "strangely immaterial" (Alaimo 2016, 150). Signifying a self-worshipping dissonant subject systematically puncturing the fabric of existence and pulling apart what was elementally threaded together in evolution, this Anthropos figure moves the Anthropocene story away from worldly particularities, imparting a unified meaning upon the lived experiences of diverse human communities. Put differently, by homogenizing humans, the Anthropocene narratives fail to account for real people, such as those living in countries that lie in low latitudes where drought predominates, "people living in poverty" in "disaster-prone areas" (Gaard 2011, 52), or refugees who are far from participating in decision-making about their fate let alone pollution problems, climate change, and strategies for survival. These subordinate groups do not figure in the picture.

Moreover, the Anthropos conceals rather than reveals the personal traumas, injustices, climate-related diseases, or even loss of habitat and "transboundary pollution" (Whitehead 2014, 9). Those who suffer the worst impacts of environmental changes, therefore, cannot be listed under the same category of this globally effective figure who is assigned the role of "a geologic, species-scale force" (LeMenager, Shewry, and Hiltner 2011, 12). Whatever the degree of complexity of the Anthropocene and its scale effects, this reality is hard to ignore, and perhaps in challenging the question of scale we can use Haraway's pertinent question: "what are the effects of bioculturally, biotechnically, biopolitically, historically situated people (not Man) relative to, and combined with, the effects of other species assemblages and other biotic/abiotic forces?" (2015a, 159). Tackling this question is one way of "de-doxifying" any sense of the Anthropos that frustrates critical attempts to confront the Anthropocene as a hybridizing mix of what Haraway calls "diverse human people" (161), and also species, geophysical forces, and material agencies that refuse to fit into totalizing categorizations.[10] Therefore, what we need instead is "scale critique to grasp what 'human' means when it names the subject of the Anthropocene" (Woods 2014, 133).

It wouldn't be wrong to assume that naming the Anthropocene subject as a geological force eventuates from the still-prized universalist idea of the human (always a white male subject) as the measure of all things and the lingering discursive specters of human exceptionalism. Even if figured rhetorically, the idea of the Anthropos is fraught with this alleged reference unwittingly locking the Anthropocene discourse in anthropocentrism. It is, however, quite ironic to situate the Anthropocene within this discourse when critical posthumanism, ecocriticism, and the environmental humanities have invalidated the traditional forms of humanism and anthropocentrism as "an inevitable mode of self-understanding" (Mitchell 2014, xviii). Based on evidence from new modes of knowledge produced by these interrelated fields, we can already see what J. Allan Mitchell, professor of medieval studies, has clearly stated: "Even where the human appears to reign over or regulate others, there are numerous surface tensions, flex points, deviations, drifts, and dense networks with which to contend. There are alternative ways of becoming, nurturing ecological ways of being among and for others" (2014, xviii). That is why the Anthropos as self-proclaimed geological agent standing over the Earth for epochs to come is problematic. It triggers indifference toward the value of human–nonhuman temporal and spatial relations and, more importantly, propagates thinking in global-scale terms. As Jeffrey J. Cohen insightfully reminds us,

> Thinking the earth in billion-year spans is utterly disorienting—and the difficulty of comprehending ecological activity over such immense durations likely underlays our inability to address climate change, to formulate the ethics of scale and Long Ecology necessary to achieve something more than the witnessing of catastrophe. (2015, 79)

It is clear that even though adopting a global scale can be practically useful in predicting future scenarios for Earth systems and in understanding the present anthropogenic planetary change, it does not adequately situate the complexities and stories of the Anthropocene when considered from close-up perspectives. There is thus "a problem with thinking about environmental problems in globalist terms alone," as Mark Whitehead, professor of human geography, also reminds us (2014, 7). Whitehead argues that although "we live in an interconnected biosphere, we experience very different fates" (7). Or, at least, one can note that geophysical forces do not veer off course only in specific places (i.e., the global South); such places, however, are more open to states of emergency and are more intensely exposed to the risks of catastrophic events that come packaged with economic exploitation. If environmental disruption and dispossession are always coupled with social dramas, cultural conflicts, and transnational politics, the Anthropocene becomes a boiling cauldron in which social and ecological dynamics intersect with compounding issues of environmental and social injustices. For that reason, environmental humanities scholars and ecocritics encourage explorations of the Anthropocene condition in terms of interactions across different scales and social regimes linked to geophysical phenomena at different time frames. Susanna Lidström and coauthors assert that "environmental problems emerge (or are 'co-produced') from dynamic, non-linear and cross-scale interactions between social, ecological, technological, economic and political relations" (2015, 2). These cross-scale interactions are matters of concern that are always intrinsically interwoven, inducing scale-problematizing concerning not only geological epochality but also an ethically complicated understanding of the Anthropocene. In fact, "geological scale diminishes the human" (Cohen 2015, 79), undermining our ability to formulate comprehensible ethics of scale. At the same time, thinking the human in the geological timescale "produces cognitive dissonance" (Midgley 2012), generating what Timothy Clark calls "a bewildering generalizing" (2015, 151) of the temporally and spatially bound perspectives of humanity, as well as a partially visible horizon of the locatedness of the human story across different sociocultural realities. "As the Anthropocene mobilises and naturalises a universal subject—'man' that is the foundational subject of humanism," Kathryn Yusoff, professor of inhuman geography, concurs, "it simultaneously negates the differences (ontological, political, sexual, and biological) that result from the uneven geographies of fossil fuel consumption" (2013, 783).

Then, defining all humans in terms of a terra-altering force "leads us astray," as aptly expressed by Alaimo (2016, 156). Bringing attention to the panoramic visuals and scientific accounts of the Anthropocene, Alaimo maintains that "focus on geology" depicts "histories of man and rock in which other life-forms and biological processes are strangely absent" (148). As her critique suggests, we need to see things from different, less spectacular, and other-than-human viewpoints that would inhabit material stories of human–nonhuman engagements in a vulnerable world. Alaimo also proposes a "scale-shifting dis/identification" (143) necessary to dissolve the disembodied, epochal species identity of the Anthropos as an exceptionally powerful figure. Humans are indeed "lethal environmental actors," Cohen concurs, "but they are coextensive with many others, including carbon, glaciers, aerial and marine currents, geographical strata, expansive biomes" (2015, 41). Significantly, the co-extensivity of material agencies and biological systems, discriminatory practices, and the ongoing ecological decline problematizes the dominant assumptions about the Anthropocene viewed over lithic time. A shift in perspective inevitably disbands it as a conceptual apparatus theorized at a distance and opens it up to a different vision of life, one that "centers on simple biological truths . . . for instance, that we are not omnipotent. We are actually a tiny part of a vast system about which, despite all our research, we really know very little" (Midgley 2012). In such a vision, the borders between human beings and more-than-human environments become continuously porous to unmask the stories of "a human-lithic world participation" in "densely sedimented temporalities" (Cohen 2015, 78). The story of the Anthropocene that transpires here is the story of natures and cultures continuously coalescing in the changing landscapes of intersecting biological, geological, chemical, climatic, economic, political, and historical forces.

This seamless link between material and social dynamics makes us more aware of the crisscrossing stories of human and nonhuman agencies grounded "within the continuum of life" and "situates the history of their embodied skills within the unfolding of that continuum" (Ingold 2011, 50). If the Anthropocene is conceived this way, it would not subscribe to an ontology that dislocates and disengages the human agency from the stuff of the living world crisscrossed by beings, elements, and forces. On this account, humans appear as the determinant actors of anthropogenic changes, but they are not acting on any passive and mute material surface waiting to be marked and cannot declare their independence from the complexity of geological and ecological processes even if they mess with them in ways that bear on standard Anthropocene discourses. The geostory, therefore, should be a story not of "hierarchically organized individual players" (Iovino and Oppermann 2014, 3) but of horizontally aligned agentic entities among which humans, like all other beings, figure as transient actors as well as authors. This is the material ecocritical horizon opening "narrative" relations between the Anthropocene agencies, humans, and the world.

Material Ecocriticism and the Anthropocene

In rethinking the conceptual geographies of the Anthropocene, material ecocriticism instigates a narrative engagement with the world beyond but not excluding the Anthropocene's emphatic geological reference. In response to the question of scale, thus, material ecocriticism does not launch a problematic critique that completely disregards the global-scale vision of the Anthropocene—in human bioturbation, for example, one can find measurable amounts of evidence to affirm the global vision. Instead, material ecocriticism turns to the shaping influence of material agencies in particular material contexts, which appear in many forms: the ozone hole, a virus, rocks, shale gas, a flower, bodies, plastic bags, a melting glacier, and even the polar vortex, a recurring cyclone with enormous power. Whether catastrophic or enticing, material agencies are woven of the same fabric of existence humans also inhabit. We are, after all, "part of that nature that we seek to understand" (Barad 2007, 67). It is through the intermingling agencies and signifying forces of cohesion and discord that we come to know the world because they all can precipitate meaningful situations by shaping and affecting the way human beings relate to the world. Being part of the Earth's body, we can never remain outside its material configurations that actively engage and intra-act with us, nor deny their generative becoming.

This conceptual horizon belies the predominant Anthropocene narratives about unified humanity causing a geological level shift in planetary history, and thus destabilizes the entrenched notion of the disembodied and yet petrified figure of the Anthropos as an epoch-making entity, even if it pays homage to the global-scale vision of environmental changes. More importantly, though, by contesting the humanist idea of inert materiality, material ecocriticism makes evident that the things we observe and with which we interact are alive and undeniably expressive. They have their own stories, showing how nature enacts entanglement, how geological forces become complicit with economic and political dynamics like human bioturbation, and how "the flesh of the world" (Tuana 2008, 198) joins the flesh of the human in material intimacy and cultural imaginary, for storying the world is also a process of relation making. Stories of the Anthropocene typically arrive from the interfaces between geophysical forces, biochemical elements, and the chronic consumer culture, all of which raise issues concerning political and economic decisions and also questions about energy, housing, factories, transport, and food production. Of course, the pernicious capitalist system operates at a planetary scale, but its effects become more tangible at regional scales as in the case of palm oil production in Malaysia at the expense of rainforests; the Chernobyl nuclear disaster in Ukraine (Whitehead 2014, 7–11), the effects of which are still felt in the Black Sea region of Turkey; and hydraulic fracking in North America for natural gas, exposure to which can cause extreme neurological damage.

It is not just against this backdrop, however, that material ecocriticism reconfigures the conceptual categories of the Anthropocene debate. Rather, material ecocriticism asks us to be attentive to the messages encoded in the activities of various creatures, elements, substances, and forces—such as microscopic organisms in our bodies—that leave traces in our lives and demand to be perceived as effective material agencies. If material agencies are our "unexpected partners" floundering in a porous bag, to use Haraway's metaphor (2008b, 160), what would be their constitutive narratives? This is one of the fundamental questions material ecocriticism asks about the Anthropocene condition. In more general terms, what are the stories of inhuman forces, elements, and nonhuman entities as active, agentic, and expressive denizens of the Earth? And how do these stories shape cultural imaginaries? Asking such questions is important not because they supplement the geological accounts of the Anthropocene but because they can change our conventional understanding of nature's majestic or microbial forces as pliable materiality that humans exploit for utilitarian purposes. In general, Earth's stories unfold from the interactions of human practices and biogeochemical forces, in which humans and nonhumans—whether biotic or not—are materially and semiotically tied.

This involves the recognition that material phenomena are not isolable from semiotic processes and that matter can be creatively expressive in bearing material stories about ecological crises interlaced with sociopolitical struggles and geophysical forces. This is key to the material ecocritical conceptualization of matter as having a storied dimension.

As I elaborated in chapter 1, emerging in articulate forms of becoming, matter in material ecocriticism is interpreted as storied matter encoded with a mesh of meanings and narrative trajectories that can challenge the cultural dominants (capitalism, humanism) of the Anthropocene. Recall that storied matter is constituted by narrative agencies that carry stories of evolution, genetic variation, and extinction; more importantly, they open possibilities for nonhierarchical, cross-scale ecological engagements and interactions between people and other entities and forces. As Haraway proposes, "we need stories (and theories) that are just big enough to gather up the complexities and keep the edges open and greedy for surprising new and old connections" (2015a, 160). Storied matter answers this need, as it promotes a kind of narrative that is attuned to material agencies and can therefore counter accusations of anthropocentrism and even anthropomorphism. Storied matter, in other words, is a way of reimagining the collective story of multiple becomings, of conflicting and intimate relationalities that enable us to think through and across not only our contemporary situation but also against the present knowledge systems that perpetuate human-centered approaches as common-sense. If, however, we see the world in terms of the narrative potentials that inhere in all agencies and understand that humans are not the only storied beings in this earthly life, we can begin to think beyond anthropocentricity and thus beyond the Anthropos as an unfathomable geological force. To counteract this disorienting framing of the Anthropocene, material ecocriticism reads the world through its narrative agencies that are thick with material-discursive archives of survivals and extinctions, always confounding the human. Material ecocriticism draws attention to what visual artist Katie Holten (2020) succinctly writes on the opening page of her essay "Stone Alphabet: "The world writes itself. It can read and be read." Indeed, this statement epitomizes the core vision of material ecocriticism, whose basic premise is that everything around us and in us is an extension of matter's expressive dynamics:

> bodies, things, elements, toxic substances, chemicals, organic and inorganic matter, landscapes, and biological entities intra-act with each other and with the human dimension, producing configurations of meanings and discourses that we can interpret as stories. . . . What characterizes them is a narrative performance. (Iovino and Oppermann 2014, 7)

Perceiving matter as a "site of narrativity," material ecocriticism debunks the claims of human superiority and thus "*the anthropocentric copyright control*," to borrow ecophilosopher Timothy Morton's befitting words (2016, 18; italics in original). If we release our copyright control, as Morton suggests, we come to realize that—to quote Holten (2020) again—"The air is seething with messages, trees are dipping with secrets, stones store stories. Language is an abbreviation of the world's readability." We also realize that humans are embedded in the Earth's storymap when interpreting the stories of matter, and these stories do not necessarily "depend upon language to be conveyed" (Cohen 2015, 36). The stories of matter are often ancient, rendered in timeless forms of language that emerge from the planet's evolving storymap. In this storymap, the human is essentially entangled with other agencies in complex negotiations and, as Anna Lowenhaupt Tsing (2015) puts it, "transformative encounters" (28). Tsing conceives of these encounters in terms of "multispecies worlds" (22) through which "divergent lifeways" gather in "multidirectional" (23) patterns and scales, and also stories. These ideas usher in a complex vision based on the complementary relationship between human and nonhuman agencies as material-semiotic actors (in Haraway's terms [2008a, 4]) in the world's creative becoming, thus contesting the belief that agency is the singular capacity of human consciousness and that the ability to be expressive, creative, and effective is unique to humans or even to biological organisms.

To illustrate, let's take shale gas—the decaying organic matter trapped in compressed rocks—as an instance of storied matter that, like oil, plays an important role in our social imaginary. Shale gas is a material text through which we can read the embodied narratives of destabilized subsurface dynamics and neoliberal economic policies, social and geological power relations, scarred and toxified lands, and also environmental injustices inflicted on nonhuman lives. Shale gas *tells a story* through these hybrid ecologies, sociopolitical crises, and environmental violence, all of which coalesce into the complexities of human bioturbation with repercussions across a range of temporal-spatial scales. Extracted from the practice of fracking, shale gas is potentially a violent actor with the insurmountable capacity of destruction when it meets poisonous chemicals used during the fracturing phase, and thus draws specific attention to the risk of their leakage to water resources and the surrounding landscape. Blasting the bedrock with explosives and pumping enormously pressurized millions of liters of water mixed with toxic chemicals to further fracture the shale rock creates boreholes that provide a channel for the gas to flow. In this process, shale gas interacts with chemicals, energy cycles, ecosystems, human politics, and economy and produces signs and meanings that we interpret as stories. In other words, this is the environment in which shale gas emerges as storied matter. Its story originates from its encounters with human bioturbation, which seems to have opened "all kinds of Pandora's boxes" (Morton 2015, 148), and previously unthinkable possibilities are now emerging from these boxes. How, then, does it speak and tell its story? Certainly not through language as we understand it, but through "nonlinguistic inscription" (in Jeffrey J. Cohen's words). "Our documentary bias," writes Cohen, "is for worlds conveyed through words. Yet the earth possesses numerous recording devices, repositories for nonlinguistic inscription" (2015, 35). Coming from the dense layers of the world's geological records, shale gas, too, is such a repository, for it holds a memorial of metamorphosing Earth. It has expressive energy and thus agency, not to be associated with the intentionality and consciousness living beings possess. Rather, this agency is a specific enactment of collective efficacy, a capacity to make something happen and a capacity to harbor narratives, stories. It is therefore a narrative agency irreducible to mere anthropomorphism for, as Cohen would say, "its plots" and "denouements are its own" (2015, 33). Narrative agencies as such enable an alternative envisioning of the Anthropocene as an articulate field of clashing and blending forces and entities.

In anthroturbation or other instances, when the genealogies of humans and nonhumans overlap, they co-create a network of relations with tensions and conflicts that we can interpret as material narratives of our storied planet. Like the Apollo–Dionysus pair in bodies, biomes, ecospheres, geological formations, microscopic realms, eruptive climates, cultural spaces, and literature, this network produces stories that may be compellingly affirmative or unexpectedly disruptive. This point applies not only to contemporary narrative agencies that produce catastrophic stories like the shale gas but also to other Anthropocene agencies sedimented within deep geological time, like rocks, shells, tree rings, minerals, bones, volcanoes, pollen, fossils, and glaciers that yield stories of ancient climate, Earth's tectonics, and vanished life.

Regardless of being perceived by the human mind or not, stories told by telluric forces, intermingling or incompatible elements, and even disturbing forms of life extend the past of the Earth into our present, determining the way all beings articulate their engagement with and relationship to the world. Even those narrative agencies of which we are unaware, such as invisible creatures inhabiting our bodies, are the coauthors of corporeal stories. Anyone attentive, even if minimally, to the living world comes to realize that we all dwell "within a community of expressive presences that are also attentive, and listening, to the meanings that move between them" (Abram 2010, 173). This way we don't simply use storied matter and its narrative agencies metaphorically but extend them to the wider material-semiotic world, enlarging our horizon of meanings.

Rethinking the storied expanse of the Anthropocene makes us more perceptive to climate patterns, chemical compounds, geological formations, and myriad other material agencies that are never silent. In their complicitous actions, they "move, rebel, ally, crush, and desire" (Cohen and Duckert 2015, 5) without subsuming their particularities in the linkage. Although the stories of material agencies are different from the stories we tell about them—the dominant stories of disposable materiality filled with economic justifications of their exploitation—they are "stories in which we participate, stories in which we are not protagonists, [but] are nonetheless in part about us" (Cohen 2015, 192). These stories come to life through one another. Life is always storied and semiotic, as biological processes involve "countless organisms that are constantly interpreting and remaking the world they inhabit" (Maran 2017). According to Wendy Wheeler, "all life—from the cell all the way up to us—is characterized by communication, or semiosis" (2011, 270). Like humans who make sense of the world through language, all biotic forms have this capacity. Human language, Wheeler claims, "is just the most recent evolutionary part of a vast global web of semiosis encompassing all living things" (2014, 71). David Abram, too, confirms this understanding in *Becoming Animal: An Earthly Cosmology* (2010): "All things have the capacity of speech—all beings have the ability to communicate something of themselves to other beings" (172). In the material ecocritical view, all material agencies—biotic or not—are engaged in sign relations, enact agentic creativity, and produce innate meanings; thus, all are storied subjects, conveying intertwined stories of their sense of being in the world. If humans and everything beyond the human participate in semiotic relations in our storied world, then everything that exists here is part of a dense tissue of stories, of matter's dynamic expressions found across all material forms. In other words, "all matter . . . is like a library of Earth's evolution, which is deeply interlaced with human mindscapes and imagination" (Oppermann 2019b, 112). In this world, life is always storied.

To see life as made of stories is to recognize creative expressions inbuilt in all matter—from atoms to bodies, from biomes to geological forces and their social imaginaries. The stories of matter are not too difficult to trace, for they are encoded in every conceivable form demanding to be perceived. All we have to do is reorient our perception to such narrative materiality that always leaves its traces in our lives. In consequence, narrative agency is not a metaphor to ascribe meaningful existence to the nonhuman. On the contrary, narrative agencies contain us as integral parts of their unfolding stories, all of which have the power to challenge our human-centered interpretations of the world.

Once in this purview, "risk, harm, and suffering," extinction, and "the liveliness of all creatures" (Alaimo 2016, 146), which Stacy Alaimo complains are undetectable in the global visual lens of the Anthropocene, become all too visible, such as the tragic story of the Laysan albatross on Midway Island in the North Pacific Ocean or the poignant story of the bluefin tuna disappearing from the waters of the Bosphorus along with marlins, lobsters, and mackerel. So do the disrupted ecologies ensuing from consumption, waste, and pollution. As Jane Bennett rightly points out, "vital materiality . . . continues its activities even as a discarded or unwanted commodity" (2010, 6). The stories of invasive species, mutating viruses, volcanic eruptions, tornadoes, and earthquakes equally bear witness to how this expressive and vital materiality dramatically shapes our daily lives, health, economy, and politics and affects bodily metabolism, air traffic, and crops in a very direct way. The COVID-19 pandemic stands out as the most recent tangible example of such stories of dramatic shaping of human and nonhuman lives. The message in the coronavirus narratives is clear: *just as you have abused and shaped ecosystems and habitats in quite a destructive way, so can we mold your lives, your health, and your economies.* Such voices are not wholly imaginary; they are the constituent voices of a dangerously unstable Earth reality whose collective weight has become impossible to ignore, and these voices share the authorship of its unmasking with the human agents. The unrolling virus narrative explains how our bodily health is interdependent on the bodily health of other species and ecosystems on both a micro and a macro level. As political ecologist Vijay Kolinjivadi (2020) reminds us, "the ease by which COVID-19 moves through human bodies, and the difficulty of containing it across any human-imposed border is a remarkable case of how humans are dependent on nature, and indeed are part of nature and cannot be separated from it." The novel coronavirus has not only dramatically troubled our daily lives but also shaped the social dynamics in a very direct way. Feminist ecophilosopher Rosi Braidotti would probably call it "the self-organizing or 'smart' structure of living matter" (2013, 57), and as such it is also a striking narrative agency acting as a "co-author that shape[s] this world and co-determine[s] our existence" (Oppermann 2018, 413).

When biological organisms, corrosive forces, and disruptive substances get together as narrative agencies, they can only project narratives of hazardous relations. Like the stories of the coronavirus, the stories of poison running through the sap of trees, for example, are also the stories of contaminated human bodies ensnared by xenobiotic substances, laying bare the porous boundaries between the social and the natural. As material ecocriticism posits, speaking of narrative encounters of human and nonhuman agencies, if we read through these narrative agencies the stories of the Anthropocene, our maps of cognition might change so that, even if gradually, disturbing tales can be replaced by less distressing ones.

It is not accidental that narrative agencies today often tell disturbing tales because they bear the burdens of systematic exploitation and contamination of the Earth's subsurface and surface ecosystems. Although these tales are coercive, they do not assume the position of self-legitimacy as irreverent, dominant human narratives do with their privileging of commerce and commodity amid anthropogenic environmental crises. Take the body of the world that narrates tales of its wounds and recoveries, how its skin erodes and cracks with volcanic and seismic activities, imprints of many epochs that it has endured, the most violent of which has, of course, come with the Anthropocene. The new wounds opened by human bioturbation are a reminder that to consent to such a harmful practice is to condone the social and economic systems of power that validate and authorize anthropocentric ideologies and forms of narrative discourse that propagate them. Thus, while the narratives of the "geology of humans" foster more anthropo*scenes* enmeshed in Cartesian dreams of control, the material agencies of more-than-human environments narrate a frighteningly imperiled world as a cautionary tale that is not outside of our mundane material existence. If every life-form moves within a grid of interlacing relationships, we cannot conceive of a notion of the outside, for the external is always internal to each entity, like bacteria and the human microbiome, or fungi and trees that compel us to see the horizon outside as the horizon inside. This is also true on the level of geological relations, "such as those between aerosol cans and the ozone layer, which come to participate in the production of the present as a time of perpetual crisis" (Denizen 2013, 27). Reading such relations as forming stories within complex networks of narrative agencies can be a counterpoint to the common Anthropocene visions fixed on the Anthropos as a geological force. The material ecocritical vision can lead us toward an understanding of the Anthropocene as plural phenomena with interlaced stories of natures and cultures congealing at multiple scales. What is unraveled here is a mesh of humans, nonhumans, geophysical forces, and toxic substances locked in multiple and often dangerous relations, disclosing a sense of an overly disenchanted world. As well as being about geological epochality, the Anthropocene is also about this "mesh": an uncanny interconnectedness "between living and nonliving forms" (Morton 2011, 22).

How, then, do we address this uncanniness and the deep "trouble" that the Anthropocene represents in ethical, sociocultural, and political worlds? Haraway suggests that since the very trouble itself contains solutions, we must "stay with the trouble" (2016, 2) so that we can cultivate our capacity to invent "new practices of imagination, resistance, revolt, repair, and mourning, and of living and dying well" (51). What "marks an Anthropocene," Shakespearean ecocritic Steve Mentz also argues, can be "defined through *resistant rereading* rather than recapitulations of the story we all think we know" (2017, 47; italics mine). In this argument, becoming aware of the means and processes by which we represent the Anthropocene allows us to recognize how the standard Anthropocene narratives are utterly inadequate in moving "us into the postcarbon future we need" (46). It is, thus, an urgent necessity to develop effective strategies to contest the dominant Anthropocene script and to rewrite it for the sake of all life-forms that struggle to stay alive under its threats, such as catastrophic and eruptive microclimates and invasive human practices (hydraulic fracking, overconstruction, overconsumption, reservoirs of poisonous chemicals, and so on).[11]

Writing New Anthroposcenarios

Such a perspective as sketched above may be the only tenable path to rewrite the Anthropocene story with nonhuman narrative agencies as potential historical actors and coauthors whose stories challenge us "to inhabit new ecologies, invent new words, and work across many knowledge practices" (Tsing et al. 2017, M23). This approach will be as far from anthropocentricism as anyone could wish, opening up the possibility to construct new narratives that will not only underscore how humans are crisscrossed by nature's recklessly disrupted majestic and microbial forces but also emphasize how our story commingles with the stories of geological forces, disappearing species, and disrupted environments. In the end, the Anthropocene will signal an ecological context in which we might learn to live well with each other and other species and understand our intersecting lives ethically, cognitively, and materially. If the current narratives of the Anthropocene storying this edifice can be reenvisioned this way, we can unsettle the conceit of the Anthropos and trigger a change in human–nonhuman relationships now overflowing with pain and trauma.

Instead of telling a science-based narrative through a radical species arrogance with a prescribed lithic inscription, the new Anthroposcenario can initially focalize narratives of changing "the quality of relationships of the human species to the natural world" (Hamilton, Bonneuil, and Gemenne 2015, 3) while at the same time highlighting the idea of the Anthropocene as something that binds all beings with interconnected stories in a common ecological fate. When stories change, the mindset connected to them changes, and so do the anthropo*sceneries* suffering under the pressure of incalculable planet-altering activities, like the burning of carbon-rich fossil fuels, drying river basins, industrial agriculture based on injecting vast amounts of nitrogen and phosphorous into regional ecosystems, and plastic production. In other words, "how we tell stories influences how we act in the world" (Harrison 2017, 458), and "narratives affect how we understand environmental problems and solutions" (459).

If we don't want the Earth to become a mere specter of ecological devastation, it becomes imperative to radically revise the Anthropocene story so that the future fossil records reveal a different Anthroposcenario in which all biological species, material agencies, elements, minerals, and everything else are allowed a life of their own. In such a scenario the world we inhabit exceeds the traditional narrative of the Anthropocene grounded in species imperiousness. Our fossil remains in this case will reveal how humanity changed course in and around the twenty-first century, beginning with "modest possibilities of partial recuperation and getting on together" (Haraway 2016, 10). The future reader will read "stories in which multispecies players, who are enmeshed in partial and flawed translations across difference, redo ways of living and dying attuned to still possible finite flourishing, still possible recuperation" (Haraway 2016, 10). Haraway's "multispecies storytelling" that promises "getting on together" (2016, 10) can also be read as "a counter-narrative to our lonely petric tales" (Cohen 2017b, 26). A counternarrative is fully implicated in the ontological dynamics of the world of which we are part, not only cognitively but also affectively. It will make us aware that as humans we are not categorically isolated beings. For example, bacteria that inhabit our gut codetermine how we feel and respond to the world, affecting our mental state, as neurobiologist Emeran Mayer explains in *The Mind-Gut Connection* (2016). But although multispecies storytelling is an alternative narrative, supplying leverage for the nonhuman, it also raises a significant question: Can the human storyteller speak from an ecologically equitable perspective, telling multispecies stories through and with other beings and things? Put differently, if we are learning to *become-with* others (as in the case of bacteria), metabolize with them, compose each other, breathe the same air, and decompose in the same soil, can we also narrate stories through and with them?

Answering this question positively is also accepting the fact that human language is still the "diagnostic reference point" (Gagliano 2017b, 87) from which we give voice to nonhuman others. However, no matter how well the other's voice is represented, multispecies storytelling remains ensconced in the literary skills of its human scribe. Even if we "envision an empirically tractable and phylogenetically neutral account of language" (Gagliano 2017b, 87) to produce environmentally just stories and their subjects, "such a strategy" would still make the emerging new story "anthropocentrically tinted, being inevitably bounded . . . to our conceptual system of metaphors" (Gagliano 2017b, 87).

There is, however, a way to get out of this impasse multispecies storytelling is confined in, which is to acknowledge that nature does not require "human literary skills to write its complexity into comprehensible format" (Kirby 2011, 87). Accordingly, all life-forms can express themselves, transmitting messages and having meaning-making abilities in their interactions with other beings, substances, and forces. This is the material ecocritical perspective that reformulates multispecies storytelling in the new Anthropocene script. Although all nonhuman stories, and storied matter itself, become visible through humans, it is important to stress again that human stories emerge through them as everything, and every life-form, participates in the world's sites of narrativity. This perspective explains why the nonhuman world and its subjects do not always need a human scribe to translate their meanings. As anthropologist Eduardo Kohn explains: "Encounters with other kinds of beings force us to recognize the fact that seeing, representing, and perhaps knowing, even thinking, are not exclusively human affairs" (2013, 1). So, everything earthly is a narrative agency that conveys stories of multispecies relationships often imbued with resilient encounters with the human dimension, like "a tomato growing in an abandoned car tire" (Gan 2017, G12). If a tomato has a story to tell (about the resilience to stay alive), it can be seen as a narrative agency, like all other storied things and beings, such as glaciers in their atrophy yielding stories of global warming, oceans transmitting stories of deoxygenation, fossils revealing stories of biological and geological evolution, and bacteria telling stories of symbiogenesis. They "all represent the different ways in which matter *expresses itself*" (DeLanda [1997] 2005, 21; italics in original) and of which humans are an obvious part.

The new multispecies Anthroposcenario integrates this material ecocritical model with stratigraphical research on physical and chemical changes and reads the Earth as a living text with sedimented stories of evolution and dissolution. Rather than drawing attention to the disruptive powers of one species, or identifying the Anthropos as the only author, it shows clearly how human and nonhuman agents are conflated in this scenario—and this, indeed, calls into question the validity of the term *Anthropo*cene itself. The reenvisioned version of the Anthropocene can make multispecies storytelling an effective strategy to eradicate the hubristic way of seeing the world as all-too-human. This allows us to rethink the conceptual geographies of the Anthropocene beyond—but not excluding—the human subject.

The messages and meanings encoded in geological forces and biochemical formations as stories help build connections with the nonhuman, and this connectivity can help reword a stratified world in narrative companionship, moving the human vision beyond the "geology of mankind" to a multispecies coexistence. The new Anthroposcenario offers an ecological anagnorisis—a recognition of awareness of connections woven into the fabric of this world. It makes us aware of the unsettling tales of nonhuman agencies, which ride on and within the waves of unstable geological forces and climate change, disclosing a disturbing truth today about our perception of and practices in the world. In telling their present story, nuclear reactors, tsunamis, acidic waters, pesticides, pathogens (viruses, bacteria, fungi, parasites), plastic products (like an estimated 150 million metric tons of plastic in the oceans), and invasive species, among other "things," exemplify this truth to show how porous the boundaries between human and nonhuman bodies and the environment are. As such, the telluric stories of earthly agencies are not figurative but material; they are fully implicated in the dynamics of human–nonhuman relations through which multispecies storytelling unfolds.

When narrative agencies convey their stories through the dense layers of the world's geological records, through their disrupted existence and present toxic embodiments, they enable "a vivid presentation of the entanglements—of the naturecultures, of the global hybrids" (Dibley 2012, 142). Narrative agencies gather in collectives of relations entailing earthly maps of transits across the permeable boundaries between natures and cultures, and humans are obvious participants in these collectives even if they play the role of adverse actors at present. Humans are never exempt from this planetary story of interlacing relationships but are always "coextensive with other actors, including carbon, glaciers, aerial and marine currents, geographical strata, expansive biomes" (Cohen 2015, 41). Reenvisioning the Anthropocene in our living world with multispecies storytelling is thus a new horizon of inquiry to disclose the stories of human–nonhuman interdependencies. And the best way to *re-story* the Anthropocene is to see it as a site of narrativity from which multispecies storytelling emerges. The new Anthroposcenario can dissolve the dominant script that has so far shaped the constitution of our reality. With dissolution comes resolution for new beginnings, and multispecies storytelling is a creative model through which the possibility of "recuperation" that Haraway speaks of evolves into a new narrative that opens our minds to becoming-with other species in the web of life. This brings along ethical obligations, for all beings who are caught spinning involuntarily in the effects of the Anthropocene demand new ethical modes of storying the Earth. If "ethical systems moderate behaviors that shape the Earth System" (Schmidt, Brown, and Orr 2016, 193), such new modes of storying the Anthropocene can help challenge the present systems of massive exploitation of limited natural resources and our liberal involvements with whatever is not human in causing global environmental changes. It is important to stress that the new Anthroposcenario points to our ethical entanglements with the nonhuman at once intimate and distant, risky and familiar, and above all unpredictable—whose presence compels us to rethink our deeds and attitudes.

Also, perhaps equally important are artistic encounters with the Anthropocene that can help modify the myopic focus on the Anthropos. Art in this sense helps us reimagine the Anthropocene in terms of affective empathy for our storied planet's human and nonhuman denizens, helping us conflate our interpretive horizon with that of narrative agencies, and to liberate our minds from anthropocentric thought toward cultivating attention to what Heather Davis and Etienne Turpin call "feeling through the Anthropocene" (2015, 3). As the authors further explain in the introduction to their edited collection *Art in the Anthropocene: Encounters Among Aesthetics, Politics, Environments and Epistemologies*,

> art provides a polyarchic site of experimentation for "living in a damaged world," as Anna Tsing has called it, and a non-moral form of address that offers a range of discursive, visual, and sensual strategies that are not confined by the regimes of scientific objectivity, political moralism, or psychological depression. To approach the panoply of complex issues that are aggregated within and adjacent to the Anthropocene, as well as their interconnections and intra-actions, it is necessary to engage with and encounter art. (2015, 4)

Engaging with art in the Anthropocene is an affirmative way of attending to the partial relations among humans, nonhumans, landscapes, and ecological forces, which eventually diminish the idea of human beings becoming geological through cultivating aesthetic sensibilities, ecological imagination, and also ethical relations with the more-than-human world. Consequently, the Anthropocene may cease to be a contested and problematic term riddled with scale issues.

Art Installation in the Anthropocene: *E-Motions* by Rahşan Düren

Art installations arguably provide ideal demonstrations of a new Anthropocene thesis, such as Turkish psychiatrist and artist Rahşan Düren's *E-Motions* (2015). Düren's installation confronts the Anthropocene by moving our attention away from the disorienting scales of geological time and cataclysmic future scenarios toward new imaginative small-scale horizons, albeit in a cautionary and ironic way.

In its standard discourse, the Anthropocene is often characterized by uncertainty and unpredictability around Earth's distress in coping with the overwhelming impact of detrimental human activities. Understandably, future scenarios are imagined for an almost unlivable Earth with either globally displaced species, including human beings, with little hope of survival, or the phenomenal extinction of life altogether. To reimagine the Anthropocene, artworks like Düren's *E-Motions* install and then subvert this characterization by retrieving a note of hope amid the dissonant horizon of disturbed ecologies and reinscribe promise in the cultural imaginary to recuperate our not-yet-totally-lost home. In this aesthetic horizon, *E-Motions* presents new imaginative vistas in confronting the Anthropocene presently charged with cataclysmic future scenarios.

In its typical etymological sense, the term *installation* refers to emplacement and settlement, but to install also means to invest, and investment suggests hope and promise in this age of the Anthropos, the universalized human agency as an epochal geoforce. Thinking with installation as part of the emerging Anthropocene lexicon problematizes such a totalizing categorization of humanity and reinstalls the subjects of the Anthropocene in the environmental imagination as *anthropoi*—plural humans, with their histories of love, strife, loss, fear, and survival. When envisioned from the perspective of the aesthetic encounters of art and the Anthropocene, art installations produce aesthetic sensibilities about whether human beings can imagine less destructive ways of interacting with the world. With its double meanings of emplacement and investment, installation expresses the hope that if we invest in changing our perceptions and ourselves, we can, as Kayla Anderson, an interdisciplinary artist and educator, notes, "transform ourselves and our technologies to fit the changing demands of the ecological and biological world we inhabit" (2015, 344). In this regard, installation enacts an aspect of Bruce Carroll's argument that ecological consciousness is "a deliberate attempt at re-directing our thinking about our habitat, about how we conceive of that habitat" (2017, 149). In aesthetic terms, installation contains geo- and biocultural meanings of changing habitats due to anthropogenic effects and processes.

Reflecting on the transience of life on an increasingly volatile planet, art installations propose "fundamental questions about extinction and survival and response," fostering "publics that learn to care, to make a difference" (Haraway 2015, 264).[12] In reimagining the Anthropocene to this end, Düren's *E-Motions* conveys such a message in Haydarpaşa, the iconic but now ghostly train station in Istanbul's Asian side, located right by the sea where the continent ends.

There are no travelers in this defunct station; instead, the whispers of the past permeate empty spaces, and echoes of the Orient Express bounce back from the gracefully painted domes. Ghostly pirouettes of the West and the East appear before instantly vanishing into the shadows again while witty seagulls and curious cats become witness to its solitary stories. Standing here feels like being poised over the threshold of the Anthropocene epoch: you want to reflect on, if not capture, its distressing silences and losses, many of which can be observed nearby in the Sea of Marmara. Gone now are swordfish, blue tuna, sturgeon, and turbot whose poignant stories lay bare "some of the complex cross-weaves of vulnerability and culpability that exist between us and other species" (Macfarlane 2016). Here the transcendent perspective of the Anthropocene is vibrant in the air, but unlike the effect of safe distance created by the aerial photography of David Thomas Smith, for example, there is also something corporeally proximal revealing the Anthropocene's impure vibrations, its disenchanted pirouettes and signs, its miasma, and its small moments, all through an art installation.[13]

Installed in Haydarpaşa's waiting lounge in October 2015, *E-Motions* consists of twenty golden dials, each 4.5 meters long, "synchronized with servo step engines producing complex and irregular movements with precision positioning" (Düren 2015) (fig. 1). The irregular movements of these dials are accompanied by sound recordings and light projections that affect the viewer visually, sensorially, and musically. They imply distress but also enact a concern for a promising message that can be felt when one of the system's seven programmed choreographies begins performing a posthuman dance in strange rhythms with the waves splashing onto the ancient stones beyond Haydarpaşa's elegant walls and with the sunlight that pours through its windows. Moving like the waves, the dials arouse intense feelings of abandonment in the solitude of Haydarpaşa, evoking a sense of a dynamic relation between motions and emotions. In such a melancholic atmosphere one is left to surmise the affective influence of unjustifiable human actions. Since our emotions strangely attune to the dials' haunting motion, experiencing this installation is indeed purely *e-motional*. It makes us ponder what it means to *feel* installed in the Anthropocene while moving in it as if we are not (fig. 2).

What turns *E-Motions* into a form of Anthropocene awareness is the plaintive tale it tells to capture the small moments of sadness embedded in the Anthropocene itself. This tale contests the hubristic visions of the Anthropocene phenomena in which humanity remains a major geological force for many millennia. The oversize gold-plated dials start moving with the switch

Fig. 1. E-Motions, Rahşan Düren, Haydarpaşa Train Station, 2015. Photo by Serpil Oppermann

of a button, implying that the human is in control; but at the same time, they seem to obfuscate human presence in quite an ironic way. Indeed, the absence of humans in this choreography is an ironic homage to the Anthropos as a catastrophic planetary agency doomed to bring about its end. But *E-Motions* also traces possibilities that are not yet fully imagined about endings while simultaneously playing with questions about what it means to be settled in a changing place while paradoxically feeling displaced.

As a meditation on loss and promise, *E-Motions* disrupts and restructures the familiar Anthropocene narratives by creating an ironic context in which emotions must be balanced with motions. There is sadness here, as we may be experiencing moments of farewells, but the message is that the environmental fate is not yet sealed. As long as the dials move, they generate the feeling of homely emplacement, the feeling that the Earth is still in place; yet the question "What if humans flip the switch?" is also unavoidable, putting the valuing of the term installation as "emplacement," or "sitting place," under critical pressure. Because the dials turn "slightly brighter when measuring happy reunions, and imperceptibly darker when registering the sorrow of departures" (Akaş 2015).

Fig. 2. E-Motions, Rahşan Düren, Haydarpaşa Train Station, 2015. Photo by Serpil Oppermann.

As I walked among the golden dials in 2015, many questions flooded my mind. Is this installation a mirror of Anthropocene-induced anxieties? Is it replaying our strained earthly becomings and displaying what we will pass on to future generations, as we attune to the dials turning "slightly brighter" and then "imperceptibly darker"? Such questions made me feel engulfed in a cloud of indeterminacies. There was no closure here in any definite sense but rather ambiguity about our species' complicated existence—like a hazy line within which was some unnamable mixture of sadness and hope. The only certainty for me as an intra-active observer was that *E- Motions* contained our stories told and untold, and our paradoxes not yet resolved. Experiencing this installation was an unexpected discernment of the Anthropocene as an open-ended process carrying some hope despite the struggles in anthropogenic landscapes shaped by the *anthropoi*.

E-Motions can be read as a projection of the Anthropocene pointing to a crumbling home but also to the idea that it is still holding. Rather than reassuring an unproblematic sense of place to dissolve our fears of being radically displaced in the future, *E-Motions* generates a feeling of hope, engaging our empathy to "invest" in the disanthropocentric meanings of the Anthropocene so that we can perhaps eliminate some of its anthropogenic manifestations. In other words, *E-Motions* not only forces visitors to inhabit this desolate world in a moment of affective pause from their daily routines but also urges them to embody the hope and sadness of the Anthropocene and what it might mean for the future of our own and many other species. This is precisely why this specific artwork was installed in an old train station. Haydarpaşa, a symbolic epitome of our home becoming dysfunctional, has served well for *E-Motions* to communicate its message of revaluing what we may lose. Thus, knowing the near future in the present, we along with all Earthly species and material agencies stand between the present and the future to ensure that the environmental fate of our storied planet should never be sealed.

Chapter 3

Migrant Ecologies of the Anthropocene

The world in which we live today is a world of migrations—processes that happen across borders and in spite of the tendency to build new frontiers, new fences. Living species, human groups, things, and goods, as well as pathogens, germs, microbes, and viruses, are constantly on the move. Some are driven by their evolutionary pathways, others by political reasons and economic deprivation; but many of them, especially the human groups, are on the move because of sectarian conflicts, regional wars, and, above all, environmental catastrophes. This chapter suggests that the stories of humans and nonhuman animals caught in the Anthropocene's conundrums are part of *migrant ecologies*. These stories are also enmeshed in our hybridized and postnatural world, which is becoming "a swirling landscape of uncertainty" (Alaimo 2011, 282). And, in the thick of many uncertainties, it is impossible to disregard the immediacy of migrant ecologies, which emerge from the negative impacts of anthropogenic climate change that has encroached on not only the lives of especially disadvantaged human populations across the world but also wildlife.[1] Hence this chapter considers migrant ecologies as one of the dire straits of the Anthropocene seen from the perspective of human storying of the world without excluding the question of the nonhuman migrants. As distressed narrative agencies who suffer the worst impacts of environmental changes, the migrant figures here are the protagonists of the traumatic tales of disrupted ecologies. Their narratives make us aware of the social and environmental injustices and climate-related traumas inflicted on human and nonhuman lives.

My objective is to present a neutral discussion of the increasingly controversial matter of refugees, migrants (both human and nonhuman), and uprooted peoples who, escaping war, climate disasters, poverty, food scarcity, economic hardships, political oppression, and other social and ecological conflicts, have given rise to the broadly controversial phenomenon of migrant ecologies in this age of the Anthropocene. The question, then, that needs to be considered here is: How are we going to respond to the stories and mutating configurations of migrant ecologies as well as to the fractures they impose on our master narratives?[2] Another particularly urgent question that follows is: How do we navigate within the entwined zones of stressed natural processes and social systems to rethink our being-in-the-world and our relations to other species in more ecologically responsible ways in the Anthropocene's dire straits? And, surely, our present reality is overloaded with scientific data on the rise in the Earth's average temperature, which reached the landmark of 1.5°C in 2016 (Huntingford and Mercado 2016); the melting of the West Antarctic ice sheet raising sea levels by several meters; and, more generally, the possibility of our daily lives being upended by planetary forces in turmoil.[3] An IPCC special report (2018) on the impacts of global warming of 1.5°C also expands on the risks, stating that "up to 10 million fewer people would be exposed to related risks, based on population in the year 2010 and assuming no adaptation" (9).[4]

Admittedly, this dark ecological picture plays a crucial role in triggering mass migrations of the most severely affected and the most vulnerable human and nonhuman populations. Add in the drastic effects on ecosystems and biotic communities of increasing plastic pollution in the oceans, toxic chemicals released into the soil and air, and mineral extraction, and you arrive in the realm of migrant ecologies embedded in the Anthropocene. Those who pay the greatest cost are the people who lose their homes, "as the land on which they live is swallowed by rising sea levels, forcing them to move elsewhere. Still, others will find that their resource base can no longer sustain them and will have to migrate in search of a different land base . . . And there are those who simply will die" (Pulido 2018, 118). I share social scientist Laura Pulido's perspective here but would add to her category of vulnerability the nonhuman species who are forced to migrate due to similar reasons and which migrant ecologies insist are the silent victims of the Anthropocene. For example, the fate of the polar bear, which I will discuss later in the chapter, is the most pronounced story of migrant ecologies as it continuously circulates in the present-day cultural memory. The polar bears' story is indeed one of the saddest stories of the warming climate in the Arctic region, which has led to decreasing food sources and thus the decrease of the polar bear population. The threats from climate change—shrinking sea ice and their tundra habitats—also affect the Arctic fox, as diminished food resources greatly decrease its chances of survival.[5]

Taking account of the shared destiny of millions of humans and nonhumans forced into migration and the magnitude of the problem, the global reach of migrant ecologies is vast and assumes multiple forms with both positive and negative dimensions. In my view, migrant ecologies contain a kind of ghostly *doubleness*, which both undermines the conventional political approaches manifesting as antipathy for immigration in the Global North but also signals the risks brought about by traveling microscopic creatures in the bodies of human and nonhuman migrants. Put differently, what gets subverted and then involuntarily reinstalled makes the discourse of migrant ecologies considerably more complicated than they appear to be. This doubleness problematizes the mode of relationality that characterizes migrant ecologies and needs to be reckoned with.

The World of Migrant Ecologies

A close look at what is going on in the world of migrant ecologies reveals that what precipitates the displacement of common people—especially those who are the most "economically, environmentally and socially vulnerable" (Vigil 2015, 44)—are the adverse effects of climate change. Although only 23 percent of United Nations reports mention a connection between climate change and migration, the term "climate refugees" is frequently used today to define people displaced by environmental factors (Fernández 2015).[6] As former president of the Earth Policy Institute Lester R. Brown explains in his book *World on the Edge: How to Prevent Environmental and Economic Collapse* (2011): "One of the defining characteristics of our time is the swelling flow of environmental refugees: people displaced by rising seas, more-destructive storms, expanding deserts, water shortages, and dangerously high levels of toxic pollutants in the local environment" (72–73). Hotter temperatures and drier conditions are also on the list; for example, between 2006 and 2010 a devastating drought in the eastern Mediterranean, especially Syria, sparked massive social unrest that resulted in an unending civil war, assuming larger and always less containable dimension with the more recent interventions of Russia, the US, and then Turkey in the conflict. Although the uprising against the regime and eventual migration from this region is not only due to drought, water shortages, and crop failures, the six million displaced people today are the representatives of migrant landscapes saturated with multifaceted social and economic conflicts. In a special report for *Scientific American*, environmental journalist John Wendle (2015) notes that "Syria's drought has destroyed crops, killed livestock and displaced as many as 1.5 million Syrian farmers. In the process, it touched off the social turmoil that burst into civil war." Initially, it was the combination of severe drought, bad government policies, and the resulting social violence that forced millions of Syrian farmers to move to cities, which led to the collapse of already-deteriorating urban infrastructures and hence to social violence driving millions of Syrians to seek refuge in Turkey. Turkish ecocrotic Meliz Ergin calls this event "drought-induced population flows in Turkey" and rightly claims that "climate induced droughts and eco-migrations are planetary problems too vast for any country to handle on their own as they often involve regional changes and transnational mobility" (2017, 258). A similar event took place in a small town in the state of Guanajuato, Mexico, in 1997. As science journalist Amy McDermott (2016) explains, the town on the river Lerma had suffered a severe drought that affected all of the crops and eventually led to the migration of local farmers and rural people. These farmers "depend on predictable weather to grow the crops they eat. When they know the rain isn't coming, or their home has been destroyed in a flood, or some other climate-fueled event has upended their lives, families face limited options: starve or move." Like in Syria, climate conditions and shrinking economic prospects are "the primary factors driving Mexicans to migrate to the United States," says McDermott. In fact, between 2005 and 2010, 1.4 million Mexicans crossed the US border. This is another exemplary story that reflects "a growing global problem. Worsening droughts, floods, wildfires, and rising seas will drive millions from their homes, all around the world" (McDermott 2016). South Asian countries such as India, Pakistan, and Bangladesh are also especially affected by floods, and environmental disasters play a major role "in this complex web of migration, mobility, inequality and generation of profit" (Samaddar 2017,189). Coupled with worsening infrastructures in many places, the effects of changing climates force impoverished people to seek resettlement in what they believe to be disaster-free places. As professor of human geography Andrew Baldwin says, "climate change will unleash unprecedented migration and displacement" (2017, 292). According to Xiaojing Zhou (2017), professor of English at the University of the Pacific, another major reason for the emergence of "ecological migrants" and "climate refugees" (274) is the collapse of "traditional rural communities and families" due to "environmental degradation" (278–79) as can be seen in China, where urban sprawl, economic globalization, and commodified lands aggravate the situation. Zhou argues that migrant ecologies become inseparable from the "impact of slow socio-ecological violence in migrant landscapes" (288). If the relations between climate change migration are riddled with economic, social, and political issues, this may create what Baldwin calls "irresolvable ambivalence" (2017, 297) concerning human mobility. According to Baldwin, "the climate change migrant designates an excess of comprehension and categorization" (298); therefore, "eco-migration," as Ergin (2017) defines migrant ecologies, "can . . . give rise to political conflict" but at the same time "solicit new venues for cooperation" (258).

In discussing climate-caused migration, many scholars thereby reference the interlocked issues of environmental changes, social inequalities, and political strife, which "deepen the distress of affected people and the natural environment" (Wright 2017, 160). Although the effects of climate change play a significant role in turning the most vulnerable people into climate change migrants, they are always entangled with poverty, regional wars, and economic needs. Yet, as Marco Armiero and Richard Tucker argue in their introduction to *Environmental History of Modern Migrations,* we should not be tempted to "reduce everything to some ecological truth. . . . Wars and poverty, two crucial causes of environmental—more specifically climate—changes" (2017, 3). That is why, the authors conclude, "it would seem irrelevant to trace impenetrable borders among environmental, economic, and political migrants as if those were parallel universes and not the intertwined socionatures of which our world is made" (4). The stories framed in migrant ecologies, then, emerge through collapsing environmental landscapes entangled with social issues and unfold through multiple effects of climate change in the world's naturecultures.

The 2016 *World Bank Annual Report* also underlines the effects of worsening climate conditions and their negative consequences leading to mass migration:

> The global community is facing challenges that are diverse in nature— economic, humanitarian, environmental—but that share key features. First, they threaten the hard-won development gains of recent decades; and second, they will not be contained within any one country's borders. Millions of people have been forcibly displaced by conflict and live in ever-more fragile areas. . . . (2)

Abram Lustgarten (2020), an environmental reporter who has been researching the most devastating consequences of climate change, estimates hundreds of millions of climate refugees due to "changing landscapes, pandemics, and mass extinctions." He interviewed economists, demographers, urban planners, insurance executives, architects, and climate scientists for a 2020 *New York Times Magazine* article:

> I traveled across four countries to witness how rising temperatures were driving climate refugees away from some of the poorest and hottest parts of the world. I had also helped create an enormous computer simulation to analyze how global demographics might shift, and now I was working on a data-mapping project about migration here in the United States. . . .
>
> In much of the developing world, vulnerable people will attempt to flee the emerging perils of global warming, seeking cooler

temperatures, more fresh water and safety. But here in the United States, people have largely gravitated toward environmental danger, building along coastlines from New Jersey to Florida and settling across the cloudless deserts of the Southwest....

Across the United States, some 162 million people—nearly one in two—will most likely experience a decline in the quality of their environment, namely more heat and less water. For 93 million of them, the changes could be particularly severe, and by 2070, our analysis suggests, if carbon emissions rise at extreme levels, at least four million Americans could find themselves living at the fringe, in places decidedly outside the ideal niche for human life. The cost of resisting the new climate reality is mounting.

Lustgarten's analysis is consistent with research conducted by climate scientists, who also predict an astounding number of displaced people on a global scale and claim that mass migration will reach global proportions, forcing nations worldwide to seek new security regimes, geopolitical alliances, and energy resources. In a research article about the planet's rapidly warming climate, "Future of the Human Climate Niche" (2020), Chi Xu, Timothy A. Kohler, Timothy M. Lenton, Jens-Christian Svenning, and Marten Scheffer proclaim that for every 1 degree Celsius (1.8 degrees Fahrenheit) of global warming, an estimated one billion people might be forced to migrate to places that offer more "favorable conditions" (11352) for their daily lives. Living in the most damaged regions of the world and already facing "declining conditions for human thriving" (11350), the likelihood of these one billion people becoming the major actors of climate-induced migrations is very high.

As conditions will deteriorate in some regions, but improve in other parts . . . a logical way of characterizing the potential tension arising from projected climate change is to compute how the future population would in theory have to be redistributed geographically if we are to keep the same distribution relative to temperature.... Such a calculation suggests that for the RCP8.5 business-as-usual climate scenario, and accounting for expected demographic developments (the SSP3 scenario [15]), ~3.5 billion people (roughly 30% of the projected global population ...) would have to move to other areas if the global population were to stay distributed relative to temperature the same way it has been for the past millennia.... (11352)

As a solution to the predicament that "climatic conditions can exert enough stress to trigger migration" (11354), Xu and coauthors suggest "climate mitigation" to "substantially reduce the geographical shift in the niche of humans" (11352). But it wouldn't be wrong to assume that climate mitigation will likely be conveniently overlooked in the present geopolitical climate. That is why explaining the causes, motives, and drivers behind migration, and especially climate change–induced migration, is never unproblematic. In the same way, defining migrants as climate refugees or ecological migrants is a complex issue, as this kind of migration is inseparable from other factors that instigate mass displacement of people as well as animals, such as Syria's mountain gazelles (*Gazella gazella*), which, fleeing from extreme violence, regularly cross the Turkish–Syrian border. Their migration stories constitute the most poignant accounts of climatic conditions and human violence.

Migration Is Not Only a Human Crisis

Drawing attention to the lack of definition relating to migration caused by ecological reasons, Oliva Dunn and Francois Gemenne write that it is difficult to isolate "environmental factors from other drivers of migration" (2008, 10). That is, environmental factors, as "a major driving force of migration," are so intricately interconnected to political instability, social unrest, and thus to security issues that the "complexity of current migration patterns also contributes to the difficulty of finding a consensus over definitions" (10). In the June 2020 issue of *Forced Migration Review*, editors Marion Couldrey and Jenny Peebles offer a compelling overview of the present situation: "Communities whose livelihoods depend on the surrounding natural resources, whether land or sea, are particularly vulnerable to the impact of the climate crisis on those resources, whether from sea level rise, inundation and salinization . . . or sudden-onset events such as flooding and storms" (1). Those communities are not just human, however, since nonhumans are often more defenseless in the face of climate change and other environmental disruptions.

Insecurity, risk, harm, pain, violence, trauma, and fear ensnare even the most innocent nonhuman actors, such as gazelles, cats, dogs, foxes, birds, and other animals who have very little chance of survival in encounters with environmental catastrophes or blood-thirsty human groups. Caught in the same maelstrom of brutal geopolitical and economic forces, the nonhuman is even more vulnerable than the human and cannot remain immune to terrorism and shattered landscapes. While we are daily exposed to media coverage of displaced persons, there is very little, if any, information about the crisis of other species that are displaced due to the barbarism of humanity—although categorizing "humanity" under such a collective label is ontologically and epistemologically highly problematic. But it serves here to make us understand that migration is not only a human crisis, and migrant ecologies do not only involve the sorrowful stories of drowned children in the Mediterranean and Aegean Seas. As Donna Haraway says, "Right now, the earth is full of refugees, human and not, without refuge" (2015a, 160). She encourages "making kin" as a life-saving strategy for the Anthropocene. Indeed, the nonhuman seeking refuge is not so different from the human seeking a relatively safe environment that holds the promise of some stability and futurity. Therefore, species migration is also part of the tragic consequence of the most adverse circumstances, environmental destruction, widespread terrorism, and violence practiced every day in geographies that kindle migrations. If we are not able to see this cross-species kinship of fates, needs, and troubles—which constitutes the core of migrant ecologies—we risk missing a huge part of the picture. As sociologists Piers Beirne and Caitlin Kelty-Huber (2015, 97) report: "Forced migration's harmful impact on the lives of non-human animals . . . tends to be grossly under-reported. While an examination of the lives of animals other than humans is worthwhile, there are many anthropocentric reasons to consider the effects of forced migration on animals." Beirne and Kelty-Huber also underline an important point, in that when displaced people set up camps in areas "which were previously unused by humans, they may deprive wild animals of critical habitat for hunting, foraging, migration and procreation. The surrounding land may be degraded as habitat through deforestation and erosion and wildlife may be hunted or poached by refugees for consumption or for trade" (98).

The stories produced by these migrations are often quite heartrending, such as the sad story of gazelles reported by Turkish journalist Yücel Sönmez:

> Following Hatay's mountain gazelles (Gazella gazella), we walk by Kırıkhan's Syrian border enclosed with a wire fence. On the other side of the border are two gazelles staring at us. Our guide, Abdullah Öğünç, who has dedicated his entire life to gazelles, has often fed the abandoned newborns with baby milk bottles, says: "They somehow manage to get past the barbed wires and come over to the Turkish side. But there are four and a half kilometers left to complete the wall they build here. Soon our gazelles won't be able to cross to our site from the land we used to send brides and grooms." I tell him: "This is human history defined by walls now." (Sönmez 2016; translation mine)

The journalist asks the tour guide if these gazelles can also be called refugees. He answers: "They resemble us so much. When they feel they are in danger, they literally shed tears. They cry as humans do. When they are very scared, they start shaking, and I have seen several die of fear too." The guide also tells the journalist that "over here in Turkey, gazelles are sacred for us, therefore they know they won't be harmed when they cross the border, and yes they migrate to our land. But we don't really know how many of them could make it, and how many perished in Syria."

Gazelles are not the only nonhuman animals that face the difficulties of migration due to environmental disturbances and increasing human pressures on their habitats. As told by environmental philosopher and anthropologist Thom van Dooren, there is, for example, the struggle of Little Penguins in Manly, Australia, entangled in and overwhelmed by "the wantonness and severity of the act of quietly destroying [their places] as though there were plenty more available coastline elsewhere" (2014, 83). Highlighting the significance of the coastline for the survival of penguins, van Dooren calls this ongoing destruction of coastlines "extinction work—perhaps not today or tomorrow, but certainly in the all-too-immediate future" (83). He underlines the need to appreciate "the entangled intergenerational fates of penguins and their storied-places" (83). Among other avian stories included in van Dooren's book *Flight Ways: Life and Loss at the Edge of Extinction,* the story of the penguins strikingly shows how the nonhuman other suffers the aggravated impact of the Anthropocene especially in consumer-invaded, instrumentalized, and destabilized coastal regions where the human and the nonhuman most frequently come together. In close encounters of this kind, the most vulnerable lives— those that are most disrupted—are not exclusively human. A disconcerted life activity can be seen among many nonmigratory animals forced into choosing between migration and extinction in once-undisturbed places now invaded by human consumers or deeply affected by changing climate conditions. Even migratory birds must change their seasonal routes as their destinations (lakes and rivers) are no longer available due to myriad social and economic processes, including excessive urban sprawl, recreational landscapes, industrial activities, "transboundary pollution" (Whitehead 2014, 49), aridity, decreasing availability of food, and the building of walls and fences along the coasts. Migration does not occur under a single set of conditions giving rise to human refugees as the only possible outcome. But the complexity involved here makes explicit what is usually left implicit in the context of climate refugees, economic migrants, or political asylum seekers, all of which predominantly foreground the human crisis. Put differently, migrant ecologies do not efface the stories of nonhuman animals caught in the same crises but self-consciously acknowledge them as equally significant "onto tales" (Bennett 2010).

Since human and nonhuman refugees cross borders (regularly or not), it must be noted that this crossing is rarely done without tension on the part of the nonhuman. It would be consistent with refugee crises to say that multispecies communities are entangled in messy social realities and ecological devastation brought about by a chain of interrelated economic and political activities that trigger environmental changes. In such a climate, becoming a refugee is almost inevitable for the nonhuman whose life is irrevocably altered and whose survival is contingent on migrating. Migration thus imposes itself as the only alternative for the continuation of what we can call "decent living" for human groups and a matter of survival for endangered nonhuman species. Migration becomes inevitable, compulsory, and thus "a world-shaping phenomenon" (Baldwin and Bettini 2017, 1). With significant effects on species whose ecosystems are under erasure due to their declining ecological niches, this phenomenon makes it almost impossible for many species to adapt to the ongoing environmental changes. If climate change–related troubles continue to negatively impact the nonhuman species who are unable to "mov[e] upward and poleward in response to warming temperatures" or are unable to undertake forced migration, they will be "at risk of extinction, especially where factors such as disease and habitat loss exacerbate the effects of climate change" (Palmer and Larson 2014, 642).

Bioethicist Samantha Noll (2018) explains forced migration as the advent of climate change entailing environmental "push factors," among which many researchers list habitat destruction, natural disasters, and changing weather that influence human and nonhuman life. There are also "pull factors" that "induce movement due to some benefit, such as a prevalence of food and water, suitable habitat.... In the ecological literature, this is frequently described as a species following their 'ecological niches' or 'climate niches'" (25). According to Noll, when these "ecological" or "climate niches . . . shift, the following options are available to species: to adapt, migrate, or go extinct" (29). Noll suggests that all displaced nonhuman species "that are induced to leave their current geographical range due to the impact of a changing climate" (26) should be included in the category of climate refugees. In this context, the plight of the polar bears, "the iconic victims of climate change" (Lewis 2013), is often cited as an exemplary case. The US Endangered Species Act lists polar bears as the most imperiled animals in the world because of the melting sea ice in the Arctic Circle. Jacob Blanchard (2020), who studies polar bears, explains that "due to climate change Polar bears have been losing sea ice to travel on very quickly. They continue to stay on land longer and have to use more body fat that was stored so they can sustain energy." Sea ice is also crucial for hunting; it is "the essential platform from which polar bears hunt. Changes in the distribution of areas of high or low biological productivity will likely alter seal distributions which will in turn result in changes in the distribution of polar bears" (Derocher, Lunn, and Sterling 2004, 167). Stories of the polar bear are ineluctably embedded in the warming climate in the Arctic as indicated by the growing body of studies that document the effects of erratic climatic cycles in Arctic ecosystems on polar bears (Stirling, Lunn, and Iacozza 1999; Stirling 2002; Post and Forchhammer 2002; Hamilton and Derocher 2019; Reid 2020). One of the most recent studies is Julian Reid's 2020 article, "Constructing Human Versus Non-Human Climate Migration in the Anthropocene: The Case of Migrating Polar Bears in Nunavut, Canada," in which Reid offers this clear warning:

> A poor community of human beings moves on account of the ways in which the climate has destroyed its habitat and they are seen to be a threat to the environments into which they move as well as the stability of the entire international system. A polar bear moves on account of the same kind of destruction of habitat and the world fears simply for the existence of the bear. (5)

Insisting on the seriousness and urgency of such onto-tales, migrant ecologies signal the need for a new direction that would return the human mindset to disanthropocentric relationalities with the physical environments, away from what Dipesh Chakrabarty calls "the futile project of human mastery" (2019, 3). The planet, says Chakrabarty, "is a site of existential concerns for those who write its histories" (4). But those stories or histories are not written only by Earth-system scientists who "have bared the planet as an entity to reckon with in debating human futures" (5). Although Chakrabarty acknowledges the nonhuman (multicellular life in particular) as "the chief protagonist of the story" (14), the disquieting onto-tales crafted by the Anthropocene's nonhuman scribes need to be included not only in the narratives of Earth-system sciences but also in the poetics and politics of migrant ecologies. These stories are important because they make us aware of the particularities and "consequential relationship" between animals and their places (van Dooren 2014, 83). They also remind us of our responsibility in communicating what is happening to the world and its inhabitants in ways, as van Dooren notes, that enable us to see the world differently, so we are "drawn into new kinds of relationships, new ethical obligations" (83). But while these stories offer insights for thinking anew the relations between mobility and place, they also contain serious ethical conflicts that need to be scrutinized carefully. For instance, one of the most hotly debated stories of forced animal migration involves "the risk of introducing a foreign species into an ecosystem that may become invasive" (Switzer and Angeli 2016, 444). As David Switzer and Nicole Frances Angeli observe, the translocation of endangered species may indeed be very problematic especially if the newcomer's "behaviors may antagonise native groups" (444), thus posing serious threats to native species, and/or may upset the balance of the host ecosystem, which "can happen rapidly and can be difficult to reverse" (447). The authors refer to the behavior of crayfish in explaining the negative impact of species translocation:

> For example, the crayfish Pacifastacus leniusculus shows aggressive behaviour that displaces native species in Japan . . . and Europe. . . . More pertinent to understanding the analogy, this same species shows less aggressive behaviour in its native range where a native congener resides . . . and therefore the animals modulate their individual behaviours to create group cultures based on the conspecific groups where they live. In higher order taxa, groups of cetaceans form their own cultures and languages, dubbed 'horizontal' cultures, allowing some cetaceans to adapt and exploit anthropogenic influences in the seas . . . (444)

Although the species migrations may cause "ecosystem destruction," Switzer and Angeli contend that characterizing translocation of endangered species as "invasive" or "alien" does indeed echo "anti-immigrant rhetoric" (445). The figure of the nonhuman immigrant thus becomes dramatized as a problem of habitat protection or ecosystem security, which raises pressing questions about who will be accountable for the flow of incoming new species and complex questions about climate injustice. As climate justice advocate Laura Geiger argues about forced human mobility, "displacement caused by the impacts of climate change always means a loss and therefore demands compensation" (2020, 21). But the major question here is: Who will compensate deer, gazelles, coyotes, polar bears, foxes, birds, and other nonhuman animals for their habitat loss? Since they all face uncertain fates, unfortunately "some will persist by shifting their range or adapting to local conditions, whereas others will be lost to extinction" (Noll 2017, 26).

Similar to those of forced human migration, the debates around nonhuman migration often invoke preserving native biodiversity, protecting the indigenous biota, and conserving the local ecosystem. Also, like much-discussed forced human migration "that demands new mechanisms for controlling 'flows' of people who, many expect, will be unleashed by climate change" (Baldwin and

Bettini 2017, 2), nonhuman mobility is viewed suspiciously in many scientific circles. In both instances, this highly complex issue requires "less idealised and more pragmatic approaches if practical solutions are to be attained" (Baldwin and Bettini 2017, 444), as well as stories that propel us to a less dystopic environmental future, one that is not full of extinction, loss, and fear. Stories, in fact, matter a great deal. We need stories that critically engage with these Anthropocene complexities, but at the same time we need to be alert that such tales should not make us lose "sight of life, in all its diverse forms, both human and nonhuman, that have shaped the planet" (Mitman 2018, 61). We should remember that "we, as humans, are but an entangled bank, a complex assemblage of animal-micro-biome interactions" and that "even the human genome is indicative of the interdependence and relationality of living forms that came together as partners in the changing development and evolution of humanity" (Mitman 2018, 67). When trying to understand our intimate "microbial relationships," as mycologist Merlin Sheldrake similarly reminds us, it is important to be aware of how these microscopic creatures change "our experience of our own bodies and the places we inhabit. 'We' are ecosystems that span boundaries and transgress categories" (2020, 91). And this becomes more complicated when we realize how intimately interconnected "we" all are in collective vulnerability. The collective "we" here, as Rosi Braidotti, puts it, "is a heterogeneous assemblage that connects 'us,' whether we are anthropomorphic humans (as opposed to uncritically anthropocentric ones) or zoomorphic ones (as in other animals)" (2020, 29). These multiple connections show that borders do not really exist in nature, which is why "weather, toxins, species all move without regard to borders" (Solnit 2007, 87). Migrant ecologies in this perspective gather stories that paradoxically enable conditions of new possibilities while apprising us of new risks posed by nonhuman migrations, especially by mobile viruses, bacteria, and microbes that defy barbwires, fences, walls, and closures. It is this *doubleness* that characterizes the sensitive narratives of migrant ecologies, which prevents us from flipping between either/or perspectives.

Surprising Stories of Migrant Ecologies

The double-coded perspective of migrant ecologies leads us to a significant observation about mischievous microorganisms: what is so astonishing in currently emerging onto-tales are the swarms of bacteria, viruses, pathogens, germs, and microbes, some of which are claimed to be making a risky comeback with the refugees.[7] More alarmingly, when animals, such as fruit bats, are forced to migrate to cooler environments, causing the disruption of the ecology of their former and new habitats, new epidemics also erupt. According to the Intergovernmental Science-Policy Platform on Biodiversity and Ecosystem Services, there are 1.7 million unidentified viruses in mammals and water birds that could be "potentially even more disruptive and lethal than COVID-19" (Settele et al. 2020). Migrations of viruses directly contribute to the spread of new diseases and, as nature writer David Quammen (2020) wrote in a *New York Times* op-ed, if we continue to disrupt ecosystems, "we shake viruses loose from their natural hosts. When that happens, they need a new host. Often, we are it." That is why "viral exchanges—first from animal to human, then from human to human, sometimes on a pandemic scale," as in the case of COVID-19. As stated in the open letter "An Environmental Humanities Response to the COVID-19 Pandemic" (2020), the novel coronavirus "carries the message of our interbeing—across bodies, species, continents."[8] Furthermore, as my colleagues and I wrote in "Through the Portal of COVID-19: Visioning the Environmental Humanities as a Community of Purpose," traveling "throughout the world, this virus is also live-streaming dire truths about the many different human conditions and contagions to which societies have become inured, from interspecies tragedies and the disproportionate injustices of gender, race, and ethnicity to the inequitable slow violence of climate change and industrial environmental poisoning" (Hartman et al. 2020). This highly mobile virus has also engendered important questions that are directly linked to migrant ecologies:

> How can we cohabit a multispecies world while negotiating and mitigating the risks of zoonotic infection and contaminations? How can we cultivate multispecies perspectives on coronavirus so that "all our relations," human and nonhuman, in the words of Winona LaDuke, may not only survive, but flourish? How do we begin thinking in multigenerational terms, or in terms of intergenerational justice and equity? (Hartman et al. 2020)

The complexity of cohabiting a multispecies world filled with risks brought about by hazardous viruses that travel across bodies conveys the double-coded messages encrypted in the discourses of migrant ecologies. Dangerous viruses can thus offer a way of understanding this problematic dimension of multispecies entanglements by rewriting the tale of climate change and migrations in the sense that not all environmentally displaced beings are victims. Apart from claiming human lives daily on a global scale, viruses like the novel coronavirus have the power to paralyze world economies, change history, influence social norms, immobilize humanity, and collapse everything that was considered normal, such as international travelling, attending school, driving or taking public transport to work, because it is "a biological threat, and it is global. Everyone has to change together to deal with it" (Robinson 2020). These words of novelist Kim Stanley Robinson point to the fact that an invisible threat can certainly "strike global civilization" and "rewrite our imaginations" but, more importantly, exacerbate the already existing inequalities.

It is an undisputed fact that the "most devastating consequences of Covid-19" pandemic are observed among "the most vulnerable . . . refugees, 85% of whom live in low and middle-income countries. Within refugee camps, self-isolation and social distancing measures are nearly impossible to implement, and people are anxious amid the spread of misinformation" (Betts, Easton-Calabria, and Pincock 2020, 73). From the perspective of migrant ecologies, the COVID-19 pandemic has not only intensified already-calcified social injustices but also amplified our biological vulnerabilities despite the species arrogance embedded in the discourses of the Anthropocene. According to ethologist Roberto Marchesini, we have been "behaving like a virus, blindly replicating through the spasmodic use of the world's resources, disorganizing its structure and saturating it with debris" (2021, 2). Although this statement may sound controversial since not all humans are guilty of traumatizing the ecosystemic processes and destabilizing the planet for economic profit, it sheds light on the emergency we are all entangled in. It might seem, however, that Marchesini is right in stating that "the planet . . . seems to be seeking immunity to the human infection, because the entire biocentric community is threatened by the ravenous aggression of humans" (2).

Defying human-made borders and infiltrating every imaginable space, the flows of mobilized harmful substances signify the dark side of migrant ecologies already replete with dismal stories of displacement. Critical plant studies scholar Michael Marder draws attention to microplastics, which are "as ubiquitous in tap and bottled water as mercury is in fish" (2019, 182). In other words, not everything that is dislodged and migrates can legitimize itself at the expense of other beings and gain acceptance unquestioningly. But it must be noted that this is not the mastering vision of migrant ecologies, which predominantly focus on the surprising tales of the multispecies world that occupy this field of inquiry.

Another surprising story in migrant ecologies involves the fate of the flora. In addition to nonhuman animals who join humans as climate refugees, some plants are included in the same category, such as the matsutake, a group of wild mushrooms much valued in Japan, which Anna Lowenhaupt Tsing brought to our attention in *The Mushroom at the End of the World* (2015). These mushrooms live in human-disturbed forests that have become a "global commodity," and they are foraged by people who are themselves displaced minorities, self-exiled poor peasants, or just plain refugees from Laos and Cambodia (Tsing 2015, 4). In plant ecology, plants that appear in nonnative places are considered to be invasive species or described as aliens even if biologists have yet to observe "the full impact of plant invasions on native biodiversity" (Stohlgren and Rejmánek 2014, 4) to conclude that plant invasion "may have some locally strong effects, but those effects may be overestimated" (4).[9]

Although plant invasion is a major concern, as Emily Grebenstein (2013) concurs,[10] biologists Thomas J. Stohlgren and Marcel Rejmánek see this as an "unsettling paradox," and argue that alien plant invasions causing extinctions or increasing diversity need more empirical evidence, because "the levels of uncertainty of ecological forecasts may be difficult to quantify, owing to uncertainties in future climates, unpredictable disturbances, species adaptations and the effects of trade and transportation bringing in enemies to alien and native species alike" (2014, 1). Biologists Kristin Powell, Jonathan M. Chase, and Tiffany M. Knight are of the same opinion:

> Many empirical studies show dramatic reductions of native biodiversity in the presence of invasive species. However, evidence that invasive species cause native species extinctions is rare, although it might be expected given the overwhelming evidence of their negative effects. Although invasive predators and parasites are known to have caused extinctions of many species, competition with invasive plants is rarely implicated in extinction. In fact, in some cases the presence of invasive plants can actually increase species richness, leading to questions about whether most invasive species are really a leading threat to the conservation of native biodiversity. (2013, 316)

There are, however, documented cases that showcase the opposite. Japanese knotweed, for example, is a plant species that can easily spread and dominate "other vegetation wherever it grows, often to the detriment of our native species," as documented by Kate Constantine (2014), a project scientist at CABI, an international environmental organization. Constantine writes that "Japanese knotweed is highly invasive and very difficult to control let alone eradicate. The plant grows and spreads via its underground stock of rhizome from which fragments break off and a whole new plant can grow—interestingly Japanese knotweed plants in the UK all originate from a single female clone."

Although ongoing scientific discussions on invasive plant species are not yet settled, their sociocultural implications occupy a good part of the arguments of those who want to accentuate socially and ecologically acceptable ways of management. To illustrate, Katharina Kapitza and coauthors (2019) foreground "the integration and understanding of social and cultural perspectives . . . on invasive species, and the consideration of biological invasions as social-ecological phenomena" (47), and they draw attention to the social and cultural dimension of biological invasions, emphasizing the necessity of having "a transdisciplinary and transparent discourse" in order have more "ecologically and socially successful, management" (48). Obviously, the related issue of the cultural dimensions of plant mobility and invasive species is how they are deployed and received in different cultural imaginaries: How are they inscribed in cultural discourses? The question of how we narrate the invasive species in cultural and literary texts inevitably joins the epistemological question of how we know them (in terms of risk, harm, precariousness, or potential benefits). Asking such questions allows us to have a different perspective, one that Brendon M. H. Larson draws attention to, namely that we need new stories about invasive species, especially about "how we relate to them in order to wend a path between the extremes of apathy and antipathy" (2010, 25). As Larson shows in his discussion, we should first avoid either/or categories in formulating new narratives about nonnative species: "To avoid the prevailing connotation that 'invasive species are our enemies,' I cannot just promote the alternative that 'invasive species are our friends.' Notice that they are still invasive species, which still activates our associations about invaders, even if unconsciously" (25). Being neither friend nor foe, invasive plant species cannot help but enact their nature like the weed in Jeremy Gadd's (2017, 37) poem "What is commonly called a weed." This short poem published in *New Shoots Poetry Anthology* (2017) captures the experiences of the weed without judgment. There is no language of alienation here, even if weeds are commonly conceived to be quite invasive in the wider political and cultural contexts due to their uncontrollable displacement and resettlement. Climbing through a narrow opening in the pavement, the weed's utmost goal is survival. Even if it is quite fragile, it will eventually "grow and expand" (37). The poem begins with the common weed pushing through a crack in the concrete to seek sunshine. Although "the tendril is weak, fragile, vulnerable," writes the poet, its stem "extruding from where its seed was blown . . . proclaims nature will one day reclaim its own" (37). He points to how the weed's roots "create cracks" in the concrete, and how those cracks "receive other migrant seeds," which continue the cycle of growth. The weed's intention to survive resembles the determination of human immigrants: both are "fragile," "vulnerable," and "blown" into new places where they are not wanted. Both inhabit tangled worlds that challenge the illusion of unity on a socio-ecological level and that at present do not tolerate defensive reactions. One can read the poem from the perspective of the weed eager to tell stories of unintended human and more-than-human entanglements humans often do not notice.

Malcolm Fisher's (2017) poem, "The Toughest Brief," in the same anthology is another rethinking of invasive plants through an ironic homage to human-induced environmental stress and degradation in a judicious narrative voice: "One plant is much the same as any another / Exotic, invasive, native, endemic / Doesn't matter," writes the poet. He asks: "How can you cherish what's unknown? / Or care for what's unloved" (95). This poem self-consciously reminds us that if we continue to be "consumers estranged from this world," we will never learn to cherish what is not on our immediate radar. Such poems ask us to look at migrant ecologies differently, to shift our awareness out of our cultural divisions (like the friend or foe binary mentioned earlier) and into that of new narratives to prevent the discourse of migrant ecologies from being conclusive and teleological. After all, if we reconsider invasive species "in terms of our changing perceptions of them," as Brendon M. H. Larson suggests, we can have "another impetus to stretch our conceptual flexibility" (2010, 33). Expanding our concepts to the nonhuman world, however, requires a capacity to do this "without smothering other life-forms with prejudice and innuendo" (Sheldrake 2020, 42).

Such an approach, as Thom van Dooren would say, "opens our world into attentiveness" (2014, 83), into the collision of human ruthlessness and nonhuman vulnerabilities, but also into "the actual ethical weight of our destructive actions" (89). Although they are unlikely to forge an immediate international political action, through such stories in plant studies and migrant ecologies we may be "drawn into new kinds of relationships, new ethical obligations" (83), which enable us to rethink and reconfigure our material and discursive practices in dealing with the migrant question. The refugee quandary itself should make it clear that holding on to a myopic vision, whether intentional or unintentional, is never a way to address, let alone solve, this crisis with intersecting dimensions.

Border Intensities

What is at stake in these migrant ecologies is also the idea that borders today are simultaneously about closure and permeability, notions that are part of the paradoxical grand narratives of migration. Rather than seeing borders as signs of closure or despair, migrants themselves have fashioned a more hybrid conceptualization that would allow at least the potential for new interpretive possibilities. Borders are material-discursive constructions that embody "narratives of injury" (Nixon 2011, 47), pain, and prolonged suffering for those who attempt to cross over to the other side (no irony intended here) and who often experience traumatic hostility. In the context of changing climates and migration, Andrew Baldwin and Giovanni Bettini write that "fences, barbwires and 'barbarians' are key visual signifiers in narratives on 'climate refugees'" (2017, 12). For Nigel Clark, professor of human geography, the border issue is related to "the experience of being 'unworlded' by environmental change" and to "the question of how we encounter those who have been 'othered' by their very world becoming strange" (2017, 134). When the world becomes strange and one is othered, making connections across people and landscapes at the border becomes increasingly difficult, and one's sense of continuity gets disrupted. Being unworlded, then, means being cast into a situation of marginality; it means being decentered and thrown into an ideologically complex form of alienation. But such an experience also challenges the idea of borders as impermeable monoliths.

The massive movements of people across the national boundaries—like Mexicans attempting to cross the Sonora Desert to reach the United States, migrants from Bangladesh at the border of India, Chinese at the Siberian border, North Africans at the Mediterranean border, and Syrians at the Turkish border—show how utterly pervious national borders are despite attempts to build fences and walls to keep them closed, and how interpenetrable the discursive borderlines can become when cultures intermingle in strife and conflict. But border interpenetrability comes with a high price. According to international relations scholar Umut Ozguc, borders are "the most violent sites of contemporary politics," which she calls "politics of death" (2020, 77). However, despite the negative framing of borders as death and destruction with "unpredictable, indeterminate, and continuously shifting forms of the seemingly fixed structure," borders for migrant ecologies represent a third space, "an in-between space" (78). Ozguc's reading of the border "as a space that gives rise to the emergence of multiple possibilities" (80) recasts the border question in terms of its "ambiguities, paradoxes, shifts, and continuities," which enable migrant ecologies to construe the border as "a socially, politically, and culturally constructed lived space" (80). Such a reading can open up multiple possibilities for human and nonhuman mobilities, including the possibility of "creatively reimagining the world as a site for democratic politics" (Baldwin and Bettini 2017, 30) even if this may sound rather unrealistic at present. These possibilities are also discussed by British climatologist Mike Hulme (2011) as "other ways of envisioning the future," which take into consideration "human creativity, imagination, and ingenuity" to "create radically different social, cultural, and political worlds in the future than exist today" (266). Although, as Baldwin and Bettini (2017)—who also find inspiration in this quotation—discreetly confess, such ideas are not likely to materialize soon. We still need to imagine a different discourse on climate change and migration to tackle the border question in a more humane way. In this sense, borders, changing climate, and migrations, involuntary or not, should be conceived and interpreted as inseparable social, political, and ecological narratives and lived experiences that derive their force more from epistemic communities of power than from any objective truth or a body of knowledge climate scientists circulate on climate metrics. Finding what Hulme calls "richer narrative contexts that enable the wisdom of different choices to be deliberated, interpreted, and judged" (2020, 311) is one way to situate these notoriously complex and manifestly interrelated problems. Hence, "when rooted in larger and thicker stories about human purpose, identity, duty, and responsibility" (311), the border question in particular demands "richer narrative contexts [that] enable the wisdom of different choices to be deliberated, interpreted, and judged" (311). Therefore, according to Hulme, solutions may be "rooted in larger and thicker stories about human purpose, identity, duty, and responsibility" (311). Seen this way, the destinies and interrelations of borders, climate change, and migrants are more often than not discursively determined and vary with time. We should also know that the border narrative can neither be seen nor solved as a discursive problem nor can it be tackled solely as a material conundrum.

In light of these ideas, I would state again that borders are material-discursive terrains that are fabricated to determine the destinies of displaced peoples. For this very reason, they are one of the most contested sociopolitical issues, as in the case of the dehumanization of Syrian refugees in 2015 at the Hungarian border and the East African refugees confined in the now-demolished Calais Jungle in France in 2015–2016. Often, but not always, borders shatter refugees' dreams of a better home—one possibly less fraught with economic, political, religious, and social conflicts, let alone ecological transformations. Borders are also ethical sites that confound save-the-day political solutions to refugee crises with unexpected stories (like Syria's gazelles) that creep across the fences built to protect insiders from being infiltrated by the outside.

From the migrant ecological perspective, ethics materialize through such stories that counter the stance of political subjects. Sedimented with so many sorrowful stories, both human and nonhuman, borders contain not only geopolitical complexities but also environmental imaginaries. In times of overwhelming distress, what we find in the border stories engrained in migrant ecologies is a desire for interlinked ecological and social change that would help with the crises, traumas, sufferings, and injustice afflicting our landscapes of life and imagination. In this context, the material is always already discursive, entailing this complex awareness that leaves us with the critical stance of seeing the migrant subject (again, both human and nonhuman) in disquieting terms of loss and dispersal and undermining received notions of this figure who won't foreclose the border question. Being a highly contested issue, in sum, the border question discloses an important dimension of migrant ecologies, which can be seen as the inevitable mangling of inside and outside when they permeate through natures, cultures, habitats, and beings of the Anthropocene. Consequently, borders are "relations between spaces," as conceptualized by Martina Löw and Gunter Weidenhaus (2017). "Whenever a border is in focus," they observe, "at least two spaces are constituted and set in relation to each other by this spatial boundary" (558). And this relationality is loaded with "complex symbolic and material implications," as Sandro Mezzadra and Brett Neilson maintain (2013, v). Relationalities, however, always depend on "who or what is in the relating" (Gan 2017, 91), which brings us to the key problematic that involves competitive relations with multiple forms of social complexities and tensions, and ambiguities and anxieties, surfacing within the current refugee crisis.

Although in this problematic space the war-torn Middle East immediately springs to mind, the refugee crisis today—and the social and environmental catastrophes triggering mass migrations of people and many nonhuman species—is not limited to this excessively disrupted terrain putting enormous social and economic stress on countries like Turkey, which is hosting an estimated nine million or more refugees from Syria, Iraq, and Afghanistan. European countries—from the Mediterranean coasts of Greece and Italy to the more affluent states of the north, now locked in a condition of unprecedented disagreement on new borders and rules—are trying to cope with hundreds of thousands of refugees and "economic migrants" flowing in from crisis-ridden parts of the world. In this regard, "the complexity of the contemporary border—its messiness, ambiguity, and unruliness" (Ozguc 2019, 1) is closely linked to the devastation caused by postcolonial struggles for the control of resources in the Middle East and Africa and devastation caused by economic turmoil in South America. For example, the controversial question of building a wall on the US–Mexico border called for a radical rethinking of what prominent feminist environmentalist Greta Gaard dubs "ecosocial contexts" (2014, 287). Such radical measures to solve the migrant problematic not only create more socially biased perceptions but also have environmental consequences. Such a wall's environmental impact on wildlife migrations—especially on endangered species like jaguars and ocelots—was eclipsed in the heated discussions focusing apprehensively on safety measures.[11] Instead, we need to affirm, as Gaard advises, "the affective mode that offers an avenue for understanding across differences" (2014, 288).

What comes within the purview of migrant ecologies are the links between climate change and social conflicts, altered landscapes and migrant species and peoples, displacement and war, and environmental degradation and urban sprawl. This is a world whose borders are in steady mutation and redefinition and whose identities are themselves "migrant" and "nomadic." In this web of not-fully-predictable relations, migrant stories of a shared experience of harm are pushed further in a moral direction that calls for concrete political measures in ethical reaction, as well as necessitating academic responses, especially from the environmental humanities scholars studying the Anthropocene's many complexities.

The Migrant Figure and Place Attachment

The borders that cannot preclude the flow of migrants yield the migrant figure as a climate refugee whose material presence subverts the notion of the Anthropos conceptualized around a disembodied human subject associated with planetary geological changes. In this framework, the migrant figure becomes even more riddled with questions, such as: How do women refugees from diverse nations, classes, regions, and incomes fit into this category? How would migrant ecologies reconfigure the narratives of the Anthropocene and change the discourse of environmental ethics and political ecology? If there is a direct link between climate change and regional conflicts, where shall we search for ecologically and socially viable solutions? How would the environmental humanities address the socioecological problems on a planet whose changing conditions affect every living being, even if the ecological crisis is not evenly experienced? How do we respond to an ever-increasing environmental and social instability of Earth and its inhabitants?

These are some of the questions we need to investigate in-depth with regards to environmental issues that demand solutions to new—socially and ontologically transversal—forms of violence. These forms include increasing toxicity and pollution in urban and natural environments, energy exhaustion, displacement of peoples, extinction of species, victims of new colonization, global redistributions of power and traditions, languages, cultural discourses, and forms of imagination. The global redistribution of culture, in particular, is a highly complex problem related to the sociocultural paradigms of geographical memory and human attachment to place as a matter of environmental belonging, which becomes gradually eroded by massive human migration specifically to the congested areas of metropolises. Consequently, human attachment to place gets replaced by economic interests dominated by socioeconomic and political concerns, especially regarding urban problems. The city overextended beyond its carrying capacity becomes stressed as it fills with new occupants who feel little or no connection to the bioregional elements around their environment and are devoid of moral responsibility to it. Lacking the natural sense of belonging to their new environment, the incoming flows of immigrants find themselves struggling over living spaces. In a very material way, Istanbul is exemplary of this, and contemporary Turkish novels specifically address this drama. One noteworthy example is Buket Uzuner's *Istanbullu* (2008), a novel that contextualizes this complex problem in a thematic questioning of the matrix of both negative and positive aspects of migrant ecologies. The erosion of social and environmental values in Istanbul is expressed by the city speaking with its own voice, displaying both urban and environmental sensitivity. Istanbul thus emerges not only as "a city of many voices, many faiths, many languages and many cultures" (Uzuner 2008, 270) but also as an exceedingly disrupted urban environment due to mass migration, which began in the 1960s with incoming villagers from Anatolia. As of 2021, Istanbul's population had dramatically increased, with 534,439 Syrian refugees settling in the city.[12]

Founded on the seven hills of a peninsula surrounded on three sides by the Sea of Marmara, the Bosphorus, and its arm called the Golden Horn, Istanbul is a typical site of migrant ecological issues. Once a city of tulips that played a significant historical role, Istanbul today is an overwhelmingly built human environment with more than fifteen million inhabitants and hosting more refugees (from Syria and Iraq mostly) than all of Europe. The ongoing degradation of Istanbul's water basins, forests, and green areas and illegal occupation of public lands exact a severe toll on the area's local ecosystem, resulting in the transformation of the natural flora and the disruption of ecological balance. Istanbul's seven hills, which were once adorned by forests with more than 2,000 species of native flora, are now largely deforested. Much of the deforestation is due to illegal settlement. Unplanned construction near the water basins, for example, seriously threatens Istanbul's water resources. As Abdurrahman Geymen and Ibrahim Baz note, this threat is quite obvious in "Elmalı, one of the dams providing drinking water to the city. This surface water source has faced pollution problems due to the change of land use. Physical, chemical and bacteriological pollution in the quality of water have stemmed, generally, from the settlements" (2008, 450). Istanbul is continually undergoing rapid urban transformation at the dangerous exhaustion of the remaining natural resources (watersheds, agricultural areas, and forests) with its population growth by migration. This is quite evident in Uzuner's novel, where one of the characters, Professor Yannis Seferis, "with a Greek name and a Turkish passport" (2008, 100), despairingly says of the immigrants: "How can they be expected to understand and appreciate the meaning of metropolis, the richness in diversity, the essence of what made Istanbul, Istanbul? It's not easy for them either; most have little or no education. What are they supposed to do, the poor things?" (98–99). The novel further references how the detrimental process of immigration led Istanbul toward conditions that resulted in a loss of sense of place and created politics of resistance to place attachment. Another character, Erol Argunsoy, the prominent architect, shares a negative, if realistic, picture of the consequences of immigration. The immigrants, he says, adopt a destructive attitude to their new environment because they lack a sense of belonging: "Now they come here just to fill their pockets by plundering and raping, by destroying and razing . . . Vandals!" (2008, 172). Place attachment "implies adaptation," as Lawrence Buell reminds us (2005, 66), which, the novel implies, the immigrants can neither feel nor experience. Instead, the immigrants reterritorialize the landscape according to their economic needs and thus remain outside the life-rhythms of a metropolis.

Set in Istanbul's 107-year-old international Atatürk Airport, which closed to commercial passenger flights on April 6, 2019, the novel fuses the diverse voices of characters from different walks of life, faiths, and cultural backgrounds who express conflicting views on globalization, immigration, commerce, identity, history, culture and art, the environment, and numerous other urban problems. Istanbul shapes their identities as they try to "benefit from the cultural offerings of the urban environment" (172), including Susan, an American woman who has chosen to become an Istanbullu (Istanbulite). Susan does not fit into the architect's description of the immigrant as she has developed a sense of place attachment with a strong sense of belonging there. She says she loves "the squawking seagulls and the drone of the ferryboats . . . the profoundly mystic colors of Sufism," and adds: "I love the openness of the people. I love it. What more can I say? What does 'homeland' mean, anyway? I'm an Istanbullu!" (114). *Istanbullu* also highlights the importance of the notion of ethics of place in a world that has become overtly transnational and where the characters struggle with community identification. The airport serves as a metaphor of a "hermetically sealed environment" and appears as "a living machine regulated and digitalized. It was a self-contained artificial city, one that produces its own air and water, one whose lifeblood flowed through pipes and along circuits" (308). The description of Atatürk airport "as a giant metal whale" (309) appropriates life-support functions of a local ecosystem through travel, trade, and commerce, as well as immigration. The airport, then, is a space marked as a product of a microcosm of globalization and immigration, where "tens of thousands of scurrying organisms, emotional creatures propelled by pain and joy, hopes and memories" (308) circulate every day. The novel allows the reader to think about problems that touch the daily lives of the Istanbulites (both the old residents and the newcomers) and challenges them to think about how these problems are implicated in the expansion of immigration policies in Turkey especially and to consider their consequences in terms of changing values in culture and identity.

Perhaps we need a careful rethinking of the social and the political representations of all these interconnected issues by which we understand not only the current state of migrant ecologies but also the totalizing narratives around them, which dissolve ethical considerations into, for instance, either security issues or safety protocols. If the prospect of the twenty-first century is the escalating refugee crisis, it is not possible to disentangle its ethical dimension from the political. Among the unresolved contradictions of migrant ecologies is, therefore, the close intertwinement of environmental, ethical, political, social, and economic pressures. For this reason alone, "separating out the geneses of today's refugees is not always easy," as rightly expressed by Lester R. Brown (2011, 81) in *World on Edge: How to Prevent Environmental and Economic Collapse*. Brown cites striking stories to call attention to this entanglement, such as the boat found by Italian authorities in 2003 carrying refugees from Africa:

> After being adrift for more than two weeks and having run out of fuel, food, and water, many of the passengers had died. At first the dead were tossed overboard. But after a point, the remaining survivors lacked the strength to hoist the bodies over the side. The dead and the living shared the boat, resembling what a rescuer described as "a scene from Dante's Inferno." (2011, 81–82)

Although it wasn't clear "whether they were political, economic, or environmental refugees," Brown notes that these refugees were believed to be from Somalia, which he describes as an "ecological basket case, with overpopulation, overgrazing, and the resulting desertification destroying its pastoral economy" (82). According to Brown, governments in developed countries should consider treating the causes of migration rather than responding to the symptoms. Given the current situation, it is indeed a wise counsel, for the whole point of migrant ecologies is not to merely represent or objectively interpret responses and actions as political theorists and cultural studies scholars do. Rather, as ecocritics and environmental humanists do in connection with the anthropogenic environmental transformations, it is better to formulate ecologically and socially viable solutions in the material practices, as well as rethink the concepts and language around totalizing impulses and totalizable discourses. Therefore, foregrounding and treating the causes of migration would keep migrant ecologies from being overshadowed by the representations of and responses to the symptoms of migration. The first step would be, as Brown suggests, "working with developing countries to restore their economy's natural support systems—the soils, the grasslands, the forests—and it means accelerating the shift to smaller families to help people break out of poverty" (2011, 83). More importantly, however, such political acts can change, to borrow Jane Bennett's terms, "the regime of the perceptible," or "provoke a gestalt shift in perception" (2010, 107). In other words, radically changing how people perceive their world, their lives, and other species through more effective strategies in economic systems and environmental policies might decrease, if not totally eliminate, suffering, harm, and eventually mass migration.

To conclude, I would like to emphasize the fact that confronting the specificities of migrant ecologies on a range of topics, geographies, and stories is not easy, but it is possible to envision solutions and offer alternative approaches if we intend to raise critical awareness about migrant ecologies in a world of porous borders that prompt a reconsideration of genuine refuge as well as a rethinking of closure. Accepting unpredictability is challenging, but the promise is also there to remind us of our humanity and of our kinship with the nonhuman communities. If we are to achieve what the leading voice in ecocriticism Scott Slovic calls "positive transformations" (2017, 102), we must come to terms with such a multifaceted phenomenon as migrant ecologies dovetailed with relative uncertainties and instabilities. We need to move knowledge forward "through the kinds of interdisciplinary engagements" that "can be mobilized by intentional *communities of purpose* to work for genuine transformative change" (Hartman and Oppermann 2020, 2; italics in original). If we want such a change in the face of worldly ambiguities, social tensions, risks, and disruption of stability, we need a new perception of the world where it becomes possible to tolerate relative stabilities. This new perception is brought to our attention by Claire Colebrook (2017), who notes that if sovereign nations "open themselves to only the very deserving few who might be genuine refugees (rather than supposedly opportunistic migrants)" (118), relative stability can be maintained. Colebrook also claims that "it is from movement and migration that relative stabilities are formed *not* in a stabilization of 'ownness' but in a relation among forces" (117).

Can we really disown our attachment to "ownness" and embrace a relational ontology, even if in theory first? I think the answer lies in the unacknowledged politics of becoming-with-each other. So, "whoever and whatever we were/are/will become," as Haraway explains, "we think, act, narrate, metabolize and come into and out of existence through each other, within each other, at stake with each other" (2015b, vii). Haraway's words not only evoke our entanglements with other beings in a striking way but also surprisingly shed light on the complex meanings and the material condition of the (un)bordered world of migrant ecologies. What we inhabit is, therefore, not distinct from what we think. What we narrate is also what we metabolize. Migrant ecologies are, for these reasons, at the stake of our earthly becomings with all that exists across "genes, species, and ecosystems to reveal a world already undergoing substantial change" (Scheffers et al. 2016, editor's summary). Heeding the surge of many uncertainties in the postnatural world where migration has a Janus face, migrant ecologies move us to a new level of understanding the interconnectedness of all things with a keen awareness of the complexities that exist within those interconnected threads.

Chapter 4

Postnatural Ecologies of the Anthropocene

As this chapter's title signals, due to the phenomenal impact of human activities on the planet, the established patterns and rhythms of "Holocene phenology" (Albrect 2016, 12) are rapidly undergoing irreversible cataclysmic changes.[1] All earthly beings are ontologically captured and exploited in this incisively configured dark ecological reality, which, as Glenn A. Albrecht points out, "correlates in human physical and mental distress" (12) and yields an anxiety-driven perspective on the prospect of possible survivals. Yet, what seems to be an intentional anthropic ignorance in economic policies consolidates anthropocentric discursive formations that shape cultural behaviors symptomatic of wider societal and ecological problems. The progressive captivity of natural environments within the destabilizing forces of capitalist greed shapes decision-making processes undertaken by governmental and private corporate actors who turn a blind eye to the Earth's aggravating metabolic disorder and social vulnerability to environmental hazards (i.e., climate anomalies, floods and droughts, bushfires, pandemics). As Henrik Enroth explains, this attitude is an "organized denial" (2020, 1) in the capitalist circles that rule the world, and this is because—to quote Kim Stanley Robinson—"we've been out of synch with the biosphere" (Robinson 2020).

Taking this concern for the postnatural discourse that addresses alarming changes happening on a planetary scale, this chapter argues that the world we exploit, consume, and want to protect nevertheless is sliding into the dangerous rhythms and disruptive cycles of *postnatures*. Unfortunately, however, as Belgian philosopher of science Isabelle Stengers observes with good reason, "we are as badly prepared as possible to produce the type of response that, we feel, the situation requires of us" (2015, 30). Despite the doom-and-gloom scenarios the term *postnature* evokes, we still inhabit a kaleidoscopic world filled with beings and things whose patterns of interconnections continue to produce meanings and stories that make it possible to imagine new accountabilities, more sustainable solutions to the planet's distress, and sustainable ethical responses. This means that we can "think through the liberatory possibilities of a messy, muddled, interspecies future" (Moore 2016, 6) to write a new geostory furnished with nonanthropocentric meanings, which can materialize with new forms of resistance, new narratives, and new lexical vocabularies. Proposing a common geostory that needs to be written collectively by "novelists, generals, engineers, scientists, politicians, activists, and citizens," Bruno Latour claims that "it will be utterly impossible to tell our common geostory without all of us" (2014,14).

This vision can inspire hope for the future because a new geostory can take into account the unheard voices of the disrupted nonhuman entities whose stories are inextricably grafted upon our stories, our lives, and our meaning-making practices. In other words, learning to pay more attention to more-than-human-environments, beings, and things that exist within, outside, and around us in an increasingly postnatural reality might help us better understand our entanglements in the world's narratives of becoming and eventually enable us to find ways out of "today's global turbulence" (Moore 2016, 1) and, thus, of postnatural ecological predicament. This predicament is captured well by ecologically oriented contemporary fictions, which represent the effects of climate change and other related ecological problems in a realistic mode by "paying close attention to what it means to live through climate shift, moment by moment, in individual, fragile bodies" (LeMenager 2017, 225). Given all the anxiety, the spreading confusion, and the ontological insecurities and fears associated with the term *postnatural*, climate change fiction (cli-fi), as the storied site of the surfacing of this reality, is useful in raising awareness about the potential dangers in this predicament. Cli-fi, in other words, might be seen to issue a warning by pointing to how postnatural ecologies unfold within broader social and political contexts.

Since climate change fictions present stories of "imminent danger and immanent resilience" (Newell, Quetchenbach, and Nolan 2020, i) encountered in postnatural environments, this chapter's last section focuses on John Burnside's *Glister* (2009) as an exemplary novel that thematizes the political, social, and psychological troubles associated with postnatural ecologies. Set against the background of a chemically poisoned land, untreatable illnesses, depression, mutant creatures, and political corruption, *Glister* shows the significance of harboring love and hope epitomized by the novel's teenage protagonist, Leonard Wilson, who refuses to be consumed by the dark reality of his postnatural predicament. Leonard's attitude reminds us of the theory of panarchy developed by ecologist Crawford Buzz Holling, who, after observing the ecology of forests, noticed that forests "have an adaptive cycle of growth, collapse, regeneration, and again growth" (Homer-Dixon 2006, 226). In his article "Understanding the Complexity of Economic, Ecological, and Social Systems," Holling explains how natural and human socio-ecological systems are "interlinked in never-ending adaptive cycles of growth, accumulation, restructuring, and renewal" (2001, 392). Like the forests' adaptive cycles that follow a process of decline and renewal through resilience in a disturbed environment, the novel's protagonist goes through a process of adaptation. Leonard's story is reminiscent of "the way catastrophe caused by such stresses could produce a surge of creativity leading to the renewal of our global civilization" (Homer-Dixon 2006, 226). Therefore, this chapter ends with a brief conclusion on panarchy, the term Holling coined after Pan, the god of nature.

Postnatural Ecologies

Bearing witness to the compromised condition of biospheric life brought about by environmentally harmful sociopolitical and economic practices, postnatural ecologies refer to often irreversible environmental changes across different biophysical systems that eventually become too unstable or overly toxified to sustain multispecies life. The term *postnatural* thus denotes a negatively transformed physical environment, ruined landscapes, and waterscapes haunted by the ghosts of their former biological assemblages. Landscapes that are burned, flooded, deforested, contaminated by toxic waste, overrun by plastic pollution, and modified by industrialized crops or invasive plants and animals are increasingly called postnatural places where endemic species struggle to stay alive. Forests, for example, become conspicuously postnatural when they stop being hubs of biodiversity.[2] Oceans, too, mutate into postnatural sites as they bear humanity's most pronounced chemical signature with increased concentration of chemicals, such as nitrogen and phosphorus flowing into oceans and promoting harmful algal blooms, which produce dangerous toxins in water and create dead zones.[3] The release of plastic waste into the ocean, which accumulates in deep sea environments as microplastics, has literally become unimaginable in scope with abundant microplastic fibers "in marine sediments on a global scale" (Gabbott et al. 2020, 36). Oceanic plastic also affects the epipelagic zone of the oceans where sperm whales live.[4] One of the most extreme examples is the 2018 newsflash of a dead sperm whale washed ashore in Indonesia with thirteen pounds of plastic trash in its stomach. But there are equally distressing stories of marine life such as sea turtles who confuse plastic garbage for food, the Mediterranean monk seals deprived of their habitats due to coastal urbanization, and coral reefs dying at an alarming rate. Oceanic pollution offers perhaps the clearest case of how "the global commons have become deeply anthropomorphized through the byproducts of human production" (DeLoughrey 2019, 101).

The vision fueling this development not only validates social and political systems of power but also infuses the majority of people's thinking and acting, bringing to the surface implicit or explicit complicity as ordinary citizens (both of the industrialized world and the Global South) become instrumental in planetary transformations. Greta Gaard describes people's complicity as "psychic numbing" and "human responses to the increasingly frightening scenarios of species extinctions, environmental 'development' and climate change futures" (2020, 225). Although plant and animal species extinctions have become the truisms of postnatural reality, the contemporary tenor of life gathered in human volition continues to make many vulnerable species defenseless, like the bleached reefs of Christmas Island in the Pacific Ocean, which have already turned into ghosts of their former vivacity. This leads to further concern. When political irresponsibility, social inequality and instability, gender, class, race-based injustices, and uneven power relations within human societies become integral to a disturbing ecological alienation, they consequently foment post-naturalization processes that reflect socio-ecological crises. These processes also signal the often-unconscious anthropocentrism of human subjects who become silent witnesses at best even if some of them suffer the consequences of their involuntary participation in planetary destabilization and postnatural expansion.

In very general terms, human beings, involuntarily or not, become what Haraway calls "messmates" (2008a, 4) in the planet's geomorphological processes and natural cycles with detrimental activities that stretch from the atmospheric heights to the planet's oceanic depths. Even those who refuse to become messmates are afflicted by a false sense of comforting distance from all that is not human. Looking through the veils of consumer lifestyles, they may be hazily cognizant of the environmental tragedies unfolding somewhere away from the "safety zones" they think they inhabit while the earthly voices continue to forewarn an almost unlivable postnatural future.

The term *postnatural* itself is quite expansive. National parks and nearby towns devastated by wildfires; pastures destroyed by poisonous chemicals that seep from underground mines; mountains harmed by mountaintop removal practices that begin with topsoil and vegetation removal;[5] and, to some extent, urban areas battered by earthquakes, hurricanes and tornadoes, floods and droughts, or traumatized by pandemics like today's COVID-19 are among the arresting examples of postnatural places. Many typical examples of the postnatural include the "hazard-prone landscape[s]" (Lewis 2019, 76) that are occupied by deadly pathogens and parasites, creating public health crises and putting urban sustainability at serious risk. As a matter of fact, postnatural landscapes are not necessarily unmitigated wastelands—especially in the case of urban settings—but disrupted living spaces entangled in inequitable social relations, which intensify "the unequal distribution of environmental risks" (Heise 2020, 125). Environmental humanities scholar Ursula K. Heise explains that "landfills, toxic waste sites, and hazardous industries are disproportionately sited near or upwind from poor communities and communities of color" (2020, 124–25). Last but not least, the postnatural is particularly recognizable in the evidence that we now have more shopping malls and synthetic products than forests and coral reefs, which seems unlikely to change in the foreseeable future. As Nicholas Ruiz III points out in *America in Absentia*, "beneath the debris of our cultures, remains the vestige of life's perennial upset" (2008, 26). If we continue to capitalize on harmful practices for the comforts they offer us in the destabilized Earth systems, we will never hear the voices of dying reefs, let alone get to know the tragic stories of multispecies life across the planet. The living world is struggling to stay alive and scientists are now tired of warning humanity. In "World Scientists' Warning to Humanity: A Second Notice," we are told that "soon it will be too late to shift course away from our failing trajectory, and time is running out. We must recognize, in our day-to-day lives and in our governing institutions, that Earth with all its life is our only home" (Ripple et al. 2017, 1028).

Another important fact to emphasize here is that for as long as humans discharge chemical compounds into lakes, rivers, and seas, they will be altering the metabolism of other species. When exposed to xenobiotic substances, damaged environments trigger biotic changes in vulnerable species, such as the androgynous fish detected in rivers. Bearing the signs of environmental toxicity, the bodies of fish become the very sites of traffic between consumer cultures and damaged natures. Since this is an entangled world of human and nonhuman interdependencies, human bodies are also caught in this traffic of pollution, waste, and toxicity. In *Toxic Bodies: Hormone Disruptor and the Legacy of DES*, environmental historian Nancy Langston provides ample evidence of toxic chemicals that "have the potential to cross the boundaries between species . . . altering the hormone systems that shape our internal ecosystems of health, as well as our relationship with the broader ecosystems around us" (2010, 2). Because these chemicals move up the food chain, bodies become internal ecosystems, Langston argues, through which poisonous material agencies gather together to constrain corporeal rhythms, sweeping them into invasive waves of internal ruin. What creates these unintended effects are the globalized transportation networks, industrial agriculture, and asymmetrical encounters between micro- and macroorganisms. Langston's examples underline the permeability of naturalcultural processes whereby toxic embodiments become quite ordinary, with bodies and environments carrying traces of xenobiotic chemicals whose residues remain long after the chemicals have been dispersed. The "geologically unprecedented transglobal species invasions and changes associated with farming and fishing" (Waters et al. 2016, aad2622) are part of this muddled ecological reality in which the all-too-familiar rhythms of time, weather, bodies, and the seasonal growth of plants and the movements of animals are thrown into disarray.

A different usage of the term *postnatural* is in relation to transgenic technologies that instigate "human-driven changes to the biology and genetics of living organisms," explained as "the purposeful and permanent modification of living species by humans through domestication, genetic engineering, and synthetic biology" (Pell and Allen 2015a, 79, 77). In discussing how the postnatural emerged in this way, Richard W. Pell and Lauren P. Allen of the Center for PostNatural History[6] draw attention to synthetic biology, which treats living entities as "reconfigurable biological machines whose genetic parts may be borrowed, hacked, and repurposed to serve new goals" (2015b, 224).

In a wider sense, the term *postnatural* signifies what political scientist Timothy W. Luke calls *denatured* environments that bear the burdens of extreme pollution, which modify the chemistry of the atmosphere, hydrosphere, and biosphere. This is how, Luke claims, "nature is turning into 'Denature'" (1997, 195). The Great Pacific Garbage Patch is a shocking reminder of the disruption of biotic life that took millions of years to evolve. It epitomizes the fundamental violence in petrochemical cultures and petroleum industries that accumulate plastics in environments and bodies. As the very symbol of the postnatural, this mass-produced durable synthetic material is like an immortal entity; it will not decompose for thousands of years, just like the radioactive waste in gas, liquid, and solid form. Therefore, we can never return to an undisrupted state of the world and fold this postnatural existence into any uncontaminated state of being. Acknowledging this problem, Simon C. Estok succinctly explains: "We will have to face this reality, a world with diminished diversity and wonders, fewer species, less of the conveniences we currently enjoy; less of the colors, flavors, smells, sights, sounds, and tastes of nature; less coral reefs and clean air, less forests and starfish" (2018, 45).

Inhabited by so many actors, biological, technological, and inorganic, this world is now swirling in toxic relations and cataclysmic changes. As geographer Noel Castree (2016) points out, "nature in its various forms has lost its former naturalness" (151), and "few serious efforts have been made to slow down the evident worldwide denaturalization of nature" (152). One can also argue that in denatured environments "nothing is natural, nothing is exactly unnatural, either," as Columbia University professor of law Jedediah Purdy does in his book *After Nature* (2015, 6). The emerging postnatural sites are emblematic of this fact: there is no nature out there independent of catastrophic human activities, and the tangles of bodies and environments at such sites help us understand the mechanisms of thickening postnatural life and species relations in our anthropocentrically fashioned world heading toward what environmentalist writer Paul Kingsnorth fears is "a planetary ecocide that nobody seems able to prevent" (2017, 142).

As such, the postnatural is part of the extensive story of the Anthropocene, making humanity's geomorphic signature on Earth's physiognomy quite exhaustive. The inescapable ecological implication of this signature in the contemporary situation is that what may have seemed unlikely in the past (before industrialization at least) is happening at present. As capitalist growth continues to interfere with the precarious balance of local and global ecosystems, which stayed relatively stable for thousands of years, the transformation of the entire planet into a postnatural celestial body is imminent. Professor of visual culture Nicholas Mirzoeff ironically observes that "capitalism has a long etiology and multiple symptoms and is resistant to cure: we might call it autoimmune climate-changing capitalism syndrome, or AICS for short" (2014, 215). Unfortunately, for as long as AICS is operative, the postnatural will gain more ground. Postnatural landscapes already bear all the marks of changes to come and project copious material signs of the Anthropocene ecologies, which include narratives of disruption, feelings of despair and fear, and even indifference if one is complicit with the system. In short, the postnatural emergence points to a scarred future dominated by forces of destruction and countless forms of violence, a future that is already taking shape here and now. For example, with their own artistry in transforming landscapes into postnatural sites, the formidable wildfires like the catastrophic fire that engulfed the town of Paradise, California, in 2018 and even a worse one in August 2020 in Death Valley with the hottest temperature of 130 degrees Fahrenheit (54.4 degrees Celsius) ever measured on Earth—disclose our vulnerabilities and fragility.[7] Fire historian Stephen J. Pyne notes that forest fires exemplify "industrialization's pyric transition from the burning of living biomass to the combustion of fossil biomass" and wrench "landscapes into new patterns everywhere" (2004, 14). This happens when human settlements encroach upon the forest areas, overtaxing the forest ecosystems and weakening the interrelated patterns of the biotic components of the forest areas that function together with the abiotic factors of the environment. Worse than this disastrous coexistence is what Anna Lowenhaupt Tsing (2018) calls "the new wild" taking over after large-scale forest fires. Often, forest regeneration becomes impossible because of the penetration of invasive plant species, making themselves a monoculture. These species "wipe out indigenous ecologies not prepared for their onslaughts" and "carve a path of destruction across the landscape" (Tsing 2018). Humans often pave the way for such a new wild with intense logging, urban sprawl, and the advance of agricultural fields. Canadian journalist Edward Struzik warns that "catastrophic fires . . . are going to happen more often because urban and industrial developments are encroaching on undeveloped wildlands at a record pace" (2017, 3). Wildlands then become postnatural landscapes filled with dispiriting stories of loss and dissolution, which actually reveals, in urban theorist Mike Davis's (2018) words, a "crazy political-economic system that so comprehensively ignores nature, ignores climate change, and continues to build houses and entire towns that will inevitably burn."

We need to be clear here: if we do not want the "end of nature" discourse to turn into a dreaded material reality in the near future, we need to find ways to discontinue what seems to be a global allegiance to the capitalist logic of more profit. This logic fosters lethal human impact on the planet's life-support systems and produces environmental injustices and social inequalities. We need to "acknowledge both material responsibility, however unevenly shared, for the escalation of extremes, and human ethical accountability to those diverse nonhuman others" (Rigby 2014, 214). To enact this responsibility, we need new analytic tools that can move us beyond the fiery waves of the Anthropocene to better conditions of livability in the emergent postnatural landscapes.

Have We Really Ended Nature?

The bleak picture sketched above emerges from reconfiguring the notion of "nature," which was first presented in a conflictual way by Bill McKibben, the leading environmentalist journalist who coined the term *postnatural* to define the "deep change" many natural environments across the planet have gone through since the time of the atomic bomb, now recognized as anthropogenic landscapes and waterscapes. Claiming that "the world will never look the same to us as it once did" (1998, 6), McKibben declared: "We have ended nature" (5). When he first announced the end of nature in his 1989 bestselling book *The End of Nature*, McKibben explained that this *end* doesn't necessarily denote the complete destruction of natural processes, which obviously have not ceased, but it signifies a conceptual erasure of the entrenched boundary between human societies and natural environments. In McKibben's words: "*But we have ended the things that have, at least in modern times, defined nature for us—its separation from human society*" ([1989] 2006, 55; italics in original).

McKibben specifically underlines the "indelible imprint" (57) of humanity that has transformed natural landscapes in such a way as to completely collapse the alleged ontological distinction between natures and cultures, which he finds utterly lamentable. While McKibben mourns the disappearance of nature as an independent force, other environmental scholars, such as Paul Wapner and Steven Vogel, criticize this line of reasoning by claiming that "the boundary between humans and nature never really existed" (Wapner 2014, 39); thus, "the end of nature might be something that . . . has *always already happened*" (Vogel 2015, 8; italics in original). According to Vogel, "finding a landscape with no history of human intervention seems difficult indeed, and every search for the imagined pristine landscape before such intervention seems destined to fail" (2015, 8). In this debate, what really ended is the common *vision* of "nature" as remote, pure, and unblemished wilderness to be replaced by the postnatural as "the (natural) human condition" (Vogel 2015, 26). For these scholars, the idea of postnature is a discursive valorization of the epistemic break between the conventional model of nature as untouched by human presence and its contemporary reconceptualization as inseparable from the social sphere.

It is, however, worth recalling that this is more of an ontological issue than a conceptual one with regard to the drastic effects of ecological disruption unleashed on a planetary scale precipitating ruined landscapes as postnatural territories. Admittedly, to see the postnatural simply as the new conceptualization of damaged environments is to see this phenomenon only partially. The postnatural is a material-discursive episode of the Anthropocene, intermingling environmental policies, extractivism, industrial agriculture, fossil fuel industries, climate disruption,[8] global pollution, landfills, toxic chemicals, wildfires, dangerous viruses, climate migrations, public health, social inertia, and environmental exploitation. Therefore, insistence on epistemic quandaries as part of what defines the postnatural is a contentious approach, because having turned into irreparably damaged and/or hybrid landscapes "with unpredictable emergent effects" (Clark 2014, 80), these ruined sites carry material threats to the health of all organisms that inhabit them. The postnatural is a messy entanglement of these factors, causing inherent anxieties and uncertainties, but it does not simply signal the end of "nature," nor the end of "a sustainable mode of earthly inhabitance" (Cohen 2013, xxi)—at least not yet. As anthropologist Werner Krauss explains, "Even in messy situations, there are possibilities for unexpected coalitions and events" (2019, 71). Although this hopeful note points to an ontological commitment to reconfiguring social relations, geopolitical alliances, and energy regimes in existing material conditions, we are far from unmaking the intensity of global environmental crisis unfolding in dark ecological scenarios. Nevertheless, succumbing to hopelessness is not an option.

In the disenchantment of the naturalcultural world, the images and visceral experiences of troubled natures frequently gather a plenitude of cataclysmic currents running wild not only in the geological strata of the planet but also in the biological systems of terrestrial creatures, including earthbound humans. The postnatural is thus a vast web of disruptive entanglements of planetary natures and cultures, biologies and technologies, and bodies and environments, all pointing toward an indeterminate ecological predicament. The postnatural can also be envisioned, in some ways at least, as an embodiment of what Timothy Morton (2016) has called "dark ecology." Morton argues that dark ecology "has the characteristics of tragic melancholy and negativity, concerning inextricable coexistence with a host of entities that surround and penetrate us, but which evolves paradoxically into an anarchic, comedic sense of coexistence" (160). Although the postnatural is implicated in Morton's vision of dark ecology, which aims to denaturalize "nature" and succeeds in so doing, it is not entirely synonymous with dark ecology. The postnatural reality itself cannot be conceptualized entirely around a "comedic sense of coexistence," even if it keeps calling this worldly particularity to our attention not only in real life but also in visual images, fictional narratives, and films that elicit a language of warning.[9]

Postnatural Transformations in the "Wasteocene"

In postnatural ecologies, the Anthropocene's technostratigraphic effects bear the mark of humanity's most recent anthropogenic signature, categorized as "technofossils" by concerned geologists (Zalasiewicz, Williams, Waters, Barnosky, and Haff 2014). They argue that concrete, microplastics, radionuclides, and inorganic carbonaceous particles not only transform the planet into a postnatural globe but also percolate through human biology and nonhuman organisms. "Technofossils are often crafted from materials that have long-term geological durability," which are "materials that either are rare in nature or do not occur naturally, like native aluminium or plastic" (Zalasiewicz, Waters, Williams, and Barnosky 2019, 144). Marking the latest phase of human modification of the composition of terrestrial minerals, technofossils are defined as "the preservable material remains" (Zalasiewicz, Williams, Waters, Barnosky, and Haff 2014, 34) of industrially produced pollutants that cause anthropogenic chemical contamination in air, soil, and water. Jan Zalasiewicz, Mark Williams, Colin N. Waters, Anthony D.

Barnosky, and Peter Haff (2014) clarify that as opposed to nonhuman fossils, which tend to be more limited, the artifacts humans produce are either very rare in nature, such as iron, aluminum, and titanium, or unknown naturally, such as vanadium and molybdenum. The authors also point to "a wide variety of novel minerals such as boron nitride, tungsten carbide, and 'mineraloids' such as artificial glasses and plastics" (36), all of which "are preservable over geological timescales" and "will contribute to the 'far-future' signal of the Anthropocene" (37). They also note that technofossils are not only sedimented in terrestrial settings but also spread to marine environments as they are "transported into deep water via shipping traffic" (38). The resultant technological pollution, accordingly, follows a catastrophist trajectory and is considered to lead to "geologically more long-lasting technostratigraphic change" (41). In sum, the number of technofossils "far outstrips current biological diversity and might now be comparable with the total of biological diversity that has ever existed on Earth" (Zalasiewicz, Waters, Williams, and Barnosky 2019, 146–47).

Since the technological pollutants are reconfiguring the atmosphere, geosphere, hydrosphere, and biosphere as waste spheres, Marco Armiero and Massimo De Angelis propose "Wasteocene" as a more proper name for the Anthropocene epoch to stress "the contaminating nature of capitalism and its perdurance within the sociobiological fabric, its accumulation of externalities inside both the human and the earth's body" (2017, 348). According to this reworking of the Anthropocene, waste determines the social and biological quality of life on the planet, challenging our abilities to find more sustainable solutions. In his recent book *Wasteocene: Stories from the Global Dump*, Marco Armiero further clarifies the term, arguing that "at the very core of every Anthropocene story lies some kind of waste" (2021, 9).

> The age of Humans is marked by a techno-stratigraphy of wasted matter, such as carbon sediments, radionuclides and microplastics, accumulating beneath the earth's surface. Waste can be considered the essence of the Anthropocene, embodying humans' ability to affect the environment to the point of transforming it into a gigantic dump. (Armiero 2021, 9)

Vividly capturing the gist of this problem, Brian Thill's epigrammatic book *Waste* also offers a snapshot of waste framed in an insightful explanation of the present-day Wasteocene:

> The world around us is filled with charred remnants and scattered filth in too many forms; too diffuse; of every size and shape and smell, ugly and

unwieldy, born of every age and temperament. It seeps into every crevice, floats down every grime-choked street, pools and piles and decays in every corner of every home and city and patch of wilderness. And there is always so much of it than we can hope to study. (2017, 3)

Most compelling, however, is literary critic Patricia Yaeger's (2008) contextualization of contaminated natures in what she calls "rubbish ecology": "First, in a world where molecular garbage has infiltrated earth, water, and air, we cannot encounter the natural untouched or uncontaminated by human remains. Trash becomes nature, and nature becomes trash" (332). If nature becomes trash, it is because, Yaeger argues, "nature is dominated, polluted, pocketed, eco-touristed, warming, melting, bleaching, dissipating, and fleeing toward the poles.... Trash is the becoming natural of culture, what culture, eating nature, tries to cast away" (338). In a world where nature is rapidly metamorphosing into rubbish ecology in which trash is becoming the cultural dominant, recategorizing the Anthropocene as the Wasteocene in its symbolic and material intensity should not be too surprising, because waste is unavoidably "an internal aspect of human condition" (Morrison 2015, 9). As prominent professor of environmental studies Myra J. Hird (n.d.) observes, "Waste has become the signifier of the Anthropocene, inaugurating the only epoch that centralizes humans." Waste can thus be customarily conceived as the signifier of postnatural ecologies that characterize the Wasteocene. Whether waste comes in the form of junk, garbage, trash, detritus, or rubbish, it is undoubtedly "one of the signatures of this time and age" (Bardini 2011, 9), signifying not only what "consumer capitalism does both to the earth and its inhabitants" (Marland and Parham 2014, 2) but also, to quote Hird (n.d.) again, "toxicity, contamination, and resource depletion our epoch created."

Whether it is discarded mindlessly or recycled, buried in landfills or reclaimed, waste saturates almost all landscapes, moves silently into the atmosphere, and settles in waterways. The resilient agency of waste permeates through human and nonhuman bodies as well, hoarding diseases that eventually culminate in tragic stories of the body's demise. When flows of toxic chemicals infiltrate biological bodies that depend on their environments for nourishment, we come to realize that the environment is "decisively no longer an environment, since it no longer just happens around us" (Morton 2010, 274). This is one of the most compact ways of representing the Wasteocene as something that defies being repressed, controlled, or even ignored. The Wasteocene, then, not only implies that the Earth is being transformed into a gigantic landfill, which is strikingly epitomized in Pixar's 2008 animated film *WALL-E* (named for the robot known as Waste Allocation Load Lifter:

Earth-class), but also points to a viable critical assessment of postnatural environments in which the illusion of externality can no longer be sustained. When the space of externality dissolves at a planetary scale, what really transpires is, as Timothy Clark proclaims, "the slow erosion of the distinction between the distant waste dump and the housing estate, between the air and a sewer, between the open road and a car park, and between the self-satisfied affluence of Sydney suburb and a drowning village in Bangladesh" (2014, 82). Clark's reckoning is exemplary of postnatural ecologies, which designate a seamless mingling of the natural and the cultural, or, as Clark puts it, "an incalculable connection between bodies, human and nonhuman, across and within the biosphere (food, water, nutrients, but also toxins and viruses), with a sense of both holism and, increasingly, entrapment" (80–81). This is as valid for nonhumans as it is for human beings as planetary-scale postnatural transformations are being "confirmed by the flesh, bones and blood of wild animals, fish and birds even in the remotest wilderness areas" (Raglon 2009, 61). Ocean acidification, for instance, lethally affects the internal chemistry of sea creatures and their metabolisms, and changes can easily be observed in the sexual morphology of fish, frogs, and salamanders. Environmentalists also draw attention to "ovapollution," "estrogenic pollution," and "chemical castration" (Di Chiro 2010, 201) among humans and animal species.[10] Moreover, birds have to endure 150 metric tons of carbon dioxide in the air. According to ecojournalist Elizabeth Kolbert (2011), the most alarming instance is "the change in the composition of the atmosphere":

> Carbon dioxide emissions are colorless, odorless, and in an immediate sense, harmless. But their warming effects could easily push global temperatures to levels that have not been seen for millions of years. Some plants and animals are already shifting their ranges toward the Poles, and those shifts will leave traces in the fossil record. Some species will not survive the warming at all. Meanwhile rising temperatures could eventually raise sea levels 20 feet or more.

These "world-altering events" (Kolbert 2014, 113) occur due to soil degradation, air pollution, and water contamination, intensifying and accelerating the ride into the postnatural. The cause of soil degradation stems from the accumulation in soils of toxic chemicals from industrial processes, which also contribute to air and water pollution. Heavy metals such as lead in petrol, hydrocarbons (the byproducts of the petroleum industries), mercury and cyanide from mining and manufacturing industries, and the radioactive substances released by the nuclear industry "reduce the ability of soils to support the ecosystem of which they are part" (Whitehead 2014, 71). In addition, artificial fertilizers such as nitrogen and phosphorus-based fertilizers are transferred from soils to rivers and eventually make their way to the oceans, where they are absorbed by phytoplankton (microalgae), prompting the growth of huge algae blooms and thus preventing the light from reaching the seafloor and creating "dead zones" (Whitehead 2014, 73). The balance of the nitrogen cycle is disrupted so drastically that nitrogen gets converted into nitrous oxides, which contribute to the erosion of the planet's ozone layer and the production of acid rains. Furthermore, "elevated levels of nitrogen can now be detected in underground aquifers[11] and high-altitude clouds" (Whitehead 2014, 73).

As these events indicate, the postnatural not only unfolds through foreseeable relationalities that now exceed human control but also mirrors industrial capitalism's violent expansion into every imaginable space, from the Canadian province of Alberta to Turkey's Mount Ida (Kaz Dağları), with violent extractive practices.[12] In reducing the biosphere to global merchandise and using "relentless extractive economies," as Stephanie Foote similarly contends, capitalists have "contaminated the quality of food, water, air, and soil, and left less tangible but no less destructive traces on the flourishing of local cultures and places" (2020, 52). The "extractive logic of a biopolitical capitalism" (Foote 2020, 52) is impressed on geophysical and social realities, producing what environmental historian Jason W. Moore has called a "world-ecological crisis today" (2017, 609), and a postnatural condition framed by dangerous microorganisms, electronic litter, and the recursive cycles of plastic production. According to feminist posthumanist scholar Cecilia Åsberg (2017), too, this is a confrontation with "accumulated toxins, mountains of e-waste, acidification, pollution, climate change, accelerated species extinction" (186), and especially "discarded pharmaceutical agents" in "food chains" (188). Thus, nature today can only be conceivably imagined as postnature in which all material agencies are entrapped with "no 'out' or 'away'" (Wood 2005, 172). Deconstructing the illusion of externality, philosopher David Wood notes that "so much of our making sense, let alone the intelligibility of our actions, still rests on being able to export, exclude, externalize what we do not want to consider. When that externality is no longer available, we are in trouble" (2005, 172–73).

There is indeed no way out, and we are in trouble as significant changes in the biogeochemical cycles of elements in the biosphere today threaten the vital conditions for the existence of life itself. The reduction of oxygen and the increase in the amount of carbon dioxide in the air, for example, "result in changes in the quantity of solar radiation falling on the earth's surface, thermal pollution of the atmosphere," and changes in the water cycle result in "the pollution of the hydrosphere and soil" (Tölgyessy 1993, 7). Because of their material enmeshment in these fundamental sources of the biosphere, human and nonhuman bodies, too, are frequently invaded by hazardous substances such as petrochemicals, neurotoxins, carcinogens, and endocrine-disruptive chemicals. Even more disquietingly, we have become "apathetic, no longer involved," and "anesthetized" to this postnatural reality, as Michael Marder (2019) aptly emphasizes. Marder's claim that "the business of the Anthropocene is one symptom of this malaise" (181) captures some of the Anthropocene's (or, more precisely, the Wasteocene's) destructive facets and, more generally, the contamination of life that characterizes postnatures. As Marder's discussion of the global dumb suggests, reckoning with toxicity is crucial at this time, not only because of the conversion of the entire planet into a massive dump site but also because humans are irrevocably entangled within networks and flows of toxic substances. Thus, we can no longer imagine any sort of demarcation between the inner and the outer worlds (the body and the biosphere) or conceive of "nature" as something external to human domains when the biophysical world is thoroughly contaminated by human debris infiltrating soil, water, and air. In Marder's words:

> The toxicity of the air, the clouds, the rain and the snow; of the oceans and their diminishing fish and crustacean populations; of chemically fertilized soil and the fruit it bears—this pervasive and multifarious elemental toxicity is also in us. The outside slips in when we inhale and ingest it, the body's "hollow" interiors, the lungs and the stomach, inexorably exposed to the atmosphere, water, and food. (2019, 182)

If the outside is also the inside, then, rather than attempting to police the permeable boundaries of postnatural forces that flow across biological and political borders easily and effortlessly, we should first strive to understand how postnatural ecologies interconnect personal, ethical, ecological, and political life through multiple concerns raised by humanity's dysfunctional relations with the planet's biospheric life. We must remember that changes observed in the atmosphere are networked to changes in hydrological cycles, which in turn manifest in the cryosphere, and the entire biosphere (the sum of all ecosystems) gets entangled in such cyclical patterns. Not surprisingly, all these changes are bound up with political, economic, and social ideations and practices that affect the ways of interacting with major planetary forces. When the human collides with the nonhuman in toxic ways, the material stories of the consequent postnatures can only disclose the dark extremities of the Anthropocene, which emerge from what Stephanie LeMenager and Stephanie Foote have called "multiple damaged ecologies that structure our world" (2013). How, then, can we fashion new forms of knowledge and foster resistance to counter this phenomenon? Perhaps accepting what David Wood refers to as the end of externality (2005, 173) is the first step to seriously consider postnatural ecologies that signal "doomsday narratives of finitude" (Lekan 2014, 195). Becoming aware prepares the mind for resistance to "instrumental perceptions of the environment" (Griffiths 2017, 145). Resistance can be potentially useful to contest the pressures of the postnatural expansion and to "negotiate life in human-damaged environments" (Tsing 2015, 131) in ways that are not fully explored for conditions of collective resistance against the imperious narratives of economic profit. Although "some groups are more prone to damage, loss and suffering in the context of differing hazards" (Wisner et al. 2004, 11), and thus more vulnerable to risks, the threats of postnatural ecologies do not, or will not, involve only those disadvantaged by gender, social class, economic position, age, disability, race, or ethnicity, especially in the future scenarios of global disasters and lethal conditions. Building resilience is therefore as important as cultivating resistance in response to the challenges of the expanding postnatural geographies.

This reality is especially intriguing for literary imagination, which struggles with the questions of how to emplot the seemingly slow collapse and find new ways of storying this unfolding reality that would encourage us to rethink the human condition together with other species, material agencies, and the Earth's biogeochemical transformations. As Australian novelist James Bradley suggests, we must find new "ways of recording and memorialising what is being lost, of resisting not just the assumptions of hypercapitalism but the amnesia it induces" (2017). Bradley also suggests that "we must find ways to communicate ideas that are not just uncomfortable and frightening but actively difficult to comprehend because they demand we accept the ideas and ideologies that structure our world are, as Marx had it, no more solid than air." Cli-fi narratives in this respect can help us better understand the world's complexities, so in the following section of this chapter, I discuss the significance of resistance and resilience in a paradigmatic novel that vividly captures a sense of what it means to endure postnatural ecologies.

Resistance and Resilience in Postnatural Ecologies and Fictions: John Burnside's *Glister*

Damaged ecologies in the postnatural figuration of the world always invite forms of resistance to reshape our impending fates. Resistance means "the refusal to accept or comply with something" (OED n.d.), and the Anthropocene's postnatural offspring is definitely something to resist and not to comply with, especially with its effects on the lives of Earth's countless inhabitants. But resistance also carries a deeper meaning: "The ability not to be affected by something, especially adversely" (OED n.d.). In this sense, resistance can be read as an art of slowing—and eventually stopping—the Anthropocene's effects on our fragile and already-wounded environments. There are also shades of resilience carried within the meanings of resistance that cannot be entirely decoupled from what resistance signifies in general. Read in this light, the postnatural ecologies that reflect the Anthropocene's dark extremities in a disenchanted world are overflowing not only with pain and trauma but also with yet-unsettled patterns of resistance and mental and/or inner forces of resilience. These forces have the potential to clear away social and psychological inertia, "to stir up potent response to devastating events, as well as to settle troubled waters and rebuild quiet places," as Donna Haraway notes in *Staying with the Trouble* (2016, 1). Taking resistance as a potent response to ecological devastation and as a refusal to accept the postnatural as the new normal has a transformative potency, especially if this response is made pervasive and enduring through creative defiance with the innovatory powers of art and literature, which offer avenues for liberating vulnerable communities from the macabre effects of human domination of the planet. Resistance is the necessary turn toward "the reality of shared concerns and collaborative world-making" (Farrier 2019, 98). Since resistance is coupled with resilience in the darkening ecologies of the Anthropocene, stories of resistance and resilience in postnatural settings show how to settle troubled natures and counter social apathy as the most undesirable response to the corrosive forces of postnatural environments. To become resilient usually means learning to survive in the uncertainty of emergency situations, managing anxieties in a precarious existence, and having endurance. Although resilience in this sense derives from *resiler* in Latin, which basically signifies "to distance oneself," resilience in modern understanding is knowing "the limits of our ability" (LeMenager and Foote 2013) but without drawing back or distancing oneself from adverse situations despite the mind-crippling feelings of uncertainty, emergency, and precarity, which may initially induce lethargy and negatively affect moods. But being resilient does not mean passive acceptance of such dispositions, to defer resolution or action, to endure conditions uncritically, or to squander time. In other words, resilience is not about enduring "pathological social relationships that are oppressive and exploitative of humans and ecosystems (life)" (Albrecht 2016, 13). Jonathan Joseph, professor of politics and international relations, relates this understanding of resilience to the "embedded neoliberalism" that predominantly relies on individual responsibility. Resilience, he argues,

> places so much emphasis on things such as individual preparedness, making informed decisions, understanding our roles and responsibilities, and showing adaptability to our situation and being able to 'bounce back' should things go wrong. These fit with neoliberal approaches that put emphasis on the responsibility of the individual to govern themselves in appropriate ways. (2013, 41)

Joseph is right here in criticizing resilience as a form of individual adaptability, which is favored by neoliberal discourse that encourages citizens to take responsibility for their own life. This logic "encourages the idea of active citizenship, whereby people, rather than relying on the state, take responsibility for their own social and economic well-being" (Joseph 2013, 42). But, as a global group of scientists have noted, even adaptation is at stake "if we continue with the unfettered destruction of our natural environment," simply because "climate change will accelerate beyond the capabilities of nature and humans to adapt" (Moomaw et al. 2020, 1). The first of the four revolutions suggested here to accelerate adaptation for climate resilience is important:

> We must adapt in the way we manage and protect natural systems. We can no longer continue to clear our forests and degrade them. Coastal and freshwater wetlands, mangroves, grasslands and coral reefs must be protected and restored for climate resilience and to accumulate more carbon out of the atmosphere. Adaptive management of agricultural lands will ensure that our food system is more resilient and productive without encroaching on natural ecosystems. (Moomaw et al. 2020, 2)

Climate resilience depends upon the protection of natural systems, but human resilience in postnatural ecologies can be conceived as "the capacity to absorb and recover from the impact of a hazardous event" (Smith and Petley [1991] 2007, 15). Being resilient also means swerving toward our evolutionary connections with all that lives on this planet to slow down the effects of the Anthropocene, with climate change its most conspicuous effect, and this can be achieved best at a collective level if there is "social cohesion" (Smith and Petley [1991] 2007, 91). To achieve social cohesion, resistance to present systems of exploitation becomes inevitable. Resilience and resistance are thus inseparable in terms of ensuring "to limit future damage" (Moomaw et al. 2020, 3).

Since the ever-expanding postnatural environments point to an unpredictable future with little or no security, crippling minds and bodies of Earthly beings, perhaps a possible way out is through stories of resistance that have the power to reorganize the discourses of the world toward nonanthropocentric epistemic changes. Such stories transmit a message that "we are parts of a living world" (Bateson 1979, 17), interconnected especially at sites of narrativity with other species, elements, and forces to attract public attention, and thus to create a web of social resistance to impending ecological collapse and spiritual degeneration. Accordingly, seeing postnatural environments as sites of narrativity that cannot be separated from their worldliness and their shared social experience engages a problematizing of anthropocentric knowledge. By contextualizing the separation between the ecological and the political, which is always conjoined with the economic and the social, these postnatural sites can be said to "translate *knowing* into *telling* (White 1980, 5; italics in original) and enable conditions of the possibility of resistance. Narrative here should be understood not as a "metacode, a human universal on the basis of which transcultural messages about the nature of a shared reality can be transmitted" (White 1980, 6), but as a shared reality of all signifying beings and things that constitute storied matter. Just as "knowing, even thinking, are not exclusively human affairs" (Kohn 2013,1), narrative, too, is not solely a form of human sense-making. In this vision, postnatural sites of narrativity, such as the dying coral reefs, toxic bodies, polluted air, and acidic oceans with their plaintive stories, show us how the Earth itself speaks about human exploitation of its very body. While the planet is sculptured with the enduring desires of humans born of technoscientific and biochemical practices, and with intricately interwoven "patterns of material, social, human, and nonhuman interaction" that "cannot be simply resisted or countered" (Mirzoeff 2014, 213), the narrative agencies point to the consequences of these patterns with their own stories of ecological degradation. They articulate a world that is in distress, but they also project resistance and resilience. The firefighters in Paradise, California, and their heroic struggle are part of such stories, but so are the deer that fought their way out of the fiery entrapment, the owl that found its way to the waterfront, and other animals (like donkeys and dogs) that defied a horrible death; so resistance is, by definition, also a more-than-human act of refusal to perish, a fight against the unpredictability of fate, and a capacity to resurge in the midst of unprecedented catastrophes. These stories can also provoke us to reimagine our future, help us see ourselves as part of a web of life, and consider what we are leaving behind for beings that will follow us.

At a more general level, the unfolding stories of postnatures enact a concern for the deteriorating condition of life in the Anthropocene. Contemporary climate change fiction also underlines this fact. In other words, the same concern is dramatized in fictional texts that focus on patterns of deterioration in naturalcultural environments, displaying "the failure of traditional social systems and the collective imagination to confront a boiling planet" (Sterling and Harrison 2020, 19). Many of the fictional scenarios in contemporary cli-fi, however, do not cultivate hopelessness despite the breakdown of social structures and darkening environmental conditions. Instead, they offer glimpses of hope in the face of catastrophic events. Taking postnatures seriously, many cli-fi novelists offer glimpses into the imminent threats of ecological disasters, alerting us to the consequences of extensive human interaction with planetary systems through a sociologically credible rather than merely fictional lens. They expose the detrimental capitalist forces in "toxic industrial society" (Albrecht 2016, 13) that relentlessly drive their inhabitants to disease and death as in British novelist John Burnside's *Glister* (2008), which is one of the best literary accounts of the consequences of anthropogenic transformations. *Glister* tells a sad story of "slow decay" of bodies and minds caught in a landscape thoroughly poisoned by a shut-down chemical plant, which is littered with dead trees and sulfuric rocks with utterly negative social side effects. It is also the story of the new ways of resistance in such destroyed habitats. The titular word "glister," as professor of comparative literature Pieter Vermeulen (2020) observes, is a "fairly obscure term—the word is more or less synonymous with 'glitter' and 'sparkle,'" but in Burnside's novel, the term "is immediately associated with the plant site (which is vast in itself and seems contiguous with the poisoned woods)" (94).

Framed within a despondent postnatural setting "in which people and the community physically and morally fall apart" (Yazgünoğlu 2019, 42), *Glister* discloses how the postnatural ecologies of the Anthropocene can easily entrap us not only within toxic environments and bodies but also within a toxic mindset. The novel also highlights the fact that resilience "is not a complete solution" (Smith and Petley [1991] 2007, 91) to the postnaturalization processes, even though it exemplifies what Turkish scholar of postnatural studies Kerim Can Yazgünoğlu calls "'natural' resilience against the backdrop of a nightmarish territory, questioning the extent to which human beings, animals, and ghosts are implicated in dark-green nature" (2019, 51). In this dark and postecological reality, Yazgünoğlu argues, the novel illustrates "a noxious world in which one cannot find a true sense of belonging but death, annihilation, and entropy" (51). According to Turkish animal studies scholar Adem Balcı (2020), who also addresses "the hazardous effects of toxicity not only on human beings and animals but also on the physical environment" (60), "the Innertown folk in *Glister* do not have socioeconomic freedom;" they are "culturally, socially, and economically marginalized others that are confined to this toxic land" (68). But that doesn't mean there is only hopelessness and despair even under such miasmic environmental conditions. Although painfully "entrapped in this malign impasse" (68), Leonard, the novel's fifteen-year-old pedantic narrator, offers small forms of resistance amid dark ecologies in which his town and its people are caught, and worse, they all have been "apathetic" to their impending fate. The novel cautions the readers against the Anthropocene's dark extremities but at the same time insists that postnatural landscapes often incite new forms of resistance against ecological degradation and environmental injustice that routinely materialize with industrial contamination, social lethargy, political corruption, and dramatic poverty.

Glister's postnatural site is a post-industrial town in the vicinity of a now-defunct chemical plant, which has poisoned the entire landscape as well as the bodies and minds of people. While the Innertown is literally rusting away, its inhabitants who worked at the plant slowly dying, the more privileged Outertown people go about their business, assuring the Innertown folk that "the danger [is] minimal" (Burnside 2009, 10) as long as they keep away from the plant. Although everyone knows that their land is poisoned by the plant, no one is quite sure about the extent of this poisoning despite the evidence "of the plant's effects on the land" (12). Leonard, however, who spends most of his time in the "poison wood," as the Innertown people call it, wants to stay with the trouble, as Haraway would say, which energizes him to live "in myriad unfinished configurations of places, times, matters, meanings" (Haraway 2016, 1). This is how he learns to become resilient to the environmental injustice and the social apathy that he witnesses every day. Leonard knows that his future is unpredictable but chooses to stay with the trouble and re-story his life with the energy of love and beauty he secretly seeks: "The chemical plant is always beautiful even when it is frightening, or when you can see how sad it is, when all the little glimmers of what was here before—the woods, the firth, the breaches—show through and you realise it must have been amazing, back in the old times. Sometimes you can still get that feeling" (Burnside 2009, 62).

Leonard's story is also a story of resistance to the decaying cultural dynamics and psychological corrosion that literally engulf everyone, including his father, whose slow death from cancer makes him a human shadow. "If you want to stay alive, which is hard to do in a place like this," Leonard says, "you have to love *something* and the one thing I love is the chemical plant" (60). Loving the plant allows the boy to be truly present instead of descending into oblivion like his father and other adults. Therefore, he declares, "I'm alive with everything that lives" (129). The underlying idea here is that being aware of the meaningful interconnections of living beings enlivens our capacity to be part of what Jessica Weir calls "connectivity thinking" (2009, 11), which

Leonard deeply cultivates. He responds to life in a spirit of openness and love despite the dark ecological reality he experiences. And, despite his young age, Leonard is also keenly aware that environmental problems are also social and cultural issues that are "deeply interwoven with economic and political agendas" (Oppermann and Iovino 2017, 3). This is epitomized in Innertown, where everything is contaminated, and not just biologically. There is bribery in high places, death threats against potential social protests, and no investigations because the authorities in big business want to keep something secret sealed up in the plant. So, the Innertown people who feel powerless to change their lot, or to look for a better life elsewhere, gradually sink into hopelessness and become engulfed in despair, denial, and an awful endemic lethargy. The worst damage is thus done to their spirit, which symbolizes the Anthropocene's dark extremities, manifesting here as the dawning of the Wasteocene, crippling the mind as badly as the bodies of people in the Innertown. The novel's hint on the Wasteocene points to a common ecological fate, not a spasmodic occurrence, and the Innertown people experience its impacts directly as shown by the toxic forces spreading out from the chemical plant, inducing a bodily crisis. But their political and economic counterparts have resulted in a large-scale spiritual infection that also engulfs the people of Outertown through political corruption. The novel is thus broadly directed at the amorality and irresponsibility of big business in its abuse of natural environments and the complicity of common people in this terrifying exploitation carried out by the local and international Consortium of agricultural and other companies.

For thirty years, the Consortium manufactured chemical substances in the plant, such as fertilizers, pesticides, fungicides, growth accelerants or retardants, and herbicides, insisting that these products are harmless. The people, however, suspect that the plant also had secret facilities producing biological weapons, a secret they believe is covered up by the authorities. After the plant is closed and becomes a government-certified zone, the Innertown becomes utterly desolate. But while "the entire land under their feet is irredeemably soured, poisoned by years of run-off and soakaway from the plant" (10), the politicians and the Consortium representatives in the Outertown want to ensure that "things ticked without too much fuss" (10). Yet the plant's effects are all too visible, especially in the poisoned wood where trees, strangely black, are "veined with dark, poisoned sap, black, but with a trace of livid in the essence of it, a green that was bitter and primordial, like wormwood, or gall" (16). There are

> avenues of dead trees, black and skeletal along the old rail tracks and access roads; great piles of sulfurous rocks where pools of effluent had

been left to evaporate in the sun. A few keen fishermen found mutant sea creatures washed up on the shore . . . and some people claimed that they had seen bizarre animals out in the remaining tracts of wood land, not sick or dying, but not right either, with their enlarged faces and swollen, twisted bodies. (11)

Like the animals in this dismal place, both adults and children develop mysterious behavioral problems, "unexplained clusters of rare cancers," "terrible diseases," "untreatable illnesses," "depression," and "blossoming madness" (12). The Innertown gradually loses its will to resist this toxified fate as all its human and nonhuman inhabitants who, like the tankers that rust in a corner, become apathetic to their miserable condition. Curiously, Leonard stands out as a beacon of hope and resilience, representing a lonely resistance to the slow death of his environment, even if he thinks the chemical plant that instigated a small apocalypse is beautiful. What initially motivates Leonard is the disappearance of his friends in the infected woods and the town's pretense that nothing unusual is happening, that the boys must have run away. The local constable, John Morrison, discovers the first boy in the woods, his body gift-wrapped and suspended from the bough of the largest tree and obviously brutally tortured to death. Morrison is under the influence of a corrupt businessman, Brian Smith, and covers up the crime and conceals the case. Instead of opening an investigation, Morrison follows Smith's orders and keeps silent about other boys who disappear in the following months. The lethargic adults lose their hopes of ever seeing their children again, but Leonard's voice supplies a glint of hope for the future: "They say that, if you want to stay alive, you have to love something. Though maybe love is the wrong word after all. Maybe you have to *be* something. . . . You just have to *be*" (251; italics in original).

Determined to solve the mystery, Leonard spends most of his time in the poisoned woods and the rusting factory, which the children use as a hunting ground and playground, but his aim is to find clues left by the murderer. Although the environment resembles "a war zone" (64), and the plant with its corrugated metal, shattered windows, and giant brick chimney (65) offers no clue, nor signs of any struggle, and thus no evidence for the five boys who disappeared, Leonard continues his search. He is aware that he has breathed the toxic air and digested the contaminated dust of the plant, but he gradually reveals another incentive that drives him into the center of the corrosive endgame. Underlying his search is a deep spiritual impulse to make everything around him holy. He feels this intensely when he meets the Moth Man, who studies butterflies and "various obscure moth species" in the poisoned woods and "who can *read* the landscape" (122). Leonard suspects that the Moth Man might be the murderer; still, he spends time with him and eventually experiences a strange sense of interconnectedness, especially after he drinks the tea the Moth Man offers him:

> I can see everything around me in perfect, almost dizzying detail, but I can also feel how one thing is connected to the next, and that thing to the next after that, or not connected, so much, but all one thing. Everything's one thing. It's not a matter of connections, it's an indivisibility. A unity. I can feel the world reaching away around me in every direction, the world and everything alive in it . . . It's all one. There isn't a me or a not-me about it. It's all continuous and I'm alive with everything that lives. (129)

Although as Pieter Vermeulen points out, Leonard's "visions of interconnectedness . . . are drug-induced" (2020, 95), the feeling of wholeness, unity, and coexistence revealed at the end of the novel empowers Leonard to be resilient to the horrors of the postnatural landscape he is born into, entailing his resistance to "the powers that be" (Burnside 2009, 10).

Unlike the Innertown people, who believe what they are told by the managers and politicians, that they were safe, and "work hard on being convinced," even smuggling "bags of the stuff" from the plant to "spread it on their gardens" (10), Leonard is aware of the plant's toxic effects. He knows that the "twisted bodies of animals" (11), "unexplained clusters of rare cancers" (12), poisoned trees, and other anomalies define their morbid existence. But, although he sees that "this wood has poison running in its veins, in the sap of every tree, in every crumb of loam and every blade of grass under my feet" (197), he initially feels powerless to fight against the mutation of his contaminated environment. He knows he is too young to lead political resistance or a protest movement, or even to change people's attitudes, yet he is quite resilient as a teenager to stay with the trouble to solve the mystery of his friends' disappearance. During his quest, he encounters violence from other children, who have gone wild in the poisoned woods, finds himself in dangerous situations which he barely escapes, and fears he might get cancer, but in the end, he comes to realize that environmental contamination, criminal activities, social attitudes, and economic and political interests all converge in the plant's secret.

Telling this story to the world, Leonard wants to believe, will initiate the dynamics of resistance and liberate the Innertown. That is why the act of storytelling stands out as the only form of resistance to the seemingly sealed fate of the Innertown. The story of disappearing and dead children, hopeless and dying Innertown people and animals, and the contaminated landscape, Leonard believes, will find a way out in the world to be recognized. In the opening of the novel, Leonard's words attest to this:

> Now that the story is finished, I want to tell it in full even as I slip away to a place before names are given or lost. I want to tell it in full even as I forget it, and so, by telling and forgetting, forgive everyone who figures there, including myself. Because *this* is where the future begins: in the forgotten, in what is lost. (1)

At the core of Leonard's storytelling lies an ethical lesson and an understanding that, in Thom van Dooren and Deborah Bird Rose's words, "telling stories has consequences: one of which is that we will inevitably be drawn into new connections and with them new accountabilities and obligations" (2017, 264). With this focus on the power of stories, *Glister* enables us to experience the arts of becoming aware of our collective ecological fate in the Anthropocene, which we can view as "a revolutionary opportunity to redefine the kinds of individuals and societies we are and want to become" (Szeman 2020, 147). This is the lesson Leonard's story of "resistance, revolt, repair, and mourning, and of living and dying well" (Haraway 2016, 51) has managed to convey to the reader, and that such stories can motivate action to bring about socio-ecological transformations.

As readers, we have already heeded the unexpected and feeble voices of the Innertown. As powerful tools of resistance, stories have the power to reorganize the discourses of the world. Even if "the world's complexities exceed their power" (Bradley 2017), stories like Leonard's help us better understand the imminent threats we may also experience in the real world. This—the storied world—is obviously where "powers that be," as Leonard calls the politicians and the corrupt businessmen with their mastery and dominant discourses, are truly contested and unmasked. On a more general level, Leonard's story is also the story of the Anthropocene mindscapes and the personal resistance they elicit through a determined way of storying the world. Leonard's sensitivity to the radical liveliness of his world, no matter how deadly it has become, is therefore significant in his storytelling as a small act of resistance. Through his narrative he transmits a message that "we are parts of a living world" (Bateson 1979, 17), interconnected via stories; but there is a more important message here, and that is the fact that the sites of narrativity are potent places to attract public attention and thus to create a web of social resistance to ecological collapse and spiritual degeneration. When these catalyzed stories of the interconnected human and more-than-human worlds disclose the toxic interchanges between corporeal beings and their postnatural environments, they create awareness about how they co-determine our storied bodies and minds. Defining an imaginable present and the futures to come, Leonard's story also holds a mirror to the anxieties experienced by many people over the toxified landscapes that are becoming increasingly postnatural.

A few questions come to mind here. In what ways can the stories of postnatures help build disanthropocentric practices in a disenchanted world? How can these stories deactivate catastrophic cycles of pollution? Can the distressing postnatural stories help implement policies of solar, water, and wind energy in the near future? To answer these questions, we need to fully understand that human beings are part of multispecies becomings despite their role as the antagonists of ongoing planetary dramas. There are no romantic solutions to these dramas, and retrieving nature from human exploitation is not possible. However, if the solutions lie in staying with the trouble, as Donna Haraway would advise, then it is time "to stir up potent response to devastating events, as well as to settle troubled waters and rebuild quiet places" (2016, 1). As she explains, staying with the trouble is about addressing trouble at present, not being tempted to make things better in an imagined future. Staying with the trouble "requires learning to be truly present, not as a vanishing pivot between awful or edenic pasts and apocalyptic or salvific futures" (2016, 1). To this, we can add *working* with the trouble to become aware of the anthropocentric means by which we construct our narratives of the world, which can be replaced with ecological narratives with human and nonhuman actors and narrators who, as Latour says, "share the same shape-changing destiny" (2014, 17). Such a perspective can bring about a shift in our ways of thinking about the world and also about how our destiny in this geostory is entangled with all that lives on this planet. This would enable us to "be free from the older modernist distinction between nature and society" (16) and also to understand that "story-telling is not just a property of human language, but one of the many consequences of being thrown in a world that is, by itself, fully articulated and active" (14). To accept this vision is to acknowledge sites of narrativity in which natural and human forces became intertwined in this shared destiny, so that "the fate of one determines the fate of the other," as Jan Zalasiewicz and his colleagues also concur (Zalasiewicz, Williams, Steffen, and Crutzen 2010, 2231). Such a vision is one way of signaling what I would call *thinking* along the solid mind of the Earth to avoid a planetary postnatural fate.

Concluding with a Note of Hope: Panarchy

Although I have argued that it doesn't seem likely we will return to an undisrupted state of the world and reverse the ongoing postnatural processes, I do not want to paint a picture of hopelessness as if all is lost, nor present a narrative that is rooted in despair and defeatism. In other words, if the expected solutions lie with us, we can, as human beings, cultivate a sense of hope by relying on our capacity for resistance and create a new "shape-changing destiny," as Latour suggests (2014, 17). In this context, *panarchy*—a term first coined by C. S. Holling in 2001, and then expanded on with Lance H. Gunderson and Donald Ludwig (2002, 5), after the god of nature, Pan, who evokes "an image of unpredictable change"—provides a new outlet for rethinking the remaining natural environments that have not yet been fully consumed by postnatural ecologies. Holling, Gunderson, and Ludwig explain that they came up with the idea of panarchy to "develop an integrative theory to help us understand the changes occurring globally . . . particularly the kinds of changes that are transforming, in systems that are adaptive" (2002, 5).

Panarchy takes Pan's destabilizing role captured in the word *panic* to refer to Earth's endangered biomes at multiple links. These links reflect a knot of intertwined relationalities, resilience, and confrontations with destructive elements like forest fires that create phenomenal postnatures. Thus, panarchy makes us aware of multiple connections between various scales and phases, such as temperature cycles in a forest system and phases of multispecies birth, growth, and maturation, and death and renewal. The changing cycles of climate produce phases of destruction and reorganization, and thus new configurations, mutations, and rearrangements of ecosystemic processes. If we think in terms of panarchy, we realize that "with each postnatural vision comes a revision of the natural. . . . But each vision persists in the others" (Cubitt [1996] 2005, 236). If we add the principle of resilience operating within the phases, in the sense of tolerating a degree of disturbances during the process of destruction, reorganization becomes possible and the ecosystem in question does not collapse into a totally dead state. Even those places that are devastated—like burned forests—may hold the seeds of renewal and thus can adapt to their changed environment.

Panarchy may carry echoes of restoring an ecosystem, which, according to Eli Clare, "means rebuilding a dynamic system that has somewhat been interrupted or broken—devastated by strip mining or clear-cut logging, taken over by invasive species, unbalanced by the loss of predators, crushed by pollution" (2014, 207). But this should not be confused with bringing back the original, which is not possible in any realistic sense; rather, restoration is about "reshaping dynamic ecological interdependencies, ranging from clods of dirt to towering thunderheads, tiny microbes to herds of bison, into a self-sustaining system of constant flux" (207). Clare also adds: "The return may be close but never complete" (207). So, instead of advocating restoration, panarchy asks us to pay attention to adaptive cycles and processes of renewal in unbalanced ecosystems, and thus carries the energy of hope. In other words, if necessary conditions are in place for adaptability, the panarchy model "accepts that components of complex systems may actively adapt to changes within their environments, creating surprising outcomes" (Boyd 2014).

In this frame of reference, we can posit that when inherent interdependencies disappear in postnatural places, the altered lands convey a stratified story of loneliness and loss but also resistance, resilience, and struggle. If resistance is an act of refusal to perish, a fight against the unpredictability of fate, and a capacity to resurge amid unprecedented catastrophes, it represents a panarchy. In "Understanding the Complexity of Economic, Ecological, and Social Systems," Holling explains how all systems, human and nonhuman, are deeply interlinked "in never-ending adaptive cycles of growth, accumulation, restructuring, and renewal" (2001, 392). All these cycles contribute to sustainability, and human beings, too, can be adaptive to changes to guarantee sustainable existence—if the changes do not, of course, lead to systemic collapse. Roger Boyd (2014), who also studies panarchy, further explicates the surprising adaptability of complex systems to changes:

> a panarchy approach accepts that components of complex systems may actively adapt to changes within their environments, creating surprising outcomes. Ecological systems are non-linear, and capable of moving from one stable state to another, very different, one. Within an overall system there are nested sets of adaptive cycles, with the larger cycles operating more slowly than the smaller ones. The different cycles can interact, with the larger ones tending to play a stabilizing role. At a critical point though, changes at different scales may interact and reinforce each other leading to systemic collapse.)

According to Holling, Gunderson, and Ludwig, the essential focus of panarchy is "to rationalize the interplay between change and persistence, between the predictable and unpredictable" (2002, 5). This interplay—especially between predictable and unpredictable changes—signifies the key dynamics of postnatural ecologies as sites of anxiety, conflicts, and existential concern because of the critical point mentioned above that may cause a total collapse of the system. Nevertheless, if a particular postnatural place can maintain resilience, it avoids being completely ruined and can evolve through time in complex states of restoration with accumulating biomass and possibly return to its earlier environmental conditions. This process, however, depends on a variety of factors, such as climate, nutrient stocks, biological diversity, and multispecies interactions that need to be engaged in mutual resistance. Hence, despite the human intervention in ecological and biological systems, and transformational changes in natural habitats, "part of the answer to the question of why the world has not collapsed is that natural ecological systems have the resilience to experience wide change and still maintain the integrity of their functions" (Holling, Gunderson, and Ludwig 2002, 18).

Seen from this perspective, Leonard's story is a good example of human resilience to maintain integrity in the face of catastrophic changes and to provide a note of hope for the present state of affairs in which the ideological and the ecological are presented as inseparable in the context of collapsing political-ecological-social conditions. This story shows that such postnatural conditions both construct and are constructed by how human beings live their role in the ecological totality and by how they deal with this reality in the existing relations of power. Leonard's story contests power relations in such a way that their implications in underlying ecological systems cannot be disregarded. His story unveils the human dimension of panarchy, highlighting, to quote Holling, Gunderson, and Ludwig again, "the interplay between change and persistence, between the predictable and unpredictable" (2002, 5).

If we can bring the very fact that "we are interconnected as a biosphere and a civilization" (Robinson 2020) into public consciousness everywhere on the planet despite the wall of social troubles in disadvantaged places, there will be hope. Although this is a gargantuan task compounded by what seem like unsolvable social, economic, and political problems, the possibility exists. If we acknowledge this collectively, the present pessimism can eventually morph into an optimism that will fuel us to imagine and construct a more livable world.

Chapter 5

The Ecology of Colors in the Anthropocene

The previous chapter ended with a note of hope, and this final chapter intends to share a brighter prospect for what the future can hold if our collective mindset is rewired toward a deeper appreciation of the vibrancy of life on Earth. Even if humanity's dark ecological entanglements in the planet's metabolism cast a shadow on this hopeful note, life's prismatic richness can catapult us away from and beyond the language of despair and the standard monochromatic discourses of green ecologies, or even beyond the colorless dark ecologies lamenting the fate of ruined landscapes. This should by no means be interpreted as turning a blind eye to the postnatural processes, to the threats of extinction and human cruelty, or to the ongoing damage multispecies interdependencies suffer from. Instead, it is a readjustment of our telescopic and microscopic lenses to notice the multiple stories of prismatic richness around us, a richness still intact amid disastrous happenings. If we want to bring a gift of hope and inspiration to the current ecological discourses, we can begin by reclaiming the colors of life shimmering "across varied forms of life" (Gan et al. 2017, G12) and through the multispecies relationalities of which we are part. As environmental ethnographer Deborah Bird Rose lyrically expresses it, "we are called into recognition: of the shimmer of life's pulses and the great patterns within which the power of life expresses itself" (2017, G61). Bringing such recognition into view, this chapter examines the entangled colors of life that not only attune us to our planet's polychromatic richness and vibrancy but also enable us to appreciate the significance of colors in affecting cognitive, perceptual, aesthetic, spiritual, ideational, and cultural experiences, and how such experiences are related to the moral appreciation of natural environments and their nonhuman inhabitants.

The entangled colors of life shimmer through bodily natures, deepen our appreciation of life's prismatic plenitude, and attune us to the animate Earth and its more-than-human entities also shimmering with life's pulses. Returning to the "verdancy of an unspoiled world" (Cohen 2013, xxi) is impossible, but life's colors hold the promise of returning humanity's attention back to the biosphere, which is now "stretched to the limit of its capacity" (Wilson 2002, 33) with the destructive currents of the Anthropocene. This return is in fact attainable through an appreciation of the world around us via its colors because we are all part of this prismatic reality. We can cultivate such an awareness even amid what Jeffrey J. Cohen highlights as "multihued contaminations, impurities, hybridity, monstrosity, contagion, interruption, hesitation, enmeshment, refraction, unexpected relations, and wonder" (2013, xxiv).

Despite the multihued environmental contaminations that create depressing currents in the present-day drama of life, the element of wonder can generate the ability to return to life's generative patterns and meaningfulness framed in the color spectrum of earthly life. It is a return to the stories of the chromatic plethora of Earth's metaphoric energies through which material realities are first contemplated in the mind's eye, literally as well as metaphorically. British poet and filmmaker Derek Jarman (1942–1994) asked a pertinent question about such contemplation in his notable book *Chroma: A Book of Color*: "Who has not gazed in wonder at the snaky shimmer of petrol patterns on a puddle, thrown a stone into them and watched the colours emerge out of the ripples, or marveled at the bright rainbow arcing momentarily in a burst of sunlight against the dark storm clouds?" (1995, 145). Marveling at the colors of the rainbow and at petrol patterns indicates how the multihued beauties and contaminations in global environments condition the possibilities of the emerging planetary realities. Needless to say, these ambiguous relationships are quite complicated and can be often accumulative, but they need not necessarily be the harbingers of the future, depending on the collective human interactions with the global environments. They simply point to the complex interconnections in the community of life. Jarman's poetic contemplation on colors is neither determinate nor clearly specified, but his poems invite us to reflect on the idea that "it is through metaphors and the imagination that reality takes on meaning" (Bachelard [1947] 2002, 49). Colors play a significant role in the meaning-making processes that shape the global cultural imaginary, and more visibly what German ecocritic Hubert Zapf calls "cultural ecology," which sees "the fundamental relations between culture and nature" as "inextricably interconnected" (2016, 82).

Material ecocriticism sees this interconnectedness between nature and culture not as the outcome of mere intertwining of two separate fields but as naturalcultural entanglements emerging through ongoing relations and creative becomings of expressive material agencies. Thus, material ecocriticism calls attention to the narrative materiality unfolding with the occasions of narrative agencies of storied matter weaving life's meanings with gestures, scents, sounds, and colors "within which the power of life expresses itself" (Rose 2017, G61). From this standpoint, earthly colors surface as the primary tools of polychrome expressions as all life-forms from the faunal to the mineral apply them with mastery to continue their existence. When it is understood that nature and culture materially, semiotically, and prismatically constitute and inhabit each other, as the compound term *naturecultures* indicates, the realization follows that colors are essential to becoming expressive. In a world of creative becomings, processes of meaning-making with colors abound, demanding to be studied in-depth and in poetic as well as scientific terms. It is not surprising that narrative agencies of storied matter also convey their stories through worldly colors, which not only shaped experiences of living beings throughout their evolutionary paths but also determined life's transformative meanings in science and human imagination. The origin of colors in scientific research might help us better understand their dynamic power in the life of images forged in art and literature, hence their valorization in terrestrial imagination.. Science lends credence to the color-dependent meaning-making processes evidenced by the signifying power of colors in the naturalcultural world. Scientific studies of how various plant and animal species use color to survive and to communicate with one another reveal that colors play a major role in sustaining life. In other words, color is a determinant factor behind ecological mutualisms for all life-forms since the beginning of evolution.

In scientific parlance, color is the absorption of certain wavelengths of white light by the atoms and molecules of biological entities, which gives grass its green color and oranges their hues between yellow and red. When the atoms of an orange, for instance, absorb light, the energy of the photons matches the energy difference in the initial and the excited state of the molecules that interact in various energy levels, including electronic energy and vibrational energy.[1] Here, the transitions induced by the absorption of light between electronic states are responsible for the colors we observe. Biological organisms also produce color by "submicroscopic structures that fractionate incident light into its component colours (schemochromes); or chemically, by natural pigments (biochromes) that reflect or transmit (or both) portions of the solar spectrum" (Brown et al. 2019).

Many material-symbolic meanings that emerge from these states of chromatic affluence comprise the discourses of the ecology of colors through which we can read earthly stories anew, even though some are quite disheartening like the moribund realms of the postnatural. Yet despite the postnatural overshadowing, the entangled colors of life always provide a more capacious understanding of global environments in human perception and experiences; they are also crucial communicative factors for narrative agencies in transmitting messages, admittedly essential in their existence. If there is both beauty and dissonance in the prismatic vision, the challenge of the human, as indicated by the Anthropocene's dark waves, is to rethink the story of life in its entangled colors. From the material ecocritical perspective, this story is embedded in plants producing configurations of meaningful expressions through colors. Like sending signals to each other under the soil to communicate with their neighbors and avoid being left in the shade,[2] changing color is also a well-regulated form of communication among plants to attract insects and birds for pollination. As horticulturalist Leonard Perry (n.d.) explains in "The How and Why of Plant Color": "Forget-me-nots (*Myosotis*) or other members of the Borage family, as well as some other flowers such as larkspur (*Delphinium*), change color between pink and blue. This usually indicates to insects that a flower has aged and is past pollination, so move on." As life-sustaining narrative agencies, plants can best express themselves chromatically. Colors, in other words, can be read as sites of narrativity through which plants display their own processes of creative becoming. The circulation of life in the plant world can only be sustained through the intimate relation between flora (all flowering and nonflowering plants and trees) and colors. We thus acknowledge that the elemental powers of life's entangled colors nourish mineral, floral, faunal, and human life and thus "the brilliant shimmer of the biosphere" (Rose 2017, G52) so that all that exists can continue to express their being in the world.

The inspiration that fuels this argument comes from an article I wrote with French philosopher Patrick Degeorges (Degeorges and Opperman 2019) and also from Jeffrey J. Cohen's edited collection *Prismatic Ecology: Ecotheory Beyond Green* (2013). In his introduction, Cohen argues that green "dominates our ecology like no other, as if the color were the only organic hue, a blazon for nature itself" (xix), but nature is polychrome, and green itself "is a composite color that arrives in a multitude of shades" (xx–xxi). Green has also been the favorite color of ecocritical analyses.

> Green analysis often focuses on the destabilizing encroachment of industrialized society into wild spaces, the restorative and even ecstatic power of unblemished landscapes, and the companionless dignity of nonhuman creatures. Woodlands, serene waterscapes, sublime vistas, and charismatic megafauna feature prominently. Blending the romantic, the pastoral, the georgic, green ecologies tend to dwell on the innate plenitude that nature offers, mourning its commodification and disruption. (Cohen 2013, xx)

Challenging this homogenizing approach, the ecology of colors projects an image of a planet of multihued biodiversity and prismatic compositions. This new discourse is informed not only by interaction with natural beauties and the moral sensibilities evoked by them and the desire to participate in the aesthetic experiences they trigger—as in the case of the Fisherman of Halicarnassus (1890–1973),[3] the Turkish writer who dwelled in the sunlit zones of the Mediterranean and Aegean Seas, discussed later in this chapter—but also by dark ecologies embedded in the porous zones of the world's naturecultures becoming increasingly postnatural. This is the story of colors that contain compelling evidence for the most enduring evolutionary development through time.

"When we sit and look at a sunset," Steven Bleicher, professor of visual arts, writes in *Contemporary Color: Theory and Use*, "we are drawn by the magic of nature's palette" (2012, 3). When, on this palette, "ecological imagination recast[s] the color spectrum into a new understanding of biodiversity" (Degeorges and Oppermann 2019), colors, like sounds, are understood to be essential to life, deeply affecting the experiences of nonhuman entities—biological, vegetal, and mineral. If the Earth is teeming with chromoscapes and soundscapes, the communicative tonality and polychrome expressions become as much an attribute of all other species as of our own. Today, however, the world's prismatic geographies are in danger of being dimmed and reduced to monochromatic maps due to the increasingly dangerous human manipulations of the planetary systems. The world's liveliness is now ironically shining through plastic waste with "hazardous luminosity . . . luring many nonhuman species to death. The world becomes dimmed. Many examples in nature show us indeed that a dying organism loses its color: humans turn pale and falling autumn leaves turn to brown and finally to black, which is commonly linked to death" (Degeorges and Oppermann 2019).

The world that is losing its colors necessitates deep change in human collective intelligence, or as Will Steffen and his colleagues put it, "to maintain the Earth System in a manageable Stabilized Earth state," we need a social transformation, which is possible if there is "deliberate management of humanity's relationship with the rest of the Earth System" (2018, 8258). For them, the necessary pathway to "the Stabilized Earth" is through "a deep transformation based on a fundamental reorientation of human values, equity, behavior, institutions, economies, and technologies. . . . Even so, the pathway toward Stabilized Earth will involve considerable changes to the structure and functioning of the Earth System" (8258). Therefore, the authors suggest "resilience-building strategies be given much higher priority than at present in decision making" (8258). To put it another way, to maintain the polychromatic affluence of life and to avoid the catastrophic and systemic consequences of the Anthropocene, we need to undergo a qualitative transformation, a collective social change. Such a transformation is possible through a "revisionist ontology," as Lawrence Buell (2013) advocates, which can "deliver a better ethics—not to mention politics—for the Anthropocene" (xi). The corollary of this way of thinking is to "reimagine the prism through which this existential challenge is framed" (Degeorges and Oppermann 2019) while facing the consequences of the Anthropocene. We can reclaim the entangled colors of life and rethink our relationship to life on Earth in terms of our intimate connections to the colorful living world. Human consciousness, after all, plays "its most significant role in the development and creative expression of the collective consciousness of nature" (Ho and Popp [1989] 1993). According to geneticist Mae-Wan Ho and biophysicist Fritz-Albert Popp ([1989] 1993), all organisms and living systems are "interlinked into a coherent whole" in a "mutually communicating universe of meaning." This means that we are enfolded in the world as a whole, and the whole is enfolded in us, in each part of itself, so to speak; in other words, "different populations enfold information not only for themselves but for all other organisms, expanding the consciousness of the whole" (Ho and Popp [1989] 1993). If we are enfolded inseparably and are integral aspects of the whole, as quantum physicist David Bohm (1988) also confirms, proposing a theory of "unbroken wholeness" (65), we cannot really adhere to the mistake that "there is merely an external 'interaction' between us and the world" (67). That is why life in its entangled colors is one continuous flow of creative expressions brought about by innumerable narrative agencies, which know how to communicate through colors their own inherent meanings, like the flowers that use colors as signals to attract potential pollinators. A flower changing its color acts as a potential narrative agency, transmitting its meanings to visitors, such as bees. This is what Bleicher affirms in *Contemporary Color*: "A single patch of color can communicate more than words themselves. That single hue can represent joy or sadness" (2012, 2). For evidence, we need look not only to flowers and bees, whose communication via the color spectrum is discernible, but also to so-called inanimate objects like stones that are imbued with the vitality of colors. Alexandrites, for example, have a unique chemical composition that allows them to change their colors. Different lighting conditions are responsible for the stones' chemical composition in absorbing light, but chromium is the element that makes for the color change in alexandrites. If changing color is a communication device, then alexandrites are the most well-known examples that can convey their stories by turning from green to blue in the daytime and to pink or purple at night. In the material ecocritical phraseology, the alexandrite is a narrative agency expressing itself with this chemical identity impressed in colors. To put it more succinctly, color is one of the most telling "material-semiotic means of relating" (Haraway 2008a, 26) for all that is more-than-human, which seems to be energetically infused into the very act of creation itself. The storied dimension of nonhuman agencies framed in colors is sedimented into the worldly processes of becoming expressive. Once we are able to pursue this claim to its conclusion, we will recognize that the entangled colors of life are always already situated at the very seat of the world as veritable invocations of story-making.

As long as life on Earth continues to be an expressive force flourishing in a unique multihued evolution, our storied planet will also continue to express itself through its prismatic foundations, and thus through the colorful prisms of biological and inorganic agencies. In a complementary direction, we will continue to reimagine the earthly prisms that can *affectively* reconnect us to our symbiotic planet, still shimmering with all of its life-forms—faunal, floral, bacterial, and mineral. Inspired by David Abram, we can also say that earthly colors have "constitutive powers that have summoned us into existence" (2010, 78), and they have played a major role in the course of our planetary evolution. In a detailed exposition of how evolution unfolded through colors, Turkish biologist Ali Demirsoy (2021) recounts how "the dance of colors" emerged when symbiotic relations between seed plants and insects began right after the planet's climate was stabilized. That is how, he writes, "fluorescence (flowering) developed with a coloration that winked at the insects from afar. So, animals from afar now understood where to search for the rich sources of nutrients" (78).[4]

Earthly Colors in Science

Earthly colors transpired when plants first began using insects and birds, and later the evolving mammals, as intermediaries. That is when the dance of colors became evident and "transformed this life-garden we call Earth into an array of bright colors" (Demirsoy 2021, 79). Ever since, earthly colors have been influencing our experiences of life and playing a constitutive part in our relations to more-than-human environments. This interpretation of earthly life provides intriguing maps of the ongoing coevolution of organisms and colors, perception, and ecological imagination. It is a prismatic vision that contests and transcends the monochromatic language of green ecology by opening to the world's polychromatic aliveness. If such colorful vibrancy is rightly understood both in its beautiful radiance and in its dark side, its aesthetic experience transcends the passive appreciation of nature and becomes a multisensorial (as well as cognitive) interaction with the material world from the human perspective. In this perspective, light, color, and liveliness always merge in the diversity of life on Earth, as explained by Ho and Popp (1989):

> We can see that sunlight is the most fundamental source of energy, which is supplied at the high frequency end, and biological systems as a whole display the natural tendency to delay the decay of this high-level energy for as long as possible. This is why the earth's natural biosphere is not a monoculture, indeed, it is the very diversity of life that is responsible for delaying the dissipation of the sun's energy for as long as possible by feeding it into ever longer chains and webs and multiple parallel cycles in the course of evolution.

Not being a monoculture, the biosphere contains all human and nonhuman hues, rhythms, perceptions, and articulations of the world. All beings are attuned to "the tenor of the world's unfolding" (Abram 2010, 173) through its varicolored vibrancies even in the face of the overshadowing effects of hybrid zones where the beautiful and the unpleasant often converge. Transcending the monochromatic language of green ecology, this prismatic vision beckons us toward an encounter with the world's chromatic aliveness without ignoring the world's dimmed colors. Creative experiences of multihued ecologies also enable us to see the world in its "life-sustaining relations" (Swanson, Tsing, and Bubandt 2017, M5). Creative experience, however, is not only a human attribute: it also fashions other beings through their multisensorial perceptions of the environment in their symbiotic relations through colors. For instance, in animals body color is ecologically significant, as color is the main determinant in species recognition and sexual selection (Tsuchida et al. 2010). Tsutomu Tsuchida and colleagues note that "many animals have color vision, recognizing their environment, habitat, food, enemies, rivals, and mates by visual cues" (1102). The authors' example of the endosymbiont relationship is the green color of the aphid's body. They contend that "the induced green color may reduce the predation risk by ladybird beetles. Notably, Rickettsiella is frequently found in co-infections with either Hamiltonella . . . or Serratia . . . endosymbionts . . . both of which are protective against parasitoid wasps and may act to offset the risk of green aphids attracting parasitoids" (1104). Another example of symbiotic relations through color is the brightly colored clownfish, which can swim among sea anemones without harm because it attracts *predatory fish* through its colors so that the anemones can catch and eat the unsuspecting fish (National Geographic 2019). These representative cases about "co-species survival" (Bubandt 2017, G136) in prismatic environments highlight the significant role color plays in the development of "ecological intelligence," or the collective ability of biological organisms to ensure their survival, as well as to effectively communicate with their neighbors.[5] This is also true for flowers, because color is an enactment of a determinate agency to express themselves and to attract pollinators. Pat Willmer and colleagues (2009) give the example of the legume *Desmodium setigerum*, which "shows a unique ability, if inadequately pollinated, to reverse its flowers' color and shape changes. Single visits by bees mechanically depress the keel and expose stigma and anthers . . . ; visits also initiate a rapid color change from lilac to white and turquoise and a slower morphological change, the upper petal folding downwards over the reproductive parts" (919). The researchers also underline how "flowers receiving insufficient pollen can partially reopen, re-exposing the stigma, with a further color change to deeper turquoise and/or lilac" (919).

To sustain the prismatic liveliness and the ecological intelligence of all beings in their chromatic interdependencies, our material and perceptual interactions with the world must be attuned to "multispecies becoming-with," as Haraway suggests, which she explains as "becom[ing] enfolded in each other's . . . lives" (2017, M35). To rephrase Haraway, although "enfolding each other" (M25) *through colors* can be both "competitive or cooperative" (M26), color, being essential to life, remains a constitutive part of all symbiotic relations. Why is this so? First, because "the biggest story of life on earth" is "symbiogenesis, the co-making of living things" (Swanson, Tsing, and Bubandt 2017, M8). Second, this story cannot be told without the role colors have been playing in its unfoldment since evolution began. Third, to understand the stories of collaborative survival through prismatic entanglements, we need "arts of imagination as much as scientific specifications" (Swanson, Tsing, and Bubandt 2017, M8).

As the underlying coding of ecological intelligence, the entangled colors of life give every prismatic being its special identity, self-consciousness, expressive competence, and existential meanings. All beings are strung together in chromatic interactions and rely on the ability to detect the correct color to ensure the continuity of life. Henceforth, every entity in its colorful becoming is differentially prismatic, producing different compositions of being in the complex ecosystem of interdependent elements. As Ali Demirsoy explains with reference to plants and insect photoperception:

> When many plants get ready to be fertilized, they begin to transmit important signals with colors and patterns in order to attract insects. For example, a white flower blackens its ovary in its middle and then furnishes it with very interesting colors and patterns. In the periods when it is not ready for fertilization, it hides itself by using the basic color, green, as much as possible. (2021, 115)

Insect vision, which is highly crucial for finding food, needs to be sensitive to plants' color configurations. Insects evolved to perceive wavelengths of from 650 to 300 nanometers, including the ultraviolet range of the spectrum but not yellow, orange, or red (Turpin 2012). Mammals, on the other hand, can perceive only three wavelength pigments (blue, green, and red), and humans can see wavelengths of the electromagnetic spectrum from 400 to 800 nanometers, from violet to red (Turpin 2012). Steven Bleicher explains this in more detail, noting that when we humans look at color what we really see is

> the action and reaction of light. White light, or the visible spectrum, is composed of wavelength, amplitude, and saturation. This may also be referred to as a visual stimulus. Wavelengths, the length of light waves, are measured in nanometers. The shorter wavelengths include X-rays and the visual spectrum of color and white light; the longest lengths include infrared. . . . Different wavelengths are also associated with different hues. Shorter wavelengths indicate violet and blue, and longer wavelengths indicate yellows, oranges, and reds. (2012, 4)

Wavelength here refers to what we humans, distinguished from other animals, see when we observe an object's color, which means that what we are really "seeing are the reflected light waves" (Bleicher 2012, 6). Animals do not see colors the way humans perceive them but use their ability "to see infrared wavelengths of color not visible to humans" (Bleicher 2012, 3). Also, different from the photosensory apparatus in plants, visual perception in animals is "mediated by specialized photoreceptor cells which absorb light and generate neural signals" (Sharrock 1992, 194). As biologist Robert A. Sharrock further explains, "the photosensory apparatus in plants is fundamentally different from visual systems in that light is absorbed by photosensitive molecules present in a wide variety of cell types that are not specifically differentiated for the purpose of light perception" (194). Insects, on the other hand, as entomologist Tom Turpin (2012) points out, can easily detect the polarization of light from the sky to navigate. Turpin also draws attention to similarities and differences between insects and humans in sight: "The most obvious is in the structure of the eye. Human eyes and the eyes of most other non-insect animals are single-lens structures. The insect eye is made up of multiple lenses and is called a compound eye."

The eye in the prismatic discourse is both a sense organ and a metaphor of coexistence; it is dependent on the world of colors, as it cannot create light by itself. Color, therefore, is a direct material engagement with the ontology of the world, a vital tool, like sound, for life navigation. Many animals, such as cuttlefish, various squid species, octopuses, spiders, frogs, and chameleons, change coloration for camouflage by producing biochromes (naturally produced pigments).[6] Coloration, as biologist Frank A. Brown and colleagues write, "is a dynamic and complex characteristic and must be clearly distinguished from the concept of 'colour,' which refers only to the spectral qualities of emitted or reflected light" (2019). To draw attention to or away from themselves, animal species use coloration, which "may serve to repel or attract other animals" (Brown et al. 2019). Coloration is used for communication, but animals also use it deceptively to create incorrect signals to reduce communication. Like animals, plants have characteristic biochromes that they use for meaningful signaling. As evolutionary ecologist Monica Gagliano explains, like olfactory signals, "colors and color patterns . . . are other prominent and well-known mediums through which plants interact and communicate. More than 450 species of plants, for example, are able to change their color, position, and shape to advertise their trading hours and even promote further business deals is inadequately pollinated" (2017b, 90). As mentioned before, recent research proves that plants use color not only as a functional tactic of sustainable communication but also as a strategic factor in "attracting and manipulating potential pollinators":

> Floral color change is commonly used to transmit this information . . . (often correlated with reduced nectar reward . . . and can be specifically triggered by pollination or visitation. By retaining color-changed flowers, plants benefit from larger floral displays but also indicate at close range which flowers are still rewarding (and still unpollinated), so that visitors forage more efficiently. (Willmer et al. 2009, 919)

Clearly, color, like agency, is not the property of humanity alone, or even unique to biological organisms. Consider stones, such as the mineral specimen alexandrite mentioned earlier, that can change hues, turning from bluish green to pinkish purple or tourmaline, and can blend multiple colors. Surprisingly, metals also carry color. As crystal healer Michael Gienger explains, "metals, particularly chromium, iron, copper, cobalt, manganese and nickel, are able to absorb certain wavelengths of light. For this reason, they are also called 'colour carriers' or 'chromospheres' (Greek *chroma*, 'colour' and *phoros*, 'carrying')" (2000, 134–35). Simply expressed, colors are in the fabric of lively matter itself in which all atoms quiver with life. Color is always bound up with a creative and expressive agency that makes the world alive in generative becomings. In this sense, a polychromatic ecological approach enables "a full-bodied alertness" (Abram 2010, 173) to human and nonhuman resonances, hues, rhythms, perceptions, and articulations of the world. Becoming familiar with all these gradations of colors, rhythms, shapes, and expressions of the inhabitants of terrestrial environments can in fact summon us back into the "creative flux of evolution" (Abram 2010, 78). This is not so difficult because, as David Abram reminds us, "we are born of this planet, our attentive bodies coevolved in rich and intimate rapport with the other bodily forms—animals, plants, mountains, rivers—that compose the shifting flesh of this breathing world" (2010, 78). This poetic account of life, however, would be incomplete without the intriguing maps of coevolution of organisms and colors, perception, and, most importantly, imagination.

Earthly Colors in Literary Imagination: The Fisherman of Halicarnassus

The prismatic approach to life that constitutes the ecology of colors was anticipated by Turkish writer known as the Fisherman of Halicarnassus[7] long before green ecology was under way, as poetically expressed in the prologue to *Ege'den Denize Bırakılmış Bir Çiçek* (*A Flower Left to the Aegean Sea* [1972]): "This deep blue sky of southern Anatolia, its violet sea, light, and land, has nourished various trees, fruits, flowers, human beings, and civilizations."[8] The significant role earthly colors play in the evolutionary story of life also colors the author's imagination, which frequently tunes in to the overwhelming beauty of the Bodrum Peninsula at the juncture of Turkey's Aegean and Mediterranean Seas.[9] Below is an exemplary passage from the Fisherman's kaleidoscopic narratives that brings attention to Bodrum's multihued topography:

> The olives in Halicarnassus, tangerines, oranges, lemons, caperberries, dates, bananas, capers, figs; in short, all the fruit trees that pantomime seasons take lessons from the aquamarine seashore's emerald green. With greens of all hues, they sing songs of green to the Aegean emerald. The tingle of this song can always be heard in the skies. (1972, 46–47)

The Fisherman knew well that the interpretations of polychromatic life on Earth enrich the ecological imagination in a vision that recasts the color spectrum perceived by both human and nonhuman eyes. He also knew that life must have evolved through colors, showing us how living connections can unfold in prismatic expressions, rhythms, perceptions, and interactive articulations of the world.

The Fisherman started developing his prismatic discourse in the 1930s, when he immersed himself in the turquoise waters of the Mediterranean Sea, which in Turkish we call *Akdeniz*—the White Sea. In *Mavi Sürgün* (*The Blue Exile* [1961]), he explains why it is the White, not the Blue, Sea: "In every cubic meter of the Mediterranean waters there exist more than forty million small creatures. In the spring and summer, they bleach the seawater at night. The whitened waters are called sea-milk" (243). He describes how miles and miles of seawater turn milky white at night with the volcano of milk erupting from the fish:

In their swimming course they lay off eggs, milk and a flood of offspring. The waves of the sea become sticky, and water stretches. Within this life-yeast, life itself boils. Their eggs are a tiny round blue lantern in the vast darkness of the sea. This discharged volcano of egg and milk stifles the seas whose choking fame is well known. At night miles and miles of sea turn milky white with these currents of fish and motherhood. The sea like Divine Light! This is the reason why the Mediterranean is called Akdeniz (The White Sea) in Turkish. (243)

But this is not a static white, because "the sea-milk shines blue and greenish some nights, and glows crimson and orange at others. But most nights it flares up like electric white, turning Akdeniz into a snow sea like the snowy nights of full moons" (246). The Fisherman emphasizes the swirling life of the Mediterranean Sea as the principal expressive force of existence in its ongoing polychromatic emergence: "The real symbol of motherhood is the sea . . . It is the sea that is the giant breast that suckles all things alive" (1961, 245–46).

The Fisherman of Halicarnassus witnessed how the sporadic Cyclades Islands that form the great archipelago accommodate nature's life-sustaining agencies and contain countless stories of human and nonhuman entanglements. "These stories are the products of . . . heavenly hands, mountains, grass, coasts, wild rocks, ruins, and open seas. I dedicate all the stories to them" (1972). These stories clearly capture a color-filled life in the crisscrossing flows of ecological and cultural forces. The Fisherman's stories of the monk seals, dolphins, countless fishes, fishermen, olive trees, donkeys, and folk songs illustrate the entangled phenomena in the Bodrum Peninsula, and the dynamics of this entanglement shimmer through the amorphous lives of these narrative agencies. They all reflect and radiate manifold prismatic meanings that can be physical, psychological, and spiritual at the same time. The reciprocal relationship between the fishermen, sponge divers, and the sea fauna are emblematic of these meanings, and the lively interactions between nature and culture on these coasts have produced, the author observes, ecologically sensitive social discourses and meanings since the ancient times.

The Fisherman was particularly interested in the well-being of the inhabitants of both human and more-than-human environments and the health of marine life in the Aegean and the Mediterranean Seas, which he understood to be part of the ecocultural evolution of the Bodrum Peninsula. He knew that for as long as animals, fish, and people coexist in a relational equilibrium, life will flourish in an enticing explosion of colors, with each being desiring to shine with its own innermost energy. The Fisherman himself lived his life accordingly in Bodrum, reproducing its rhythms and colors, and expressed it quite humorously: "The sun that ripens the oranges breeds nice people here" (1972, 47). He appreciated the archipelago as a storehouse of polychromatic expressions, as a colorful spectrum of life, and as a majestic display of natural beauties that enchanted him. "That Sea, those islands were ten times more beautiful than the wildest imagination can conjure up heaven. Especially that lucent sky, how placid it was so far away! I could hear the sea, the whisper of the vine leaves" (1961, 182). The dynamic intensity of Homer's wine-dark sea, the astonishing blue of the sea, "a sapphire or navy of infinite depth" (quoted in Williams 2013, 75), shaped the Fisherman's ecological imagination. As British journalist Roger Williams (1947–2019) wrote, quoting the Fisherman: "Bodrum, the Aegean, the Mediterranean all seemed an eternal blue. *The sea and sky cannot be more blue than they are in Bodrum.* 'Blue explodes, absolute, deafening, infinite'" (2013, 80; italics in original). It was as if this ancient sea, the Mediterranean, was communicating its timeless stories to the Fisherman. One of the most stunning passages of his intense communion and relations with the old sea is in *The Blue Exile*:

> Here was a sense of profoundness enveloping us in its infinity. The great Archipelago, darkening in the turquoise of the evening—*the old sea*—showed me its majestic presence. The sea cracked upon the horizon without warning like a vast blue thundering infinity. It was a deep blue roar . . . I felt like watching infinity from the hill I was standing on. (1961, 172)

As famous environmentalist Mitchell Thomashow explains, such moments are indeed "moments of great awareness and serendipity, when you feel that you are deeply touched by something unfathomable" (2002, 212–13). Evoking a deepening wonder about forms of creativity that pervade the aquatic environments, these sublime experiences were the major sources of inspiration for the writer's stories. They enhanced his ecological imagination, making him feel as if he was imbued by the blueness of the entire sea and as if the immense beauty of the blue sea was disclosing its inner being to him as an awe-inspiring narrative agency. The wondrous blue of the Mediterranean is thus intertwined with the craft of his writing, endowing his narratives with symbolic vitality. The blue, in other words, was the metaphoric ink that the Fisherman used to compose his stories: "If that blue is the sea's own, then dip your pen into it and write blue, blue on sheets of white" (quoted in Williams 2013, 74).

Indeed, dipping his pen into this impassioned blue, the Fisherman demonstrates how ecological sensibility can be made coterminous with narrative art and aesthetics, creating a clear-sighted recognition of connections between the immanent vitality of aquatic habitats and the dynamism of human poetics—and, in a more expansive sense, between nature and culture. Roger Williams cites the story of journalist Ian Crawford's encounter with the Fisherman in Bodrum, published in *New Scientist* in 1977. Crawford found the Fisherman "lying on his boat in the bay with the tiller between his feet." As quoted by Williams, Crawford wrote:

> He was a handsome old man, who spoke seven or eight languages with commanding fluency, wit and erudition. He talked of Homer as if he had just left him in a pub down the road, of how the hexameter had been born of a dance rhythm formed with the fingers of one hand, and of Pegasus on a petrol station sign blushing from head to toe at being used in an advertisement. (Williams 2013,14)

Equally significant in the ecological dimension is the cultural facet of colors in the Bodrum Peninsula. Here, the stories of humans and nonhumans have become so densely interwoven that the ever-unfolding ecocultural heritage never ceased to fascinate the author. In the Fisherman's stories, the songs of the gray bottlenose dolphins and the monk seals blend with the spirited *viva voce* of the loggerhead and green turtles, and fuse with the stories of fishermen, of cypress, lemon, and olive trees, and of donkeys, goats, and other animals. He was fascinated by how they were joined together to create a prismatic constellation of biocultural forces, inviting a new interpretation of nature as a remarkable polychromatic agency. In the Fisherman's eloquent words: "In Halicarnassus, all the olives, tangerines, oranges, lemons, palm trees, capers, bananas, figs—in short, all the trees that entitle the fruits to have their parade, take their lessons from this coast's sea-green. They sing their multigreen songs to the emerald green of the Aegean Sea" (1972, 47). As it is spoken on these coasts, Turkish, he continues, is dressed in their colorful songs. Like the folk dances modeled on the white-feathered dancing demoiselle crane—a sacred symbol in Turkish mythology—the human culture around here echoes the evolutionary rhythms of interconnected beings, of the sea and its elemental forces. The Fisherman never saw Bodrum's multihued ecological formation as separable from its cultural and historical significance. In such an astonishing mingling of history and ecology, "there is no border where evolution ends and history begins, where genes stop and environment takes up, where culture rules and nature submits, or vice versa" (Haraway 2004, 2).

The Fisherman saw Bodrum's biocultural rhythms and reflexes as creative affirmations of a prismatic choreography ceaselessly forging enduring naturalcultural patterns. He was quite emphatic about such choreography that was born out of the creative materiality, vitality, and expressiveness found in all species, abiotic material entities, elements, and forces. Using narrative as a means for "plumbing ecological interpenetration" (Cohen 2014, 55), the Fisherman recounted ongoing energetic creativity within the folds of these watery zones. He intuitively knew that the marine mammals and the Mediterranean fishes were effective narrative agencies even though they would never develop intentionality, cognition, and full consciousness like the human agency; nevertheless, they were all signifying agencies. He was convinced that the sea creatures he was familiar with, such as the cuttlefish, the bluefish, and the sea bream, were capable of expressing themselves and had stories to tell. Observing their process of communication via colors as their tool, he realized that the polychromatic semiotic connections determine how marine life evolves. In his essay "Akdeniz Balıklarının Marifetleri" (The Craftsmanship of the Mediterranean Fish), he explains how the cuttlefish communicates using coloration, which is indispensable to its evolution:

> You all know about the cuttlefish. You know how it leaves a trail of ink behind. You think it colors the sea black to escape its enemies. Not so at all! This rowdy character is more cunning than you can imagine. Think that a bluefish, or sea bream, its deadly enemy, is chasing after it. No master chameleon can match the cuttlefish in shape shifting. Now it is intensely red, then it suddenly turns deep green. When chased by the bluefish it becomes pitch black. But can it really escape from under the

noses of bluefish, sea bream, sea bass, leer fish, and dolphins? It may get caught. But when it realizes the situation, it suddenly turns cotton white and tries to get away. Moving sideways it leaves its ink, explodes it one after the other. Then the enemy sees eight or ten holes of darkness. The cuttlefish has escaped in its sheer whiteness while its follower is snapping at empty darkness. (2002a, 51–52)

In addition to the cuttlefish and other creatures in the Mediterranean and Aegean Seas that inspired the stories and songs of sponge divers and fishermen, there are many other examples of how the colors of nature fashion the cultural imaginary and social discourses all over Anatolia. The tulip prose in Turkish literature is one such example, dating back to the Tulip Age in the eighteenth-century Ottoman Empire, as it conspicuously reflects the naturalcultural enmeshment, particularly in Istanbul. For Turks, the tulip is not just a beautiful flower. The Ottoman seals incorporated the tulip, and today it is inscribed in every ceramic tile, marble artwork, tourist map, and brochure, as well as many other artifacts. Tulips frequently feature in contemporary Turkish literature as well, as in Buket Uzuner's novel *Istanbullu*: "If Istanbul was a flower, it was most certainly a tulip" (2008, 377). Tulips in their multicolored variety spotlight the intensity of our entanglements with prismatic ecologies, not only materially but also narratively. When the city speaks with a voice of its own in the novel, it highlights the naturalcultural significance of its native flowers and plants in their chromatic richness: "I am Istanbul; I am in the Judas tree, in acacia, in lavender; I am turquoise! I am the unfathomable; the muse of possibility, vitality, creativity" (2). Calling itself "mistress of metropolises, community of poets, seats of emperors, favorite of sultans, pearl of the world" (1), Istanbul also envisions itself in terms of its ecological aspects, as "the smell of earth, the tag of sea, the stuff of dreams" (3). But due to ongoing urban sprawl, the chromatic vibrancy of Istanbul's forests has at present faded to dusty gray.

Colors reveal their secrets in the scope of plastic arts and narratives, but they are also "written into" physical forms, housing meanings, stories, histories, and memories, like Homer's wine-dark sea that enchanted the Fisherman, or like minerals, rocks, and bodies. "Following colors in their materiality" (Cohen, 2013, xxiii) opens up so many entries into the intricacies of naturalcultural domains. The color spectrum of biological entities and ecosystems is an inextricable part of human aesthetic/symbolic palettes. From the Turkish perspective, the electric blue of the Aegean and the Mediterranean Seas, the lush green of forests saluting the Black Sea, the lonely maroon of the Taurus Mountains, the passions of the multicolored tulips of Istanbul, and the spectral white snow on Mount Ararat have all been central agents in constructing the symbolism of the aesthetics and poetics of culture in Anatolia. If "human culture is inextricably enmeshed with vibrant, nonhuman agencies," as Jane Bennett underlines (2010, 108), a mutual destiny unfolds with ethical commitments on the part of the human in a shared existence. Knowing this well, and cruising the multihued currents of life in Bodrum, the Fisherman believed that humans and nonhumans shared a mutual destiny. In his essay "Knidos Afroditi" (Aphrodite of Knidos) in *Ege'den Denize Bırakılmış Bir Çiçek* (*A Flower Left to the Aegean Sea*), he writes: "Life is such that the mutually created should love one another. Because if they do something else than love one another, they will be the executioners of one another" (1972, 23).

Although Bodrum is nothing like what it was in the Fisherman's lifetime, it still stands out, with its turquoise coasts, as Homer's land of eternal blue, inspiring reverence and aesthetic appreciation but also deep concern for the region's marine ecosystems as well as its historical and cultural heritage, which are under serious threat today. It is not just the excesses of tourism that threaten the Fisherman's beloved sites; it is pollution caused by oil spills, and tons of refuse flowing into the sea. His warning in the quotation above takes us back to the ecology of colors' inclusion of dissonances lurking within the material-discursive prisms. Dissonances yoke together questions of ontology, epistemology, and ecology to reorient our attention toward border crossings between aesthetic and critical stances and toward the hybrid zones of the postnatural.

The Dissonances of Earthly Colors: Dark Ecological Disruptions

The colors of this world do not always speak of the vibrant beauties of nature. Though not totally alien, there is a new world of colorful forces, objects, and substances that are endowed with the power of destruction: synthetic matter, chemicals, toxins, migrating viruses, microbes, pesticides, and plastic in varying densities cohabitate in natural and urban environments. All these dark material substances dwell in the most intimate recesses of the Earth's bodily natures and are now linking together stories of environmental injustices, violence, and environmental and social catastrophes. And they come in an amazingly multicolored diversity and collectively invade life. Covered with plastic trash, Kamilo Beach on the Big Island of Hawaii is famously emblematic of this harmful chromatic phenomenon, with countless plastic objects in various sizes, some as small as the beach's grains of sand. The "coexistence of these strangers and their strange iridescence" (Morton 2013a, 312) signals cyclical conjunction of repression launched by the global human. Kamilo Beach is a beautifully colored, lethal zone for seals, seabirds, sea turtles, and many species of fish.[10] Like the albatross on Midway Island in the North Pacific Ocean, brought to public attention by Chris Jordan's film *Midway: Message from the Gyre* (2009), they consume macro- and microplastics as attractive food and die. Kamilo's story, like Midway's dismal narrative, is one of a pervasive environmental tragedy; it presents the life of *materia color*—beautiful yet dangerous, plastic twisting itself into the digestive tracts of sea creatures and birds. The beautiful ambiance of plastic prism occupying such places explodes into a horrifying choir of death songs at the nonhumans' irreversible moments of contact with toxic human products. Clearly, all is not well in nature's colorful expanses. And in the afflictions of the Anthropocene, color is never innocent or benign. It has the power to kill and cause emotional pain. Anyone who has seen the tragic story of the Laysan albatross dying amid colorful plastic objects on Midway Island can recognize the pernicious influence of color on nonhuman bodies. Color is not always innocent even if it possesses aesthetic power.

If the entangled colors of life move toward hazardous luminosity—as in the case of the deadly lure of plastic waste suffocating life in the oceans and lands— the colorful vibrancy of being alive turns to life-under-erasure as if it is gradually crossed out but not totally erased. The landscapes that are less colorfully appealing, such as swamps and deserts, are of course exempt from the process of dimming of colors as they unexpectedly help the human imagination to go beyond green. For instance, in his introduction to *Getting over the Color Green: Contemporary Environmental Literature of the Southwest*, Scott Slovic (2001) cites Wallace Stegner to underline this point. To really appreciate the inhuman scale at large, "you have to get over the color green," says Stegner, and Slovic agrees, pointing to "the value of vast sprawls of land devoid of human forms and lacking in the verdant, accommodating color green" (xvii). Slovic's inspiration comes from the allure of the desert aesthetic foregrounded by American nature writers who have been attentive to the ecological values of not-so-aesthetically-beautiful places like arid landscapes. What needs to be developed here, Slovic claims, is "a tendency to 'appreciate the unappreciated'" (xix).

However, at this time of colossal environmental degradation, it is not enough to hold on to the aesthetic justification and apprehension of arid landscapes alone. Doing so would simply reenact the taxonomy of green environmentalism in a more capacious but still incomplete way; such a form of thought would contort the entangled colors of life with a melancholic loss. We already see this melancholy in the fading colors of massively polluted places. How are we going to revalue or cope with the environments lost to industrial toxicity, agricultural conquest, and other exploitative human practices? While this perspective may seem counterintuitive to the aesthetics of the entangled colors of life, it calls forth a new ecology beyond green that would shed critical light on aesthetic and ethical responses to a trashed planet where not all the colors are natural.

Taking us through the postgreen territories in which other species' responses to the beauty of colors—especially shining through plastic refuse—cause their demise, the ecology of colors asks the crucial question of how our appreciation of nature would change if we were to consider the more-than-human-environments choking under human detritus. Similar to life-forms, ecosystems are not immune to waste and debris recycling poisonous particles into the air, water, and soil. The postgreen vision offers a new framework for an ecological aesthetic that is inclusive of nonhuman perceptions and experiences of more-than-human environments. Our perceptual awareness, like that of many other species, is multisensory even if we do not realize how our cells interact with the food we consume or the air we breathe, while our eyes are focused on a green lawn or the vast loneliness of the desert brown.

In fact, whether on an island or in the woods, in a city park or on a mountain, a chorus of muddy-colored impurities have become simultaneous with *natura color*, calling forth a sensory, critical, and moral attentiveness to environmental transformations. As Patricia Yaeger explains: "In a world where molecular garbage has infiltrated earth, water, and air, we cannot encounter the natural untouched or uncontaminated by human remains. Trash becomes nature, and nature becomes trash" (2008, 332). But even if "we can keep waste at a distance, dump it in a natural environment that doesn't touch us, doesn't intrude on our organizations and codifications and decisions, doesn't trump our agency, doesn't trouble our fantasy that we alone have agential dominion," as Simon C. Estok says, it is "all-permeable in our worldings" (2018, 147). There is no place on this planet that human trash and garbage cannot infiltrate, and our waste is never outside us either. As ecocritic Heather I. Sullivan also notes, thinking that waste is out there somewhere away from us is inherited from "Modernity's anti-dirt campaigns," which "include efforts made to remove or conceal bodily filth, waste, and the sweaty labor of agricultural processes" (2012, 526). It is thus commonsensical to claim that our world is no longer a self-contained, primal, pastoral, or unspoiled "Green Eden," as it used to be imagined, but a composite one with "human and non-human actors operating in alliance as well as at odds with each other" (Cohen 2013, xxiv). The significance of this composite world is that it triggers a potentially traumatic tension between ecological aesthetics as embedded in the prismatic world and environmental ethics invoking a sense of great problems in this embeddedness determined by global contamination. If we do not want human pollutants dimming the colors of nature, we need to reconsider the dynamics of our interdependence with all the environments in ways that enhance responsiveness and responsibilities. As Bill McKibben notes in his 2006 introduction to his classic book *The End of Nature*: "It is the contrast between the pace at which the physical world is changing and the pace at which the human society is reacting that constitutes the key environmental fact of our time" ([1989] 2006, xv).

Being profoundly altered by Anthropocene-induced climate change and massive pollution, the Earth today is a mesh of humans, biological organisms, and humanly made substances transcorporeally connected in multifarious and often dangerous relations. One need not travel far to Kamilo Beach or to Midway Islands to decode a dark ecology; the biochemistry of our bodies equally discloses such relations with the number of microplastics accumulating in our organs and tissues, which can damage the immune system. Based on a growing body of evidence, one research review by Kieran D. Cox et al. (2019) demonstrates that

> microplastics are being integrated into widely consumed food items via animals ingesting microplastics in the environment, contamination during production, and/or contamination by plastic packaging. Microplastic particles (MPs) less than 130 μm in diameter have the potential to translocate into human tissues, trigger a localized immune response, and release constituent monomers, toxic chemicals added during plastic production, and pollutants absorbed from the environment, including heavy metals and persistent organic pollutants like PCBs and DDT. Despite increasing evidence that microplastics contaminate a large variety of food and beverages, in addition to outdoor and indoor environments, and the possibility of deleterious effects on human health following ingestion and/or inhalation, an investigation into the cumulative human exposure to MPs has not occurred. (7068)

The varieties of postgreen ecologies, including dark ecology, that emerge in the aftermath of such entanglements with toxic chemicals and "cumulative human exposure to MPs" are quite distinct, demanding sustained attention for at least two reasons. First, although dark ecology "possesses aesthetic power," as Cohen observes, "we may well find ourselves in a gray and brown space of stumps, fumes and sludge" (2014, 58). We simply cannot seal out its harmful effects. Second, our enmeshment in dark ecology invites a reparative stance rather than one that ignores its gray and brown hues. Dark ecology asks us to cultivate a sensibility that attunes us more critically to ourselves and nonhuman natures mutually caught up in its tornadoes. Importantly, this is not a shift away from the aesthetic appreciation of natural beauties of our color-filled Earth but rather an opening up of a different orientation toward the questions of pollution, toxicity, climate change, and environmental degradation. The dark side of postgreen ecology is like a wake-up call for a new engagement that extends beyond the allure of beautiful colors. It compels us to recognize the maps of intersections between the beautiful and the perilously colorful elements because the ecological health of our planet and its human and nonhuman inhabitants is at stake. It follows that from the blueness of the Mediterranean to the multihued dance of auroras in the Canadian and Norwegian skies, the chromatic complexity around us presents an amazing diversity and beauty alongside grief and tragedy. As anthropogenic processes continue to produce cascading effects on our ecologies, creating cracks in the aesthetic tableau of global natures, the ugly is bound to coexist with the beautiful, as diffuse and discrete as the auroras.

In the discourse of the entangled colors of life, the vistas of sylvan charm found in nature narratives are important, but equally crucial are critical accounts of plastic debris, parasites, chemical refuse, and our daily pollutants, intervening directly in the biosphere, "making decisive contact with humans" (Morton 2013a, 313). Comingling with biological organisms, these corrosive forces and disruptive substances spill onto the planet's life-support systems and bodily natures. Consider the oil spills in the Niger Delta, in the Gulf of Mexico, and off the coast of Rhode Island or the ongoing ecological devastation caused by the Great Pacific Garbage Patch. The prismatic approach, therefore, wants us not to turn a blind eye to what Cohen calls "volatile knots of human and inhuman actors operating in alliance as well as at odds with each other" (2013, xxiv). Being attentive to all earthly colors, including the dimming ones, the ecology of colors clarifies various threads of our coexistence, as well as our dark ecological alterity. Rather than debunking this reality, it cultivates a realistic attitude toward it while at the same time advocating for a reenchantment of the Earth's multihued life. The ecology of colors is the critique of "the disenchantment of nature," which according to David Ray Griffin, means "the denial to nature of all subjectivity, all experience, all feeling. Because of this denial, nature is disqualified" (1988, 2). It also means, as Griffin quotes Max Weber, "taking the magic out" (2). In the parlance of the ecology of colors, disenchantment means nature losing its polychromatic richness and becoming a disoriented dance of ghostly colors divorced from their former lucency.

With intensifying environmental insecurities, it is obvious that our polychrome world is turning pale, like the moribund realms of gray or like the melancholic mindscapes of black. As Levi Bryant, the leading theorist of object-oriented ontology, concurs, absorbing light and not emitting it, black embodies "melancholy existential connotations" (2013, 292). Being nonreflective, though, black "helps us move beyond anthropocentrism" (293). Reminding us of snakes, fish, and insects that "encounter the world through infrared," a spectrum in which the black bodies can be seen, Bryant argues that black is important for understanding the perspectives of many nonhuman beings. Because, he adds, black "invites us to explore the perspectives of *other* entities, investigating how the world is encountered *for them,* thereby overcoming the anthropocentric perspective that focuses on how things are *for us*" (293; italics in original). So conceived, these postgreen ecologies are segments of the ecology of colors, which navigates on a continuously redrawn map by the forces of *harmonia* and *dissonantia*. In the face of environmental crises, the boundaries between them become more porous, necessitating a more critical assessment of the chromatic magnetism of life. As Estok reminds us, our future "is situated on ground overwrought and overrun with various irreversible invasions (cultural, species), shifting and unstable soils in which profound power struggles continue to play out" (2014, 221). Although Estok says this is the future, it is in fact the very ground—the *dissonantia* plane of postgreen ecologies—where our present reality is being redrawn.

In his essay "At the Edge of the Smoking Pool of Death," Timothy Morton implicitly concurs with this view. He writes that "we have entered the gigantic fjord of the next moment of history, without even knowing it" (2013b, 25). This is an apt metaphor for the age of the Anthropocene. Humans are now altering almost every feature of the planet, and these changes occur at a global level, such as the yearly release of 160 million tons of sulfur dioxide into the atmosphere, the massive increase in ocean acidification, and the toxification of the soil through artificial fertilizer applications. As cultural anthropologist Stefan Helmreich notes, life scientists "assess large-scale changes in the ocean by looking at the sea's smallest inhabitants: marine microbes. Such microbes are looped into massive planetary processes" (2010, 50). Not too different is the result of research conducted on the phenomenon known as colony collapse disorder (CCD) among bees or the alarmingly rapid rates of disappearing honeybees. Scientists have discovered that neonicotinoids, widely used insecticides that kill bees at an exponential rate, are the direct cause of CCD. The consequences of the loss of bee populations are grave, as CCD is directly linked to our food chain (Hagopian 2014).[11]

Although we cannot always produce scientific certainties about the complexity of environmental transformations, we can say with conviction that social, political, and cultural factors have a great impact on these changes that take place from the oceans to the atmosphere. In the simplest sense, there is no easy alliance in human–nonhuman encounters. If there is "biospheric connectedness" (Heise 2008, 62), it is certainly to the detriment of the nonhumans today, as in the case of the bees and marine life, among others. Therefore, it is important to develop new types of ecological thinking and economic practices and to find better ways of interacting with nonhuman others. Going beyond green is one of the viable ways to achieve peace with the Earth and its nonhuman denizens; or in slightly modified words of French philosopher Patrick Degeorges, prismatic ecologies can direct us to "the arts of re-establishing the conditions for Peace with the Earth" (2021, 4).

It is in this light that the prismatic lens offered by the ecology of colors enables us to explore in a more thoughtful way what Peter Quigley, professor of English at University of Hawaii, Manoa, calls "radical forces of nonhuman energy" (2012, 10) and what anthropologist Terre Satterfield and ecocritic Scott Slovic describe as "the complexity and wonder of all forms of intelligence" (2004, 103). These forms are teeming with layers of interesting stories and multiple levels of meaning to be unearthed, and today the storied world is filled with the entanglements of the beautiful and the horrific. In these "entangled tales," as Karen Barad observes, "each is diffractively threaded through and enfolded in the other" (2012b, 207). That being the case, while beauty is an indispensable aspect of the ecology of colors, as showcased in the Fisherman's Mediterranean tales, pollution and devastation cast a shadow of skepticism over this vision. However, "if skepticism is taken too far and is an unrelenting end unto itself," as Quigley quite rightly warns against an excessive skepticism, "one ends up in a paralyzing, corrosive, nihilist, realm of the absurd, looping endlessly on a draining, politically obsessed, hamster wheel" (2012, 13).

Fortunately, the ecology of colors would never get onto that wheel, but it will emphasize nature today as a hybrid or mixed space housing the biological and the synthetic, and the natural and the manufactured in critical entanglements. According to Jeffrey J. Cohen, Latour's term *kakosmos* best describes this "tangled, fecund, and irregular pluverse" (2013, xxiii), which is indeed useful in broadening the conceptual arguments over the protean meanings of nature. Inherently irresolute, nature's meanings are never culture-free, biology-free, and technology-free, nor are they ever going to be story-free universal truths. Environmental historian William Cronon once proclaimed that "nature will *always* be a contested terrain. We will never stop arguing about its meanings" (1996, 52). In a horizon like this, the world becomes a prism through which the pure and the impure hybridize, and the dynamics of this hybridity necessitate nonanthropocentric ecologies so that a more meaningful, less pernicious, and more accountable human participation in the more-than-human world can be made possible.

To epitomize how such participation can be envisioned in a nonanthropocentric way, I would like to draw attention to the Fisherman of Halicarnassus's encounter with a seal at a cave, which he writes about in "Foklar, Yunuslar" (The Seals and Dolphins) in the collection *İmbat Serinliği* (*The Coolness of the Breeze* [2002b]). One night, while watching the sea's phosphorescence in total darkness, the Fisherman is startled when he hears someone sneezing. He then notices a dark shadow near him and hears a heavy panting that sounds like *hoh* and finally recognizes that this is his seal friend he had met at a cave.

> On the Black Island in Bodrum near the sea, there is a cave with flowing sulfur water. I used to stand on top of this cave. In the winter when there was no one, a seal would regularly visit the cave. We used to have intimate eye contact and gaze at each other for a while. When he didn't see me, I would send him my greetings calmly saying hello. Then he would turn around and look me in the eye. His eyes were so innocent. (2002b, 145)

Human participation in multispecies life need not always be invasive; if we want to cultivate ecological sensibility and maintain an ethically balanced co-presence of human and nonhuman elements on land and the sea, we can begin with the arts of noticing human–nonhuman relationalities as the Fisherman did. When such multispecies relations and entanglements with nonhuman others become part of our visceral and felt experiences, we come to realize that "we are all of us ... interdependent constituents of a common biosphere, each of us experiencing it from our own angle, and with our own specific capabilities, yet nonetheless all participants in the round life of earth" (Abram 2010, 143). This is also how we can notice our participation in the story of a wider life in its entangled colors that always enfold us in their iridescent flow, which is an inbuilt tendency to navigate the currents of life in the multihued ecologies of our storied planet. The ecology of colors, in this sense, makes us realize that although we are afflicted by the dark ontologies of the Anthropocene and its epochal swirls, we are also enmeshed in the prismatic ecologies that comprise this world. It is time to reconnect with the storied planet and with life as an expressive force filled with colors.

It is possible to reimagine the prism through which the ecology of colors can *affectively* connect us to our symbiotic planet and contribute to the expanding ecological thought of conceptualizing ways of knowing multispecies creativities and expressivity (of all material agencies) through colors. In doing so, the ecology of colors utilizes transdisciplinary approaches and engages with both scientific and aesthetic research about colors in their multitude of relations to ever-unfolding life on this planet. To pay deeper attention to the entangled colors of life is also to pay attention to our own and other species' existential experiences, within which colors play a central role. All life stories are embedded in colors, in the unfolding of meaningful signs, and in the onto-tales that actively environ, condition, and engage every one of us, both human and nonhuman, more often than not reflexively. The entangled colors of life pervade and mediate our understanding of the world as well as help us and everything that exists to navigate its labyrinths. Co-determining one another, colors and life will continue to be entangled despite the Anthropocene's dimming effects, and they will disseminate seeds of life, or "the gifts of life," as Deborah Bird Rose (2018) would say, sustaining the planet's lifeworlds so that narrative agencies can persevere.

Coda

Thinking with the Storied Planet

We stand at a critical moment in Earth's history, a time when humanity must choose its future. As the world becomes increasingly interdependent and fragile, the future at once holds great peril and great promise.
   —*The Earth Charter*

In the preamble of *The Earth Charter*—the website dedicated to "a mindset of global interdependence and shared responsibility"—there is a warning message to humanity.[1] If we are "one human family and one Earth community with a common destiny," then we should hear the clarion call for "a change of mind and heart" and restore our connection to the Earth, change our conceptual frameworks (what we think and know about the world), and remember that we are fundamentally interconnected—in a material sense—with all that exists in an expansive web of life, which is what defines coexistence. This web of life needs to be understood in terms of "an interfolding network of humanity and nonhumanity" (Bennett 2010, 31). In intermingling with other life-forms and material agencies in extensive networks of production and consumption, "we humans are fully in nature. And nature is fully in us" (Åsberg and Braidotti 2018, 1). In my discussions, I have also emphasized what physicists David Bohm and David F. Peat have revealed from the quantum mechanical perspective, that "there is no absolutely sharp 'cut' or break between consciousness, life, and matter, whether animate or inanimate" (1989, 211). *Ecologies of a Storied Planet in the Anthropocene* has emerged from the lively debates on these points of intersection that constitute the basis for relational ontology, which is "premised on the causal correlations and co-constitutive relationships among all entities and meaning-making processes" (Oppermann 2013, 65). As theorized by Barad (2007), relational ontology entails the recognition that the material-discursive entanglements, of which we are part, are the consequences of a dynamic relationality between naturalcultural practices and material configurations of the world. In this climate of diverse relationalities, and crossing the sciences and the humanities, the stories of the new Anthroposcenarios, migrant and postnatural ecologies, and the ecology of colors trouble the narratives of anthropocentrism, opening us to the entanglements and complexities of "more-than-human rhythms" (Gan et al. 2017, G12) of the animate world. These stories comprise the core of relational ontology.

Addressing multiple concerns about environmental transformations in multispecies life, ruined landscapes, and biodiversity loss, but also "reinforcing our contact zones with the nonhuman world" (Oppermann and Iovino 2017, 7), this book has turned to ways of reopening the sense of interconnectedness among biotic and nonbiotic matter, humans and nonhumans. It is of course hard to internalize this understanding without subverting the dominant vision behind the conventional representations of the planet as lifeless, voiceless, and mindless, and thus as a mere resource for human welfare. Behind such subversion lies a major shift in our ways of thinking about culture and nature; human, nonhuman, and material agencies; and the world. Such a shift in our mindset not only helps deconstruct human exceptionalism but also enhances the prospects for thinking with the storied planet, calling to our attention a world of signifying forces endlessly generating a mélange of living stories—the "meaning-making *activity* at the core of every form of life, whether human or not" (Gagliano 2017, 87). We must avoid fixing our notion of the Earth as lifeless and devoid of agentic capacity. Our access to the nonhuman world of experiences and their meaning-making processes, however, has so far been mediated by the power and limit of our anthropocentric ideological codes and narrative representations, and by social systems of power that have not only conditioned our set of attitudes but also validated human exceptionalism. Nonetheless, being entangled with others, living and not, humans can no longer be defined in terms of what I have previously called "the conjectural singularity" linked to the "impulse of exploiting the coexisting sphere of the nonhuman" (Oppermann 2016a, 276).

Surfacing today in multifarious ways, such as migrant and postnatural ecologies, the aftershocks of anthropocentrism have also deeply affected the evolutionary colors of life so dramatically that "life-enhancing entanglements disappear from our landscapes" (Gan et al. 2017, G4). That is why I have insisted on building new modes of knowledge by crossing the sciences and humanities, which have engendered the progressive conceptions of nonhuman communication, expressive creativity, and storied matter with its narrative agencies. It is indeed true that humans are not the only life-forms to communicate and process information. "Everything in the world does it, like us" (Serres 2012, 172). According to Eduardo Kohn, this is the "semiotic quality of life" (2013, 78). It is perhaps clearer now why I have claimed that the world can be recoded in terms of storied matter comprised of narrative agencies, which "requires arts of imagination as much as scientific specifications" (Swanson et al. 2017, M8). The usefulness of this theoretical framework is obvious in dealing with the complexities of the Anthropocene that demand of us the awareness of what has been done to planet Earth through extensive exploitation by modern industry, as well as a self-conscious turning toward the "wild stories of more-than-human attempts to stay alive" (Gan et al. 2017, G 6). As Kohn reminds us, "coming to terms with this realization change(s) our understandings of society, culture, and indeed the sort of world that we inhabit" (2013, 1).

In the interplay of many voices—as I write in conversation with other environmental humanities scholars, ecocritics, and scientists—I have specifically attempted to conjure up the often-silenced voices of more-than-human beings and things and to foreground their stories in a poetics of worlding. The complementarity between human, animal, vegetal, and abiotic agencies is articulated across a range of scientific and literary texts, and across the stories generated by narrative agencies. In these stories, however, as Anna Lowenhaupt Tsing would say, "hope and despair huddle together" while "life and death haunt each other" (2005, 268). My aim has been to point to how the narrative agencies of our storied planet communicate these facts in various modes of expressive becomings within which we—as humans—are participatory actors even if we are the only ones responsible for inscribing "despair" on the biological world.

Thinking with the storied planet, as I have done throughout this book, enables me to envision life as a boundless sea of agency infused with integral relationships and existential entanglements, which urge us to acknowledge the fact that "we are in *and of* the world, materially embedded in the same rain-drenched field that the rocks and the ravens inhabit," as David Abram poetically reminds us (2010, 72). It is in such an environmental context that the agentic capacity in the more-than-human environments can be recognized as an inherent vitality embedded in both organic and inorganic matter. Again, as Abram puts it, material agencies are "expressive presences that are also attentive, and listening to the meaning that moves between them" (2010, 173). The human body is also part of these interconnected expressive presences as "an assemblage of microbes, animals, plants, metals, chemicals, word-sounds, and the like" (Bennett 2010, 120–21). Similarly, the traffic of wind, pollen, bees, insects, flowers, honey, and animals moving between human and nonhuman bodies attests to the irreducible interconnections that comprise life on this planet, indicating how humans and nonhumans coalesce in producing action. Calling all organisms "autonomous agents," biologist Stuart Kauffman provides a convincing example: "The quite familiar, utterly astonishing feature of autonomous agents—*E. coli*, paramecia, yeast cells, algae, sponges, flat worms, annelids, all of us—is that we do, every day, manipulate the universe around us. We swim, scramble, twist, build, hide, snuffle, pounce" (2003, 54). The idea of the human agent acting upon the world and imposing meaning upon matter is refuted in this new materialist understanding. In granting emphatic value to the notions of agency, experience, expressivity, and narrative, material ecocriticism also contributes significantly to the new materialist thought by "reconfiguring the subjects of the Anthropocene," and by dismantling our "self-deceptive dream[s]" of domination and exploitation (Oppermann and Iovino 2017, 12). If the human is always already constituted by numerous nonhuman others, even if they are all microscopic in size, and if nature is within us, then all self-deceptive dreams unavoidably dissolve.[2] This focal point is memorably made by Haraway in an interview with Nicholas Gane: "Human beings have always been in partnership. To be human is to be a congeries of relationalities, even if you are talking about *Homo erectus*" (Gane 2006, 147).

It is this vision that needs to be anchored in all layers of our storied planet undergoing so much stress with environmental and social tragedies. Experienced differently at regional scales, multiple challenges—such as refugee crises, social violence, political instabilities, environmental injustices, and the processes of climate change with deeply felt tremors—present a bleak picture. But we need to be resilient and courageous in charting sustainable courses in global climate mitigation efforts, spreading environmental awareness with new narratives to address the impacts of changing climates in the global cultural imaginary. And here stories offer a helping hand because stories help forge "relationships"; they are "about learning to see and understand, and as a result about being drawn into new obligations and responsibilities" (van Dooren 2020, 2). This is about what Jessica Weir calls "connectivity thinking" (2009) so that we come to realize the world as "multiply storied worlds" (van Dooren and Rose 2017, 261). According to Thom van Dooren and Deborah Bird Rose, storytelling is "an ethical practice," and "the stories that we tell are powerful contributors to the becoming of our shared world" (2017, 263–64). Stories are also effective tools of resistance, and storying the world anew in environmentally just ways is as important as scientific efforts in finding solutions to the planetary threats that we, along with all earthly agencies, are facing. Stories can be a catalyst for hope amid the ecological uncertainties emerging today from the planet's geomorphological processes and natural cycles put in disarray with detrimental global human activities, which have refashioned the current *epoch* as the Anthropocene, the human age.[3] We are all called into forming new stories, "new histories and descriptions, crossing the sciences and humanities" (Gan et al. 2017, G12).

For the planet's ecological health, it is time to hit the brakes because the human impact on planetary ecosystems, as I have been arguing, emerges from a mélange of capitalist-consumerist and colonialist ideologies (the major culprits here), which almost unmoor life from its foundations. But no species can survive if the Earth turns into *terra ignota*. Earth system scientists warn us that there is a high probability we are heading "to a very different state of the Earth System, one that is likely to be much less hospitable to the development of human societies" (Steffen et al. 2015, 737). This is also a dire truth for the oceans. Marine anthropologist Stefan Helmreich warns us that "the oceans will not wash away our sins but rather drown us in them" (2009, 14), which reminds me of the common metaphor "We are all in the same boat." Even if this metaphor is disliked in the ecocritical community (Who are *we*? How can victims and oppressors equally occupy an all-encompassing category as *we*?), it has a speculative truth value in the global cultural imaginary. You know the argument: when the ship sinks, everyone will eventually drown, but those holding first-class tickets get a better ride longer. Those who exploit natural resources, destabilize Earth systems, and capitalize on environmentally harmful technologies ironically escape the worst horrors of the world they destroy.[4] They may secure a place for themselves in the lifeboat, but even in that lifeboat, they will find it hard to survive if the Earth transforms into *terra ignota*.

It is easy to imagine such a dark ecological scenario, but as I have argued in this book, the agential world of the storied planet may stimulate our imagination to move us beyond the mundane troubles of the modern individual lulled by fossil-fuel economies. I believe it is important for all of us to learn to listen to the world—maybe imaginatively first—in these momentous times of environmental troubles. We may live in an impossible present, but we can learn to be more attentive to the vibrant life full of stories, a colorful life that still exists in the more-than-human environments, holding a mirror to our shared vulnerabilities in the planetary ecosystems. The Earth beckons us to think with its narrative agencies. And, ultimately, this is what this book is about: to speculate about how "stories make worlds" and "worlds make stories" (Haraway 2016, 12). Thinking with the storied planet, we may realize how Haraway's words are in accordance with reality and recognize that we *are* the storied world in the form of a human being, just like everything that exists is similarly a story. Since cosmologists are also cognizant of the storied world, perhaps intuitively, I would like to conclude with Brian Swimme and Mary Evelyn Tucker's words from *Journey of the Universe*:

The great discovery of contemporary science is that the universe is not simply a place, but a story—a story in which we are immersed, to which we belong, and out of which we arose.

This story has the power to awaken us more deeply to who we are. For just as the Milky Way is the universe in the form of a galaxy, and orchid is the universe in the form of a flower, we are the universe in the form of a human. (2011, 2)

Acknowledgments

This book began its journey when the novel coronavirus made a grand entry to the world in 2020. But it was not simply this deadly virus that caused unending painful moments during the writing process. It was something worse. My father's fall and hip surgery in early January 2020 gave rise to a series of life-disrupting events: my mother's progressive dementia, my father's deepening distress, hospitals visits, lockdowns, curfews, followed by more family drama and hospital visits, all made worse by COVID-19, which tragically culminated in my mother's transition to higher dimensions in July 2021, leaving me and my father in total desolation. There were also moments that put a smile on my face, such as my friends congratulating me on my galactic mind, which they said I must have in these dark times of mental distress I daily witnessed in my parents' home. Whether or not I, or anyone else, can have a galactic mind is a matter of pure speculation, but I extend my gratitude to my family members and my friends who were always there, extending emotional support and encouraging me to go on when I felt like Samuel Beckett's unnamed character, repeating, "I can't go on, I'll go on."

I must first mention my family members whose presence and emotional support helped me to stand firm during so many storms, both discursive and emotional! My deepest gratitude goes to my spouse, Michael, whose emotional support was a true blessing and most essential during this time. Thank you, Michael, for being there! I also extend my heartfelt thanks to my nephews: Mert Tunç, my pacific and compassionate nephew, graduate student of computer science at METU; and my younger caring nephews, Hasan Tunç and Hüseyin Tunç, who always listened to my stories of distress and provided me with rational methods to go on. I especially thank my aunt Gürsen Tunç Karesioğlu, who, as a retired nurse, never refrained from providing emotional assistance, and my father, Basri Tunç, who always encouraged me to go on.

And among my friends and colleagues who were always there for me are Nurten Birlik, professor of English at METU; Nevin Özkan, professor of Italian at Ankara University; N. Berrin Aksoy, professor of translation and interpretation studies at Atılım University; Steven Hartman, visiting professor at the University of Iceland and executive director of the BRIDGES Sustainability

Science Coalition; Scott Slovic, distinguished professor of environmental humanities at the University of Idaho; Simon C. Estok, professor of English and ecocriticism at Sungkyunkwan University, South Korea; Greta Gaard, professor of English and coordinator of the Sustainability Faculty Fellows at the University of Wisconsin–River Falls; Helena Feder, associate professor of literature and environment at East Carolina University; Stephanie Foote, Jackson and Nichols Professor of English at West Virginia University; M. Sibel Dinçel and Sinan Akıllı, assistant and associate professors of English at Cappadocia University; Alev Alatlı, chairperson of the board of trustees at Cappadocia University; Funda F. Aktan, coordinator of the board of trustees at Cappadocia University; Dr. Başak Ağın, Dr. Gülşah Göçmen, Dr. Hatice Çelikdoğan, Dr. Adem Balcı, Sevda Ayva, my former graduate students from Hacettepe University. I am fortunate to have such amazing intellectual friends. In this circle, my dearest friend and colleague Serenella Iovino, professor of Italian studies and environmental humanities at the University of North Carolina, Chapel Hill, holds a special place in my heart. I am most grateful to all of them for comforting me at my time of grief and immense sorrow on the loss of my mother.

I also extend my gratitude to the following colleagues who invited me to participate in their book projects and special journal issues: Scott Slovic and Peter Quigley, Swarnalatha Rangarajan and Vidya Sarveswaran, Jeffrey J. Cohen and Stephanie Foote, Cymene Howe and Anand Pandian, Rosi Braidotti and Maria Hlavajova, Iris van der Tuin, Hubert Zapf, Axel Goodbody and Carmen Flys Junquera, Stacy Alaimo, and Barış Ağır. I also owe special thanks to precious colleagues and friends who have always inspired me and continue to do so: Karen Barad, Donna J. Haraway, Jane Bennett, David Abram, Lowell Duckert, Cecilia Åsberg, Heather Sullivan, Louise Westling, Karl Steel, Bronislaw Szerszynski, Astrida Neimanis, Douglas Vakoch, Laura Wright, Rob Nixon, Marco Armiero, Matthew Calarco, Anne Fisher-Wirth, Cate Sandilands, Dorion Sagan, Margarita Carretero Gonzales, Juan Carlos Galeano, Imelda Martin Junquera, Jan Zalasiewicz, Elizabeth DeLoughrey, Ursula Heise, Adam Dickinson, Stephanie LeMenager, Eileen Joy, Steven Mentz, Saraj Jaquette Ray, Paul Levi Bryant, Clare Colebrook, Timothy Morton, Patrick Degeorges, Thomas Bristow, Julia Kuznetski, Monika Rogowska-Stangret, Boris Previšić, Nathan Kowalsky, Boris Previsic, Thom Van Dooren, William Ripple, Dana Bönisch, Cassandra Laity, Jesper Olsson, Pasquale Verdicchio, Robin Chen-Hsing Tsai, Chia-ju-Chang, and many others in the academic realm, at EASLCE and ASLE.

I am also grateful for the gracious comments and gentle critiques I received from the reviewers, which helped me revise the last chapter. So thank you to all who have been my human angels of motivation, and to all the narrative agencies of our storied world who have been the true sources of inspiration.

Last but not least, I warmly thank Stephanie Foote, the editor of the Salvaging the Anthropocene series at West Virginia University Press, for welcoming this book as part of the series. I let my heartfelt thanks flow not only to Stephanie but also to Derek Krissoff, who were so understanding with me during the writing process. I also thank Charlotte Velloso, Rachel Fudge, and Sara Georgi for their editorial support and everyone else on the production team. It was a pleasure to work with you.

Some chapters of this book have appeared in partial form in the following places. I have considerably expanded on these previous publications and thank the editors and publishers for giving me the opportunity to update my previous ideas and statements.

A large part of chapter 1 was originally published as "Nature's Narrative Agencies as Compound Individuals," in *Neohelicon* (Speculative Materialism Contexts and Paradigms for Ecological Engagement, guest edited by Robin Chen-Hsing Tsai) 44, no. 2 (December 2017): 283–95. Reprinted with permission.

Chapter 2 appeared in an earlier version as "The Scale of the Anthropocene: Material Ecocritical Reflections," in *Mosaic* (special issue on Scale), 51, no. 3 (September 2018): 1–17. Reprinted with permission. Other portions of chapter 2 originally appeared as "Installation," in "The Living Lexicon" section of *Environmental Humanities* 10, no. 1 (2018): 338–42. It was also published in a different version in *Anthropocene Unseen: A Lexicon*, edited by Cymene Howe and Anand Pandian (Punctum Books, 2020). Part of chapter 2 was also drawn from "Envisioning a New Anthroposcenarios," published in *NANO: New American Notes Online* (Special issue on the Anthropocene, edited by Kyle Wiggins and Brandon Krieg) 13 (December 2018), https://nanocrit.com/issues/issue13/Envisioning-a-New-Anthroposcenario.

Chapter 3 is an expanded version of "Introducing Migrant Ecologies in an (Un)Bordered World," which was originally published in In *ISLE* (Special Cluster: Migrant Ecologies in an (Un)Bordered World) 24, no. 2 (Spring 2017): 243–56.

A large part of Chapter 5 was originally published as "Nature's Colors: A Prismatic Materiality in the Natural/Cultural Realms," in *Ecocritical Aesthetics: Language, Beauty, and the Environment*, edited by Peter Quigley and Scott Slovic, 157–71 (Bloomington: Indiana University Press, 2018).

Notes

INTRODUCTION

1. Concerning "representations," Levi Bryant argues in *The Democracy of Objects* that "we get a variety of nonhuman actors unleashed in the world as autonomous actors in their own right, irreducible to representations and freed from any constant reference to the human where they are reduced to our representations" (2011, 23).
2. I am inspired by the title of the book *Arts of Living on a Damaged Planet*, edited by Anna Tsing, Heather Swanson, Elaine Gan, and Nils Bubandt (2017).

CHAPTER 1

1. Although Alaimo (2012) rightly claims it is "difficult to capture, map, and publicize the flows of toxins across terrestrial, oceanic, and human habitats" (477), the agentic material formations have visible social and economic consequences. Alaimo herself refers to the disruptive effects of toxic substances in the food chain, and the consequent medical expenditure of restoring health, and to the economic consequences of the increasing anthropogenic threats on local and global ecosystems. This natural-cultural dynamic necessitates not only ethical but also political reflection and thus a change in discursive practices—all prompted by manifold material agencies.
2. "Nature-culture" was first introduced by Bruno Latour in *We Have Never Been Modern* (1993) and then used by Donna Haraway without the hyphen in *The Companion Species Manifesto* (2003) to denote the ontological inseparability of nature and society.
3. The biosphere is the zone of life on Earth, extending from the surface up to the atmosphere and down to the oceans. It is a relatively thin layer forming a boundary between the atmosphere, hydrosphere, and lithosphere. Water, air, soil, plants, animals, raw materials, and solar radiation are the essential components of the biosphere (Tölgyessy 1993, 3–13).
4. For readers who are not scientists, Deren Quick's (2011) article "Scientists Make First Step Towards Bringing Life to Inorganic matter," in *New Atlas,* provides a clear explanation.
5. For further reading, see the twenty articles written by biologists in response to Gibson et al. (2010).
6. I am referring to Jeremy Konner's (2014) mockumentary, *The Majestic Plastic Bag*, narrated by Jeremy Irons. This ironic short film is about the story of a plastic bag, represented as petroleum species, which struggles to reach its final destination of

the Great Pacific Plastic Patch. This is an area of plastic waste within the North Pacific Gyre, estimated to be twice the size of Texas and growing.
7. As Patrice Haynes (2014) explains, the baseline of relational ontology "is not discrete things but rather the network of relations in and through which varying agential sites (i.e., things) emerge" (134).
8. Whitehead's organic realism is about actual existence defined as a process of becoming. In *Process and Reality*, Whitehead posits that the world is comprised of "actual entities"—also termed "actual occasions" ([1929] 1978,18), and the principle of actual existence is creativity. Actual entities are foundational elements of reality, which manifest in four grades of "occasions of experience." The first grade is about processes, such as electromagnetic waves; the second grade comprises the so-called inanimate matter; the third grade involves living organisms; and the fourth grade refers to subjective experience seen in animals and humans as primary individuals who exercise purposive causation. Primary individuals are organized as (a) compound individuals, such as animals, and (b) nonindividuated objects without any subjectivity, such as stones. There is no ontological dualism here but an "organizational duality." All individuals, however, as David Ray Griffin observes, interact with others in terms of "efficient causation" (1988, 23).
9. According to Whitehead, perception is not limited to humans or animals but is the property of all entities. His term *prehension* expands the scope of perception from a conscious perceiving of the environment, as in the case of humans and animals, to the unconscious way of perceiving it, as in the case of low-grade individuals such as cells, molecules, and even electrons. In *Science and the Modern World*, Whitehead defines "prehension" as *"uncognitive apprehension,* by which he means "apprehension which may or may not be cognitive" ([1925] 1948,70). In *Process and Reality,* he writes: "That the first analysis of an actual entity, into its most concrete elements, discloses it to be a concrescence of prehensions, which have originated in its process of becoming" ([1929] 1978, 23).
10. "Ocean of grief" is the expression the narrator uses when he encounters the dying albatross on Midway island. See Chris Jordan's 2009 documentary film, *Midway: Messages from the Gyre.*

CHAPTER 2

1. See "Decision IPCC/XLV-2, Sixth Assessment Report (AR6) Products, Outline of the Special Report on climate change and oceans and the cryosphere": https://www.ipcc.ch/site/assets/uploads/2018/11/Decision_Outline_SR_Oceans.pdf.
2. See Alliance of World Scientists for further information: https://scientistswarning.forestry.oregonstate.edu. See also Lenton et al. (2019), in which the authors note that "the evidence from tipping points alone suggests that we are in a state of planetary emergency: both the risk and urgency of the situation are acute" (595). Also see the inaugural issue of *Ecocene: Cappadocia Journal of Environmental Humanities* I edited together with Steven Hartman in 2020 (https://ecocene.kapadokya.edu.tr/index. php/ecocene/issue/view/1), which offers noteworthy responses from leading environmental humanities scholars to "World Scientists' Warning to Humanity: A Second Notice" (Ripple et al., 2017) and the "World Scientists' Warning of a Climate Emergency" (Ripple et al., 2020).
3. *Storyworld* is a term invented by cognitive narratologist David Herman (2018), who

defines it as "the worlds projected by narrative texts and inhabited by the agents, nonhuman as well as human, with which a given narrative is concerned" (9).
4. See the results of the binding vote by AWG, released on May 21, 2019: http://quaternary.stratigraphy.org/working-groups/anthropocene.
5. See *Newsletter of the Anthropocene Working Group*, vol. 10: Report of activities 2020 (December 2020), http://quaternary.stratigraphy.org/wp-content/uploads/2021/03/AWG-Newsletter-2020-Vol-10.pdf. Also see vol. 11, Report of activities 2021 (February 2022), http://quaternary.stratigraphy.org/wp-content/uploads/2022/03/AWG-Newsletter-2021_final.pdf.
6. See, for example, Dannenberg and Zitzelsberger (2019), who claim that damages caused by climate change can be "limited directly by solar geoengineering." The authors analyze the views of 723 scientists "who are involved in international climate policy-making and who will have a considerable influence on whether solar geoengineering will be used to counter climate change."
7. By "some people," I am referring, for example, to Scott Pruitt, the head of the US Environmental Protection Agency during the Trump administration, who thinks carbon dioxide is not an engine of climate change. See Chiacu and Volcovici (2017).
8. Geomorphology is "the study of the nature and origin of landforms, particularly of the formative processes of weathering and erosion that occur in the atmosphere and hydrosphere. These processes continually shape the Earth's surface, and generate the sediments that circulate in the Rock Cycle. Landforms are the result of the interactions among the geosphere, atmosphere and hydrosphere." See "Weathering and Erosion" and "Introduction to Geomorphological Processes" (Hong Kong Geological Survey [2009] 2021).
9. I use *worlding* in the sense of being-in-the world both materially and discursively.
10. The term *doxa* denotes what Roland Barthes (1994, 47) called the public opinion, or dominant ideology appearing as "the Voice of Nature." *De-doxifying* what is taken for granted as the Anthropos means resisting the self-implanted meaning of this doxa.
11. A microclimate is a local atmospheric zone with a different climate from the surrounding area.
12. Haraway here is referring to the crochet coral reef project, which brought together seven thousand people in twenty-five locations to crochet coral reefs. Their artwork is produced as installations in different places "responding to climate change, an exercise in applied mathematics, and a wooly experiment in evolutionary theory." See "Crochet Coral Reef: An Ever-Evolving Nature-Culture Hybrid," https://crochetcoralreef.org.
13. David Thomas Smith's (n.d.) "Anthropocene Photographs" can be seen in *LensCulture*, https://www.lensculture.com/articles/david-thomas-smith-anthropocene.

CHAPTER 3

1. "The impacts of climate change are faced by all, but poor and vulnerable communities and groups are the most affected." See "Earth Observations for Climate Action" section of the GEOSS Platform (The Global Earth Observation System of Systems' Platform), which provides reliable, up-to-date, and historical information on atmospheric, oceanic, and terrestrial processes. Earth observation data, information, and knowledge from all over the world can be accessed at the

GEOSS portal. There is also data available about specific geolocations: https://www.geoportal.org/?m:activeLayerTileId=osm&f:dataSource=dab.
2. See the essays that seek answers to this question in *ISLE*'s "Special Cluster: Migrant Ecologies in an (Un)bordered World," 24, no. 2 (Spring 2017): 243–325. The four essays in this cluster envision various solutions and offer alternative approaches.
3. For more climate information and to view the updated data, see NASA Earth Observatory: https://earthobservatory.nasa.gov/world-of-change/global-temperatures. Also see the National Centers for Environmental Information, part of the US National Oceanic and Atmospheric Administration: https://www.ncdc.noaa.gov.
4. For IPCC reports, see: https://www.ipcc.ch/reports.
5. See "The Arctic Meltdown" at Center for Biological Diversity, https://www.biologicaldiversity.org/programs/climate_law_institute/the_arctic_meltdown/slideshow_text/arctic_fox.html.
6. See also the special issue on "Disasters and Displacement in a Changing Climate" in *Forced Migration Review* (May 2015): https://www.fmreview.org/climatechange-disasters/contents.
7. For example, even though the Turkish Ministry of Health had disclaimed such news, mainstream media have reported that infectious diseases such as malaria, tuberculosis, measles, typhus, brucella, and many others believed to be a thing of the past have made a deadly comeback in the southeastern regions of Turkey with millions of Syrian refugees who settled in Turkey.
8. See "An Environmental Humanities Response to the COVID-19 Pandemic: An Open Letter," *Bifrost Online*, June 8, 2020, https://bifrostonline.org/environmental-humanities-response-to-covid-19. To sign the letter, visit the dedicated website hosted by the Environmental Humanities Center at Cappadocia University: https://ehc.kapadokya.edu.tr/sign-the-letter.
9. The most obvious example of an invasive plant is kudzu, which can climb over trees so quickly it suffocates and kills the branches and trunks it shades from the sun. See Frank (2015).
10. Referring to several examples (e.g., Japanese honeysuckle, Norway maple, English ivy, kudzu), Grebenstein (2013) notes: "Non-native plant species pose a significant threat to the natural ecosystems of the United States. Many of these invasive plants are escapees from gardens and landscapes where they were originally planted. Purchased at local nurseries, wholesale suppliers and elsewhere, these plants have the potential of taking over large areas, affecting native plants and animals and negatively changing the ecosystem. In recent years an increase in travel and international trade has rapidly introduced many new non-native species to the United States."
11. On January 20, 2021, US President Biden issued an executive order to stop the construction of the border wall (Hill 2021).
12. This number is provided by the Refugee Association in Turkey (October 23, 2021), and refers only to the registered Syrians: https://multeciler.org.tr/turkiyedeki-suriyeli-sayisi/.

CHAPTER 4

1. Phenology is the study of seasonal natural phenomena in relation to climate, plant, and animal life.

2. The World Wildlife Fund lists eleven regions of the world where total forest loss is expected by 2030, such as the Atlantic forest (spanning parts of Paraguay, Brazil, and Argentina), one of the richest rain forests in the world, with richer biodiversity per acre than the Amazon. See Schwartz (2015). These forests are turning into postnatural territories with cattle ranching, mining, oil extraction and dam-building, logging, and agriculture, which are the direct human causes of deforestation. See Rainforest Concern (n.d.).
3. Another factor here is ocean acidification "through the absorption of atmospheric CO_2 with open-ocean surface pH declining by a range of 0.017–0.027 pH units per decade since the late 1980s, threatening the survival of particularly soluble organisms, such as aragonitic pteropods. Increasing acidity may raise the calcium carbonate compensation depth (CCD) in the deep ocean, causing the demise of carbonate-shelled deep-water benthic organisms" (Syvitski et al. 2020).
4. The epipelagic zone, which reaches from the sea surface down to approximately 200 meters (650 feet), is home to whales, dolphins, sharks, billfishes, tunas, and jellyfish.
5. Jenna R. Jambeck et al. (2015) have calculated that "275 million metric tons (MT) of plastic waste was generated in 192 coastal countries in 2010, with 4.8 to 12.7 million MT entering the ocean" (768). Moreover, as Syvitski et al. (2020) note, "microplastics are increasingly being transported by aeolian vectors, permitting true global distribution, even to Arctic snowfields, forming a near-ubiquitous and unambiguous marker of Anthropocene strata" (7).
6. See Center for PostNatural History: https://www.postnatural.org
7. For details, see Lustgarten (2020).
8. John Holdren, a science advisor to President Barack Obama, advocates for the term "climate disruption" as a more descriptive term for climate change caused by global warming (Griffin 2015, 16).
9. Some American and British fictional examples include Richard Powers's *Gain* (1998), Maggie Gee's *The Ice People* (1998) and *The Flood* (2005), David Mitchell's *Cloud Atlas* (2004), Sarah Hall's *The Carhullan Army* (2007), Jeanette Winterson's *The Stone Gods* (2007), Saci Lloyd's *Carbon Diaries* (2008), Joseph D'Lacey's *Garbage Man* (2009), Liz Jensen's *The Rapture* (2009), Marcel Theroux's *Far North* (2010), Peter Heller's *The Dog Stars* (2012), Nathaniel Rich's *Odds Against Tomorrow* (2013), JL Morin's *Nature's Confession* (2015), Jenni Fagan's *The Sunlight Pilgrims* (2016), and Craig Russell's *Fragment* (2016). Among films and documentaries, striking examples are Roland Emmerich's *The Day after Tomorrow* (2004), Al Gore's *An Inconvenient Truth* (2006), Jennifer Baichwal's *Manufactured Landscapes* (2006), Leila Conners Petersen and Nadia Conners's *The 11th Hour* (2007), Franny Armstrong's *The Age of Stupid* (2009), Jeremy Irons's *The Majestic Plastic Bag: A Mockumentary* (2010), Mark Monroe's *Before the Flood* (2016), Jeff Orlowksi's *Chasing Coral* (2017), *Plastic Ocean* (2017), and Jennifer Baichwal and Nicholas de Pencier's *Anthropocene: The Human Epoch* (2018).
10. Giovanna Di Chiro is critical of this rhetoric on chemical pollution, which she claims appeals to cultural fears concerning "the future existence of *natural masculinity*" (2010, 201), and thus serves heterosexist arguments. However, the fact remains that chemical pollution affects all bodies regardless of gender.
11. An underground bed or layer of permeable rock, sediment, or soil that yields water.
12. Alberta's oil sands operation is the world's largest industrial project, razing the boreal forest to mine bitumen from the ground in immense open pits. The gold

mine project on Mount Ida (on the Biga peninsula of northwestern Turkey) is carried out by the Canadian gold company Alamos Gold Inc, which cut approximately 195,000 trees on Mount Ida. It is a holy site in Turkish cultural memory. Turkish tribes that settled in the region in the fourteenth and fifteenth centuries named it Goose Mountains (Kaz Dağları), after the sacred bird favored by the Sky God (Gök Tengri) in Tengrist/Shamanist belief. (See Oppermann and Akıllı 2021.)

CHAPTER 5

1. There is a vibrational energy flow within and between polyatomic molecules, which governs their reactivity. This is known as intramolecular vibrational energy redistribution in isolated molecules. According to V. P. Gupta (2016): "The transitions between vibrational states of a molecule are observed experimentally via infrared and Raman spectroscopy. These techniques can be used to determine a molecule's structure and environment since these factors affect the vibrational frequencies. Vibrational spectroscopy provides important information about the nature of chemical bond, intramolecular forces acting between the atoms in a molecule, and intermolecular forces in condensed phase" (248).
2. See Devlin (2018).
3. The Fisherman of Halicarnassus is the pen name of Cevat Şakir Kabaağaçlı, who in 1925 was sentenced to exile for three years in Bodrum (Halicarnassus in ancient times), then a remote fishing village. When he arrived in Bodrum, a small picaresque town at the junction of the Aegean and the Mediterranean Seas, he fell in love with the place and adopted the name "The Fisherman of Halicarnassus." He spent most of his time with the local fishermen and sponge divers, listening to their stories of the sea creatures. He was deeply impressed by the cultural heritage on the shorelines of the Mediterranean and the Aegean and began writing on Bodrum's human and nonhuman inhabitants, as well as the colorful life he admired in the turquoise seas he sailed with his boat. For a detailed account of his life and works, and a historical sketch of the region, see Williams (2013).
4. All translations from Ali Demirsoy are mine.
5. I borrow the term *ecological intelligence* from American psychologist Daniel Goleman (2010), who uses the term for human beings only as an "all-encompassing sensibility" that allows us to "see the interconnections between our actions and their hidden impacts on the planet, our health, and our social systems" (44). I extend this to be more inclusive of all biotic systems.
6. Biochromes create color by the differential reflection and absorption of solar energy. See Brown et al. (2019).
7. The Fisherman's oeuvre focuses on the history and ecology of the Bodrum Peninsula, which he saw as a gateway to the great antiquity of Anatolia where the roots of Western Civilization lie. Bodrum, he observed, represented the multihued rhythms of Anatolian cultures and natures. He also realized that an impressive ecological culture had existed for centuries here. The Fisherman's lyrically written tales evoke the vibrant chromatic life he witnessed on land and in the sea. He deliberately creates a color-conscious discourse anticipating the ethical and narrative spaces of "ecology of colors." His Mediterranean narratives in this regard give expression to what Cohen calls "polychromatic, ecstatic ecology" (2013, xvii).
8. All translations from the Fisherman's texts are mine.

9. The Bodrum Peninsula is in Southeast Turkey where the Aegean Sea meets the Mediterranean. It is surrounded by thirty-two islands and islets that form a 174-kilometer coastline. Homer described this exceptionally beautiful site as the land of the eternal blue. The town of Bodrum (Halicarnassus) was founded by the Carians in the eleventh century BC as a union of six cities. It became the capital of the kingdom of Caria (meaning "steep country") during King Mausolos's rule in the fourth century BC. The name Bodrum is used by the Turkish cartographer, geographer, and admiral of the Ottoman fleet Piri Reis in his book *Kitab-ı Bahriye* (Book of Navigation, 1521, 1525), which contains his famous and mysterious map of the world, the oldest and the most accurate world atlas drawn in 1513.
10. For a detailed account of the plastic-covered beach, see Martinez (2011).
11. See also Walia (2014). For those interested in reading the scientific account behind these posts, see Jeffery S. Pettis et al. (2013), who expose the fact that pesticides and pathogens interact in deadly ways "to have strong negative effects on managed honey bee colonies. Such findings are of great concern given the large numbers and high levels of pesticides found in honeybee colonies. Thus, it is crucial to determine how field-relevant combinations and loads of pesticides affect bee health."

CODA

1. See https://earthcharter.org/read-the-earth-charter/preamble.
2. Ed Yong (2016) explains well those microscopic entities that become part of the human body: "The average human swallows around a million microbes in every gram of food they eat" (145).
3. Like Jan Zalasiewicz, I have used the term *epoch* provisionally, because its formal status and potential stratigraphic unit has not yet been officially defined. See Zalasiewicz (2017, 118).
4. Harmful technologies include extraction of rare minerals and precious metals, such as cobalt and lithium, for electronic devices, which end up as electronic waste in landfill sites.

References

Abram, David. 1997. *The Spell of the Sensuous: Perception and Language in a More-Than-Human World*. New York: Vintage Books.
———. 2010. *Becoming Animal: An Earthly Cosmology*. New York: Vintage Books.
Akaş, Cem. 2015. "Movement, with Feeling." *Rahşan Düren: E-Motions*. Accessed February 4, 2020. http://rahsandurenhaydarpasa.com/eng/movement-with-feeling.html.
Alaimo, Stacy. 2010. *Bodily Natures: Science, Environment, and the Material Self*. Bloomington: Indiana University Press.
———. 2011. "New Materialisms, Old Humanisms: or, Following the Submersible." *NORA: Nordic Journal of Feminist and Gender Research* 19, no. 4: 280–84.
———. 2012. "States of Suspension: Trans-Corporeality at Sea." *ISLE: Interdisciplinary Studies in Literature and Environment* 19, no. 3: 476–93.
———. 2016. *Exposed: Environmental Politics and Pleasures in Posthuman Times*. Minneapolis: University of Minnesota Press.
Albrecht, Glenn A. 2016. "Exiting the Anthropocene and Entering the Symbiocene." *Minding Nature* 9, no. 2: 12–16.
"An Environmental Humanities Response to the COVID-19 Pandemic: An Open Letter." *Bifrost Online*, June 8, 2020. https://bifrostonline.org/environmental-humanities-response-to-covid-19.
Anderson, Kayla. 2015. "Ethics, Ecology, and the Future: Art and Design Face the Anthropocene." *Leonardo* 48, no. 4: 338–47.
Appel, H. M., and R. B. Cocroft. 2014. "Plants Respond to Leaf Vibrations Caused by Insect Herbivore chewing." *Oecologia* 175, no. 4: 1257–66.
Armiero, Marco. 2021. *Wasteocene: Stories from the Global Dump*. Cambridge: Cambridge University Press.
Armiero, Marco, and Massimo De Angelis. 2017. "Anthropocene: Victims, Narrators, and Revolutionaries." *The South Atlantic Quarterly* 116, no. 2: 345–62.
Armiero, Marco, and Richard Tucker. 2017. "Introduction: Migrants in Environmental History." In *Environmental History of Modern Migrations*, edited by Marco Armiero, 1–16. London: Routledge.
Åsberg, Cecilia. 2017. "Feminist Posthumanities in the Anthropocene: Forays Into the Postnatural." *Journal of Posthuman Studies* 1, no. 2: 185–204.
Åsberg, Cecilia, and Rosi Braidotti. 2018. "Feminist Posthumanities: An Introduction." In *A Feminist Companion to the Posthumanities*, edited by Cecilia Åsberg and Rosi Braidotti, 1–22. Cham, Switzerland: Springer Nature.
Åsberg, Cecilia, Redi Kooback, and Ericka Johnson. 2011. "Beyond the Humanist Imagination." *NORA: Nordic Journal of Feminist and Gender Research* 19, no. 4: 218–30.

Askin, Ridvan. 2016. *Narrative and Becoming*. Edinburgh: Edinburgh University Press.
Atwood, Margaret. 2012. "Rachel Carson's Silent Spring, 50 Years On." *The Guardian*, December 7, 2012. https://www.theguardian.com/books/2012/dec/07/why-rachel-carson-is-a-saint.
Bachelard, Gaston. (1947) 2002. *Earth and Reveries of Will: An Essay on the Imagination of Matter*. Translated by Kenneth Haltman. Dallas: The Dallas Institute Publications.
Balcı, Adem. 2020. "Spinning Toxic Yarns of Matter: Material Environments and Marginalized Toxic bodies in Latife Tekin's *Berji Kristin: Tales from the Garbage Hills* and John Burnside's *Glister*." *Middle Eastern Literatures* 23, no. 1–2: 59–78.
Baldwin, Andrew. 2017. "Postcolonial Futures: Climate, Race, and the Yet-to-Come." *ISLE: Interdisciplinary Studies in Literature and Environment* 24, no. 2: 293–305.
Baldwin, Andrew, and Giovanni Bettini. 2017. "Introduction." In *Life Adrift: Climate Change, Migration, Critique*, edited by Andrew Baldwin and Giovanni Bettini, 1–21. London: Rowman & Littlefield.
Barad, Karen. 2007. *Meeting the Universe Halfway: Quantum Physics and the Entanglement of Matter and Meaning*. Durham. NC: Duke University Press.
———. 2008. "Living in a Posthumanist Material World: Lessons from Schrödinger's Cat." In *Bits of Life: Feminism at the Intersections of Media, Bioscience, and Technology*, edited by Anneke Smelik and Nina Lykke, 165–76. Seattle: University of Washington Press.
———. 2012a. "Intra-Actions." Interview by Adam Kleinman. *Mousse* 34: 76–81.
———. 2012b. "On Touching—The Inhuman That Therefore I Am." *Differences: A Journal of Feminist Cultural Studies* 23, no. 3: 206–23.
Bardini, Thierry. 2011. *Junkware*. Minneapolis: University of Minnesota Press.
Barthes, Roland.1977. "Introduction to the Structural Analysis of Narratives." In *Image Music Text*. Essays selected and translated by Stephen Heath, 79–124. London: Fontana Press.
———. 1994. *Roland Barthes by Roland Barthes*. Translated by Richard Howard. Berkeley: University of California Press.
Bateson, Gregory. 1979. *Mind and Nature: A Necessary Unity*. New York: E. P. Dutton.
Beirne, Piers, and Caitlin Kelty-Huber. 2015. "Animals and Forced Migration." *Forced Migration Review* 49: 97–98.
Bennett, Jane. 2010. *Vibrant Matter: A Political Ecology of Things*. Durham, NC: Duke University Press.
———. 2012. "Powers of the Hoard: Further Notes on Material Agency." In *Animal, Vegetable, Mineral: Ethics and Objects*, edited by Jeffrey Jerome Cohen, 237–69. Washington, DC: Oliphaunt Books.
Betts, Alexander, Evan Easton-Calabria, and Kate Pincock. 2020. "Refugee-Led Responses in the Fight against COVID-19: Building Lasting Participatory Models." *Forced Migration Review* 64: 73–76.
Birch, Charles. 1988. "The Postmodern Challenge to Biology." In *The Reenchantment of Science: Postmodern Proposals*, edited by David Ray Griffin, 69–78. Albany: State University of New York Press.
Blanchard, Jacob. 2020. "Migration of Polar Bears Southwards." *ArcGIS StoryMaps*, March 13, 2020. https://storymaps.arcgis.com/stories/ee3094c82e234fc28e2fb0e30522fc3b.
Bleicher, Steven. 2012. *Contemporary Color: Theory and Use*. New York: Delmar Cengage Learning.

Bohm, David. (1980) 1995. *Wholeness and the Implicate Order*. London: Routledge.
———. 1988. "Postmodern Science and a Postmodern World." In *The Reenchantment of Science: Postmodern Proposals*, edited by David Ray Griffin, 57–68. Albany: State University of New York Press.
Bohm, David, and B. J. Hiley. 1993. *The Undivided Universe: An Ontological Interpretation of Quantum theory*. New York: Routledge.
Bohm, David, and F. David Peat. 1989. *Science, Order and Creativity*. London: Routledge.
Boyd, Roger. 2014. "Panarchy: Implications for Economic and Social Policy." *Resilience*, December 12, 2014. https://www.resilience.org/stories/2014-12-12/panarchy-implications-for-economic-social-policy-2.
Bradley, James. 2017. "Writing on the Precipice." *Sydney Review of Books*, February 21, 2017. https://sydneyreviewofbooks.com/essay/writing-on-the-precipice-climate-change.
Braidotti, Rosi. 2013. *The Posthuman*. Cambridge: Polity Press.
———. 2020. "'We' May Be in This Together, but We Are Not All Human and We Are Not One and the Same." Special Issue: "Environmental Humanists Respond to the World Scientists' Warning to Humanity." *Ecocene: Cappadocia Journal of Environmental Humanities*.1, no. 1: 26–31. https://doi.org/10.46863/ecocene.31.
Brown, Frank A., Edward Howland Burtt, George S. Losey, and Denis Llewellyn Fox. 2019. "Coloration." *Encyclopedia Britannica*, February 7, 2019. https://www.britannica.com/science/coloration-biology.
Brown, Lester R. 2011. "Environmental Refugees: The Rising Tide." In *World on the Edge: How to Prevent Environmental and Economic Collapse*, 72–83. New York: Earth Policy Institute/Norton & Company.
Bryant, Levi R. 2011. *The Democracy of Objects*. Ann Arbor, MI: Open University Press.
———. 2013. "Black." In *Prismatic Ecology: Ecotheory Beyond Green*, edited by Jeffrey Jerome Cohen, 290–310. Minneapolis: University of Minnesota Press.
Buell, Lawrence. 2005. *The Future of Environmental Criticism: Environmental Crisis and Literary Imagination*. Oxford: Blackwell.
———. 2013. "Foreword." In *Prismatic Ecology: Ecotheory Beyond Green*, edited by Jeffrey Jerome Cohen, ix–xii. Minneapolis: University of Minnesota Press.
Bubandt, Nils. 2017. "Haunted Geologies: Spirits, Stones, and the Necropolitics of the Anthropocene." In *Arts of Living on a Damaged Planet: Ghosts of the Anthropocene*, edited by Anna Lowenhaupt Tsing, Heather Swanson, Elaine Gan, and Nils Bubandt, G121–41. Minneapolis: University of Minnesota Press.
Burnside, John. 2009. *Glister*. London: Vintage.
Callaway, Ewen. 2016. "Race to Design Life Heats Up." *Nature* (News in Focus) 531: 557–58. https://www.nature.com/news/polopoly_fs/1.19633!/menu/main/topColumns/topLeftColumn/pdf/531557a.pdf.
Carranza, Nancy. 2018. "Agency." *Critical Posthumanism: Genealogy of the Posthuman*, April 24, 2018. http://criticalposthumanism.net/agency.
Carroll, Bruce. 2017. "A Role for Art in Ecological Thought." *Concentric: Literary and Cultural Studies* 43, no. 1: 145–64.
Castree, Noel. 2016. "Nature." In *Keywords for Environmental Studies*, edited by Joni Adamson, William A. Gleason, and David N. Pellow, 151–56. New York: New York University Press.
Chaisson, Eric. 2005. *Epic of Evolution: Seven Ages of the Cosmos*. New York: Columbia University Press.

Chakrabarty, Dipesh. 2012. "Postcolonial Studies and the Challenge of Climate Change." *New Literary History* 43, no. 1: 1–18.

———. 2019. "The Planet: An Emergent Humanist Category." *Critical Inquiry* 46, no. 1: 1–31.

Chiacu, Doina, and Valerie Volcovici. 2017. "EPA Chief Pruitt Refuses to Link CO_2 and Global Warming." *Scientific American*, March 10, 2017. https://www.scientificamerican.com/article/epa-chief-pruitt-refuses-to-link-co2-and-global-warming.

Clare, Eli. 2014. "Meditations on Natural Worlds, Disabled Bodies, and Politics of Care." In *Material Ecocriticism*, edited by Serenella Iovino and Serpil Oppermann, 204–18. Bloomington: Indiana University Press.

Clark, Nigel. 2010. "Volatile Worlds, Vulnerable Bodies: Confronting Abrupt Climate Change." *Theory Culture Society* 27, no. 2–3: 31–53.

———. 2017. "Strangers on a Strange Planet on Hospitality and Holocene Climate Change." In *Life Adrift: Climate Change, Migration, Critique*, edited by Andrew Baldwin and Giovanni Bettini, 131–49. London: Rowman & Littlefield.

Clark, Timothy. 2014. "Nature, Post Nature." In *The Cambridge Companion to Literature and the Environment*, edited by Louise Westling, 75–89. New York: Cambridge University Press.

———. 2015. *Ecocriticism on the Edge: The Anthropocene as a Threshold Concept*. London: Bloomsbury.

Cobb, John B., Jr. 1988. "Ecology, Science and Religion: Toward a Postmodern Worldview." In *The Reenchantment of Science: Postmodern Proposals*, edited by David Ray Griffin, 99–113. New York: State University of New York Press.

Cohen, Jeffrey Jerome. 2013. "Introduction: Ecology's Rainbow." In *Prismatic Ecology: Ecotheory Beyond Green*, edited by Jeffrey Jerome Cohen, xv–xxxv. Minneapolis: University of Minnesota Press.

———. 2014. "Elemental Relations." *O-Zone: A Journal of Object-Oriented Studies* 1: 53–61. https://www.academia.edu/7028259/Elemental_Relations.

———. 2015. *Stone: An Ecology of the Inhuman*. Minneapolis: University of Minnesota Press.

———. 2017a. "Drown." In *Veer Ecology: A Companion for Environmental Thinking*, edited by Jeffrey Jerome Cohen and Lowell Duckert, 246–67. Minneapolis: University of Minnesota Press.

———. 2017b. "Posthuman Environs. In *Environmental Humanities: Voices from the Anthropocene*, edited by Serpil Oppermann and Serenella Iovino, 25–44. New York: Rowman & Littlefield.

Cohen, Jeffrey Jerome, and Lowell Duckert. 2015. "Introduction: Eleven Principles of the Elements." In *Elemental Ecocriticism: Thinking with Earth, Air, Water, and Fire*, edited by Jeffrey J. Cohen and Lowell Duckert, 1–26. Minneapolis: University of Minnesota Press.

Colebrook, Claire. 2011. "Matter without Bodies." *Derrida Today* 4, no. 1: 1–20.

———. 2014. *Death of the Posthuman: Essays on Extinction*. Vol. 1. Ann Arbor, MI: Open University Press.

———. 2017. "Transcendental Migration: Taking Refuge from Climate Change." In *Life Adrift: Climate Change, Migration, Critique*, edited by Andrew Baldwin and Giovanni Bettini, 115–29. London: Rowman & Littlefield.

Constantine, Kate. 2014. "Japanese Knotweed—Could a Tiny Insect Tame the Monster?" *Ecologist: The Journal for the Post-Industrial Age*, October 17, 2014.

https://theecologist.org/2014/oct/17/japanese-knotweed-could-tiny-insect-tame-monster.

Coole, Diana. 2010. "The Inertia of Matter and the Generativity of Flesh." In *New Materialisms: Ontology, Agency, and Politics*, edited by Diana Coole and Samantha Frost, 92–115. Durham, NC: Duke University Press.

Coole, Diana, and Samantha Frost. 2010. "Introducing the New Materialisms." In *New Materialisms: Ontology, Agency, and Politics*, edited by Diana Coole and Samantha Frost, 1–43. Durham, NC: Duke University Press.

Cooper, Geoffrey J. T., Philip J. Kitson, Ross Winter, Michele Zagnoni, De-Liang Long, and Leroy Cron. 2011."Modular Redox-Active Inorganic Chemical Cells: iCHELLs." *Angewandte Chemie* 50: 10373–76.

Cox, Kieran D., Garth A. Covernton, Hailey L. Davies, John F. Dower, Francis Juanes, and Sarah E. Dudas. 2019. "Human Consumption of Microplastics." *Environmental Science & Technology* 53: 7068–74.

Couldrey, Marion, and Jenny Peebles. 2020. "Climate Crisis and Local Communities." *Forced Migration Review* 64: 1–4.

Crist, Eileen. 2013. "On the Poverty of Our Nomenclature." *Environmental Humanities* 3, no. 1: 129–47. https://doi.org/10.1215/22011919-3611266.

Cronon, William. 1996. "Introduction: In Search of Nature." In *Uncommon Ground: Rethinking the Human Place in Nature*, edited by William Cronon, 23–56. New York: Norton.

Crutzen, Paul, and Eugene F. Stoermer. 2000. "The 'Anthropocene.'" *IGB Global Change NewsLetter* 41: 17–18.

Cubitt, Sean. (1996) 2005. "Supernatural Futures: Theses on Digital Aesthetics." In *FutureNatural: Nature, Science, Culture*, edited by George Robertson, Melinda Mash, Lisa Tickner, Jon Bird, Barry Curtis, and Tim Putnam, 237–55. London: Routledge.

Dannenberg, Astrid, and Sonja Zitzelsberger. 2019. "Climate Experts' Views on Geo Engineering Depend on Their Beliefs About Climate Change Impacts." *Nature Climate Change* 9: 769–75. https://www.nature.com/articles/s41558-019-0564-z#article-info.

Davis, Heather, and Etienne Turpin. 2015. "Art & Death: Lives Between the Fifth Assessment & the Sixth Extinction: Introduction." In *Art in the Anthropocene: Encounters Among Aesthetics, Politics, Environments and Epistemologies*, edited by Heather Davis and Etienne Turpin, 3–29. London: Open University Press.

Davis, Mike. 2018. "Letting Malibu Burn." An Interview with Suzi Weissman. *Jacobin*, February 12, 2018. https://jacobinmag.com/2018/12/california-fires-let-malibu-burn-mike-davis-interview.

Degeorges, Patrick. 2021. "Making Peace with the Earth—The Diplomatic Turn." *Ecocene: Cappadocia Journal of Environmental Humanities* 2, no. 1: 1–6.

Degeorges, Patrick, and Serpil Oppermann. 2019. "Reclaiming the Entangled Colors of Life in the Face of the Anthropocene." *Bifrost Online*. https://bifrostonline.org/reclaiming-the-entangled-colors-of-life-in-the-face-of-the-anthropocene.

DeLanda, Manuel. (1996) 2012. "An Interview with Manuel de Landa." By Konrad Becker and Miss M. In *Future Non Stop: A Living Archive for Digital Culture in Theory and Practice*. http://future-nonstop.org/c/bad189cc715b73b2e88626a072d17a64.

———. (1997) 2005. *A Thousand Years of Nonlinear History*. New York: Zone Books.

---. 2003. "Self Organizing Markets." In *Anarchitexts: Voices from the Global Digital Resistance: A Subsol Anthology*, edited by Joanne Richardson, 279–83. New York: Autonomedia.

DeLoughrey, Elizabeth M. 2019. *Allegories of the Anthropocene*. Durham, NC: Duke University Press.

Demirsoy, Ali. 2021. *Canlılığın Oluşum Öyküsünde Renklerin Dansı* (The Dance of Colors in the Formation Story of Aliveness). Ankara: Akılçelen Kitaplar.

Denizen, Seth. 2013. "Three Holes: In the Geological Present." In *Architecture in the Anthropocene: Encounters Among Design, Deep Time, Science and Philosophy*, edited by Etienne Turpin, 25–42. Ann Arbor, MI: Open Humanities Press.

Derocher, Andrew E., Nicholas J. Lunn, and Ian Sterling. 2004. "Polar Bears in a Warming Climate." *Integrative and Comparative Biology* 44: 163–76.

Derrida, Jacques. 1987. "Semiology and Grammatology: Interview with Julia Kristeva." In *Positions: Jacques Derrida*, translated by Alan Bass, 15–36. London: The Athlone Press.

Devlin, Hannah. 2018. "Plants 'Talk To' Each Other through Their Roots." *The Guardian*, May 2, 2018. https://www.theguardian.com/science/2018/may/02/plants-talk-to-each-other-through-their-roots.

Dibley, Ben. 2012. "'The Shape of Things to Come': Seven Theses on the Anthropocene and Attachment." *Australian Humanities Review* 52: 139–53.

Di Chiro, Giovanna. 2010. "Polluted Politics? Confronting the Toxic Discourses, Sex Panic, and Eco-Normativity." In *Queer Ecologies: Sex, Nature, Politics, Desire*, edited by Catriona Mortimer-Sandilands and Bruce Ericson, 199–230. Bloomington: Indiana University Press.

Dickinson, Adam. 2015. "Anthropocene." *ESC: English Studies in Canada* 41, no. 4: 21.

Dillard, Annie. 1988. "Teaching a Stone to Talk." In *Teaching a Stone to Talk: Expeditions and Encounters*, 67–76. New York: Harper and Row Press.

Doerr, Anthony. 2014. "The New You." *Orion Magazine*. https://orionmagazine.org/article/the-new-you.

Dunn, Oliva, and François Gemenne. 2008. "Defining Environmental Migration." *Forced Migration Review* 31: 10–11.

Düren, Rahşan. 2015. *E-Motions* (Installation). October 2015. rahsandurenhaydarpasa.com/eng.

Ellsworth, Elizabeth, and Jamie Kruse. 2013. "Introduction. Evidence: Making a Geologic Turn in Cultural Awareness." In *Making the Geologic Now: Responses to Material Conditions of Contemporary Life*, edited by Elizabeth Ellsworth and Jamie Kruse, 6–26. New York: Punctum Books.

Enroth, Henrik. 2020. "Declarations of Dependence: On the Constitution of the Anthropocene." *Theory, Culture & Society* (December 16): 1–22. https://doi.org/10.1177/0263276420978283.

Ergin, Meliz. 2017. "Drought-Induced Migrations in Syria and Turkey." Special Cluster: Migrant Ecologies in an (U)nbordered World, coordinated by Serpil Oppermann, Serenella Iovino, and Zhou Xiaojing. *ISLE: Interdisciplinary Studies in Literature and Environment* 24, no. 2: 257–91.

Estok, Simon C. 2011. *Ecocriticism and Shakespeare: Reading Ecophobia*. New York: Palgrave Macmillan.

---. 2014. "Afterwords. Beckoning with Irreversibilities in Biotic and Political Ecologies." Special Issue: A Review of International English Literature

Postcolonial Ecocriticism among Settler-Colonial Nations. *Ariel* 44, no. 4: 219–32.

———. 2018. *The Ecophobia Hypothesis.* New York: Routledge.

———. 2021. "The Global Poltergeist: COVID-19 Hauntings." In *Haunted Nature: Entanglements of the Human and the Nonhuman,* edited by Sladja Blazan, 181–95. Cham Switzerland: Palgrave/Macmillan.

Farrier, David. 2019. *Anthropocene Poetics: Deep Time, Sacrifice Zones, and Extinction.* Minneapolis: University of Minnesota Press.

Fedrizzi, Alessandro, Rupert Ursin, Thomas Herbst, Matteo Nespoli, Robert Prevedel, Thomas Scheidl, Felix Tiefenbacher, Thomas Jennewein, and Anton Zeilinger. 2009. "High-Fidelity Transmission of Entanglement over a High-Loss Freespace Channel." *Nature Physics* 5: 389–92.

Fernández, María José. 2015. "Refugees, Climate Change and International Law." *Forced Migration Review* 49: 42–43.

Fishel, Stefanie R. 2017. *The Microbial State: Global Thriving and the Body Politic.* Minneapolis: University of Minnesota Press.

Fisher, Malcolm. 2017. "The Toughest Brief." In *New Shoots Poetry Anthology: Poems Inspired by Plants,* edited by Ella Skilbeck-Porter, 95. New South Wales: Redroom Company. http://redroomcompany.org/projects/new-shoots.

Fisherman of Halicarnassus (Cevat Şakir Kabaağaçlı). 1961. *Mavi Sürgün* (The Blue Exile). Istanbul: Bilgi Yayınevi.

———. 1972. *Ege'den Denize Bırakılmış Bir Çiçek* (A Flower Left to the Aegean Sea). Istanbul: Bilgi Yayınevi.

———. 2002a. "Akdeniz Balıklarının Marifetleri" (The Craftsmanship of the Mediterranean Fish). In *İmbat Serinliği* (The Coolness of the Breeze), 51–53. Istanbul: Bilgi Yayınevi.

———. 2002b. " Foklar, Yunuslar" (The Seals and Dolphins). In *İmbat Serinliği* (The Coolness of the Breeze), 145–49. Istanbul: Bilgi Yayınevi.

Foote, Stephanie. 2020. "The Sense of Place at the End of the World." *Ecocene: Cappadocia Journal of Environmental Humanities* 1, no. 1: 52–58. https://doi.org/10.46863/ecocene.34.

Frank, Priscilla. 2015."The Dangerous Beauty of One of the World's Most Invasive Plants." *HuffPost,* December 16, 2015. https://www.huffpost.com/entry/kudzu-photos-helene-schmitz_n_56704e47e4b0fccee1700578.

Gaard, Greta. 2011. "Global Warming Narratives." In *The Future of Ecocriticism,* edited by Serpil Oppermann, Ufuk Özdağ, Nevin Özkan, and Scott Slovic, 43–64. Newcastle upon Tyne: Cambridge Scholars Press.

———. 2014. "What's the Story? Competing Narratives of Climate Change and Climate Justice." *Forum for World Literature Studies* 6, no. 2: 272–91.

———. 2020. "New Ecocriticisms: Narrative, Affective, Empirical and Mindful." Special issue: "2020 Ecocriticism: In Europe and Beyond," edited by Axel Goodbody, Carmen Flys Junquera, and Serpil Oppermann. *Ecozon@* 11, no. 2: 224–33.

Gabbott, Sarah, Sarah Key, Catherine Russell, Yasmin Yohan, and Jan Zalasiewicz. 2020. "The Geography and Geology of Plastics: Their Environmental Distribution and Fate." In *Plastic Waste and Recycling: Environmental Impact, Societal Issues, Prevention, and Solutions,* edited by Trevor M. Letcher, 33–63. London: Elsevier.

Gabet, Emmanuel J., O. J. Reichman, and Eric W. Seabloom. 2003. "The Effects of Bioturbation on Soil Processes and Sediment Transport." *Annual Review of Earth Planetary Sciences* 31: 249–73.

Gadd, Jeremy. 2017. "What Is Commonly Called a Weed." In *New Shoots Poetry Anthology: Poems Inspired by Plants*, edited by Ella Skilbeck-Porter, 37. New South Wales: Redroom Company. http://redroomcompany.org/projects/new-shoots.

Gagliano, Monica. 2017a. "The Mind of Plants: Thinking the Unthinkable." *Communicative & Integrative Biology* 10, no. 2: e1288333-1–4. http://doi.org/10.108 0/19420889.2017.1288333.

———. 2017b. "Breaking the Silence: Green Mudras and the Faculty of Language of Plants." In *The Language of Plants: Science, Philosophy, Literature*, edited by Monica Gagliano, John C. Ryan, and Patricia Vieira, 84–100. Minneapolis: University of Minnesota Press.

Gan, Elaine. 2017. "Timing Rice: An Inquiry into More-than-Human Temporalities of the Anthropocene." *New Formations: A Journal of Culture/Theory/Politics* 92: 87–101.

Gan, Elaine, Anna Tsing, Heather Swanson, and Nils Bubandt. 2017. "Introduction: Haunted Landscapes of the Anthropocene." In *Arts of Living on a Damaged Planet: Ghosts of the Anthropocene*, edited by Anna Tsing, Heather Swanson, Elaine Gan, and Nils Bubandt, G1–12. Minneapolis: University of Minnesota Press.

Gane, Nicholas. 2006. "When We Have Never Been Human, What Is to Be Done? Interview with Donna Haraway." *Theory, Culture & Society* 23, no. 7–8: 135–58.

Geiger, Laura. 2020. "Climate Crisis and Local Communities in South East Asia: Causes, Responses and Questions of Justice." *Forced Migration Review* 64: 18–21.

Geymen, Abdurrahman, and Ibrahim Baz. 2008. "Monitoring Urban Growth and Detecting Land-Cover Changes on the Istanbul Metropolitan Area." *Environmental Monitoring and Assessment* 1, no. 36: 449–59.

Gibson, Daniel G., et al. 2010. "Creation of a Bacterial Cell Controlled by a Chemically Synthesized Genome." *Science* 329: 52–56. https://science.sciencemag.org/content/329/5987/52.

Gienger, Michael. 2000. *Crystal Power, Crystal Healing: The Complete Handbook*. Translated by Astrid Mick. London: Blanford.

Glick, Daniel. 2019. "The Big Thaw." *National Geographic*, September 23, 2019. https://www.nationalgeographic.com/environment/global-warming/big-thaw.

Goleman, Daniel. 2010. *Ecological Intelligence: The Coming Age of Radical Transparency*. London: Penguin Books.

Grebenstein, Emily. 2013. "Escape of the Invasives: Top Six Invasive Plant Species in the United States" *Smithsonian*, April 19, 2013. https://www.si.edu/blog/escape-invasives-top-six-invasive-plant-species-united-states.

Greiner, Clemens, and Patrick Sakdapolrak. 2013. "Translocality: Concepts, Applications and Emerging Research Perspectives." *Geography Compass* 7, no. 5: 373–84.

Griffin, David Ray. 1988. "Introduction: The Reenchantment of Science." In *The Reenchantment of Science: Postmodern Proposals*, edited by David Ray Griffin, 1–46. New York: State University of New York Press.

———. 1998. *Unsnarling the World-Knot: Consciousness, Freedom, and the Mind-Body Problem*. Berkeley: University of California Press.

———. 1989. "Hartshorne's Postmodern Philosophy." In *Hartshorne, Process Philosophy, and Theology*, edited by Robert Kane and Stephen H. Phillips, 1–33. Albany: State University of New York Press.

———. 2001. "Process Philosophy of Religion." *International Journal for Philosophy of Religion* 50: 131–51.

———. 2015. *Unprecedented: Can Civilization Survive the CO2 Crisis?* Atlanta: Clarity Press.

Griffiths, Matthew. 2017. *The New Poetics of Climate Change: Modernist Aesthetics for a Warming World.* New York: Bloomsbury Academic

Grosz, Elizabeth. 2010. "Feminism, Materialism, and Freedom." In *New Materialisms: Ontology, Agency, and Politics,* edited by Diana Coole and Samantha Frost, 139–57. Durham, NC: Duke University Press.

Grusin, Richard. 2017. "Anthropocene Feminism: An Experiment in Collaborative Theorizing." In *Anthropocene Feminism,* edited by Richard Grusin, vii–xix. Minnesota: University of Minnesota Press.

Gupta, V. P. 2016. *Principles and Applications of Quantum Chemistry.* London: Elsevier.

Hagopian, Joachim. 2014. "Death and Extinction of the Bees." Global Research: Centre for Research on Globalization, March 28, 2014 (rpt. 2019). https://www.globalresearch.ca/death-and-extinction-of-the-bees/5375684.

Hamilton, Clive, Christophe Bonneuil, and François Gemenne. 2015. "Thinking the Anthropocene." In *The Anthropocene and the Global Environmental Crisis,* edited by Clive Hamilton, Christophe Bonneuil, and François Gemenne, 1–13. London: Routledge.

Hamilton, Stephen G., and Andrew E. Derocher. 2019. "Assessment of Global Polar Bear Abundance and Vulnerability." *Animal Conservation* 22, no. 1: 83–95.

Haraway, Donna. 2003. *Companion Species Manifesto: Dogs, People, and Significant Otherness.* Chicago: Prickly Paradigm Press.

———. 2004. "Introduction: A Kinship of Feminist Figurations." In *The Haraway Reader,* 1–6. New York: Routledge.

———. 2008a. *When Species Meet.* Minneapolis: University of Minnesota Press.

———. 2008b. "Otherworldly Conversations, Terran Topics, Local Terms." In *Material Feminisms,* edited by Stacy Alaimo and Susan Hekman, 157–87. Bloomington: Indiana University Press.

———. 2015a. "Anthropocene, Capitalocene, Plantationocene, Chthulucene: Making Kin." *Environmental Humanities* 6: 159–65.

———. 2015b. "Preface: Cosmopolitical Critters." In *Cosmopolitan Animals,* edited by Kaori Nagai et al., vii–xiv. London: Palgrave Macmillan.

———. 2016. *Staying with the Trouble: Making Kin in the Chthulucene.* Durham, NC: Duke University Press.

———. 2017. "Symbiogenesis, Sympoiesis, and Art Science Activisms for Staying with the Trouble." In *Arts of Living on a Damaged Planet: Monsters of the Anthropocene,* edited by Anna Tsing, Heather Swanson, Elaine Gan, and Nils Bubandt, M25–50. Minneapolis: Minnesota University Press.

Harrison, Summer. 2017. "Environmental Justice Storytelling: Sentiment, Knowledge, and the Body in Ruth Ozeki's *My Year of Meats.*" *ISLE: Interdisciplinary Studies in Literature and Environment* 24, no. 3: 457–76.

Hartman, Steven, Joni Adamson, Greta Gaard, and Serpil Oppermann. 2020. "Through the Portal of COVID-19: Visioning the Environmental Humanities as a Community of Purpose." *Bifrost Online,* June 8, 2020. https://bifrostonline.org/steven-hartman-joni-adamson-greta-gaard-serpil-oppermann.

Hartman, Steven, and Serpil Oppermann. 2020. "Seeds of Transformative Change." *Ecocene: Cappadocia Journal of Environmental Humanities*. 1, no. 1: 1–18. https://doi.org/10.46863/ecocene.29.

Hartshorne, Charles. 1936. "The Compound Individual." In *Philosophical Essays for Alfred North Whitehead*, edited by F. S. C. Northtrop et al., 193–220. New York: Russel and Russel.

———. (1967) 1989. *A Natural Theology for Our Time*. La Salle, IL: Open Court Publishing Co.

———. 1970. *Creative Synthesis and Philosophic Method*. La Salle, IL: Open Court Publishing Co.

Hassan, Nora, Streit Cunningham, Martin Mourigal, Elena I. Zhilyaeva, Svetlana A. Torunova, Rimma N. Lyubovskaya, John A. Schlueter, and Natalia Drichko. 2018. "Evidence for a Quantum Dipole Liquid State in an Organic Quasi–Two-Dimensional Material." *Science* 360, no. 6393: 1101.

Hayles, N. Katherine. 2005. *My Mother Was a Computer: Digital Subjects and Literary Texts*. Chicago: University of Chicago Press.

———. 2017. "The Cognitive Nonconscious and the New Materialisms." In *The New Politics of Materialism: History, Philosophy, Science*, edited by Sarah Ellenzweig and John H. Zammito, 181–99. New York: Routledge.

———. 2020. "Novel Corona: Posthuman Virus." *Critical Inquiry*, In the Moment (blog), April 17, 2020. https://critinq.wordpress.com/2020/04/17/novel-corona-posthuman-virus.

Haynes, Patrice. 2014. "Creative Becoming and the Patiency of Matter: Feminism, New Materialism, and Theology." *Angelaki: Journal of the Theoretical Humanities* 19, no. 1: 129–50.

Head, Lesley. 2014. "Contingencies of the Anthropocene: Lessons from the 'Neolithic.'" *The Anthropocene Review* 1, no. 2: 113–25.

Heise, Ursula K. 2008. *Sense of Place and Sense of Planet: The Environmental Imagination of the Global*. New York: Oxford University Press.

———. 2016. *Imagining Extinction: The Cultural Meanings of Endangered Species*. Chicago: University of Chicago Press.

———. 2020. "Environmentalisms and Posthumanisms." In *The Bloomsbury Handbook of Posthumanism*, edited by Mads Rosendahl Thomsen and Jacob Wamberg, 117–28. New York: Bloomsbury Academic.

Hekman, Susan. 2010. *The Material of Knowledge: Feminist Disclosures*. Bloomington: Indiana University Press.

Helmreich, Stefan. 2009. *Alien Ocean: Anthropological Voyages in Microbial Seas*. Berkeley: University of California Press.

———. 2010. "Human Nature at Sea." *AnthroNow* 2, no. 3: 49–60.

Heringman, Noah. 2015. "Deep Time at the Dawn of the Anthropocene." *Representations* 129, no. 1: 56–85.

Herman, David. 2018. *Narratology beyond the Human: Storytelling and Animal Life*. New York: Oxford University Press.

Hill, Jessica. 2021. "Fact Check: Biden Executive Order Halts Border Wall Construction, Redirects Funding." *USA Today*, February 3, 2021. https://www.usatoday.com/story/news/factcheck/2021/02/03/fact-check-joe-biden-executive-order-trump-border-wall-construction/4337994001.

Hird, Myra. J. n.d. "Waste Flows." *Discard Studies*. Accessed May 20, 2020. https://discardstudies.com/discard-studies-compendium/#Wasteflows.

Ho, Mae-Wan, and Fritz-Abert Popp. (1989) 1993. "Gaia and the Evolution of Coherence." Paper presented at the 3rd Camelford Conference on "The Implications of The Gaia Thesis: Symbiosis, Cooperativity and Coherence." November 7–10, 1989. The Wadebridge Ecological Centre, Camelford, Cornwall. Revised October 8, 1993. https://ratical.org/co-globalize/MaeWanHo/gaia.html.

Holling, C. S. 2001. "Understanding the Complexity of Economic, Ecological, and Social Systems." *Ecosystems* 4: 390–405.

Holling, C. S., Lance H. Gunderson, and Donald Ludwig. 2002. "In Quest of a Theory of Adaptive Change." In *Panarchy: Understanding Transformations in Human and Natural Systems*, edited by Lance H. Gunderson and C. S. Holling, 3–22. Washington, DC: Island Press.

Holten, Katie. 2020. "Stone Alphabet." *Emergence Magazine: Ecology, Culture, and Spirituality* 5. https://emergencemagazine.org/story/stone-alphabet.

Homer-Dixon, Thomas. 2006. *The Upside of Down: Catastrophe, Creativity, and the Renewal of Civilization*. Washington, DC: Island Press.

Hong Kong Geological Survey. (2009) 2021. "Hong Kong Geology: A 400-Million-Year Journey." Last revised March 18, 2021. https://hkss.cedd.gov.hk/hkss/eng/education/GS/eng/hkg/chapter4.htm.

Hulme, Mike. 2011. "Reducing the Future to Climate: A Story of Climate Determinism and Reductionism." *Osiris* 26, no. 1: 245–66.

———. 2020. "One Earth, Many Futures, No Destination." *One Earth* 2, no. 4: 309–11.

Hunter, Lawrence E. 2009. *The Processes of Life: An Introduction to Molecular Biology*. Cambridge, MA: MIT Press.

Huntingford, Chris, and Lina M. Mercado. 2016. "High Chance That Current Atmospheric Greenhouse Concentrations Commit to Warmings Greater Than 1.5 °C over Land." *Scientific Reports* 6, no. 30294: 1–7. https://www.nature.com/articles/srep30294#introduction.

Ingold, Tim. 2011. *Being Alive: Essays on Movement, Knowledge and Description*. New York: Routledge.

Iovino, Serenella, and Serpil Oppermann. 2014. "Introduction: Stories Come to Matter." In *Material Ecocriticism*, edited by Serenella Iovino and Serpil Oppermann, 1–17. Bloomington: Indiana University Press.

IPCC (Intergovernmental Panel on Climate Change). 2018. *Global Warming of 1.5°C: An IPCC Special Report on the Impacts of Global Warming of 1.5°C Above Pre-Industrial Levels and Related Global Greenhouse Gas Emission Pathways, in the Context of Strengthening the Global Response to the Threat of Climate Change, Sustainable Development, and Efforts to Eradicate Poverty*. Switzerland. https://www.ipcc.ch/sr15.

———. 2019. *Special Report on the Ocean and Cryosphere in a Changing Climate*. September 25, 2019. https://www.ipcc.ch/srocc.

Jacques, Vincent, et al. 2007. "Experimental Realization of Wheeler's Delayed-Choice Gedanken Experiment." *Science* 315: 966–68.

Jambeck, Jenna R., et al. 2015. "Plastic Waste Inputs from Land into the Ocean." *Science* 347, no. 6223: 768–71.

Jarman, Derek. 1995. *Chroma: A Book of Color*. New York: The Overlook Press.

Jordan, Chris, director. 2009. *Midway: Messages from the Gyre*. Documentary film. http://www.midwayfilm.com.

Joseph, Jonathan. 2013. "Resilience as Embedded Neoliberalism: A Governmentality Approach." *Resilience* 1, no. 1: 38–52.

Joy, Eileen. 2014. "Living (Playful) Process: No, David Graeber, You Did Not Invent a New Law of Reality, and Yes, Barbara Ehrenreich, That Science Does Exist." *Figure/Ground Communication*, March 1, 2014. http://figureground.org/living-playful-process.

Kapitza, Katharina, Heike Zimmermann, Berta Martín-López, and Henrik von Wehrden. 2019. "Research on the Social Perception of Invasive Species: A Systematic Literature Review." *NeoBiota* 43: 47–68. https://neobiota.pensoft.net/article/31619.

Kaplan, Sarah. 2020. "Climate Change Affects Everything—Even the Coronavirus." *Washington Post*, April 15, 2020. https://www.washingtonpost.com/climate-solutions/2020/04/15/climate-change-affects-everything-even-coronavirus.

Kauffman, Stuart. 2003. "The Emergence of Autonomous Agents." In *From Complexity to Life: On the Emergence of Life and Meaning*, edited by Niels Henrik Gregersen, 47–71. Oxford: Oxford University Press.

———. 2008. *Reinventing the Sacred: The Science of Complexity and the Emergence of a Natural Divinity*. New York: Basic Books.

Kerry, John. 2014. "Remarks on Climate Change." US Department of State: Diplomacy in Action. Indonesia. February 16, 2014. https://2009-2017.state.gov/secretary/remarks/2014/02/221704.htm.

Khan, Yusuf. 2019. "Goldman Sachs Released a 34-Page Analysis of the Impact of Climate Change and the Results Are Terrifying." *Insider*, September 25, 2019. https://www.insider.com/goldman-sachs-climate-change-threatens-new-york-tokyo-lagos-cities-2019-9.

Kingsnorth, Paul. 2017. *Confessions of a Recovering Environmentalist and Other Essays*. Minneapolis: Graywolf Press.

Kirby, Vicki. 2011. *Quantum Anthropologies: Life at Large*. Durham, NC: Duke University Press.

Kohn, Eduardo. 2013. *How Forests Think: Toward an Anthropology Beyond the Human*. Berkeley: University of California Press.

Kolbert, Elizabeth. 2011. "Enter the Anthropocene—Age of Man." *National Geographic*, March 2011. https://www.nationalgeographic.com/magazine/2011/03/age-of-man.

———. 2014. *The Sixth Extinction: An Unnatural History*. New York: Picador.

Kolinjivadi, Vijay. 2020. "This Pandemic IS Ecological Breakdown: Different Tempo, Same Song." *Uneven Earth*, April 2, 2020. http://unevenearth.org/2020/04/this-pandemic-is-ecological-breakdown-different-tempo-same-song.

Konner, Jeremy. 2014. *The Majestic Plastic Bag*. Vimeo video, 04:11. https://vimeo.com/21714944.

Krauss, Werner. 2019. "Postenvironmental Landscapes in the Anthropocene." In *The Routledge Companion to Landscape Studies*, edited by Peter Howard, Ian Thompson, Emma Waterton, and Mick Atha, 62–73. New York: Routledge.

Kristensen, Erik, Gil Penha-Lopes, Matthieu Delefosse, Thomas Valdemarsen, Cintia O. Quintana, and Gary T. Banta. 2012. "What Is Bioturbation? The Need for a Precise Definition for Fauna in Aquatic Sciences." *MEPS: Marine Ecology Progress Series* 446: 285–302.

LaCugna, Catherine M. 1991. *God for Us: The Trinity and Christian Life*. San Francisco: HarperCollins.

Langston, Nancy. 2010. *Toxic Bodies: Hormone Disruptors and the Legacy of DES*. New Haven, CT: Yale University Press.

Larson, Brendon M. H. 2010. "Reweaving Narratives About Humans and Invasive Species." *Études rurales* 185: 25–38.
Latour, Bruno. 1993. *We Have Never Been Modern*. Translated by Catherine Porter. Cambridge, MA: Harvard University Press.
———. 1999. *Pandora's Hope: Essays on the Reality of Science Studies*. Cambridge, MA: Harvard University Press.
———. 2004. *Politics of Nature: How to Bring the Sciences into Democracy*. Translated by Catherine Porter. Cambridge, MA: Harvard University Press.
———. 2010. "An Attempt at a 'Compositionist Manifesto.'" *New Literary History* 41, no. 3: 471–90.
———. 2014. "Agency at the Time of the Anthropocene." *New Literary History* 45, no. 1: 1–18.
Leakey, Richard, and Roger Lewin. 1996. *The Sixth Mass Extinction: Biodiversity and Its Survival*. London: Phoenix.
Lekan, Thomas M. 2014. "Fractal Earth: Visualizing the Global Environment in the Anthropocene." *Environmental Humanities* 5: 171–201.
Llywelyn, Morgan. 1993. *The Elementals*. New York: TOR.
LeMenager, Stephanie. 2017. "Climate Change and the Struggle for Genre." In *Anthropocene Reading: Literary History in Geologic Times*, edited by Tobias Menely and Jesse Oak Taylor, 220–38. University Park: Pennsylvania State University Press.
LeMenager, Stephanie, and Stephanie Foote. 2013. "Editor's Column." *Resilience: A Journal of the Environmental Humanities* 1, no. 1: n.p.
LeMenager, Stephanie, Teresa Shewry, and Ken Hiltner. 2011. "Introduction." In *Environmental Criticism for the Twenty-First Century*, edited by Stephanie LeMenager, Teresa Shewry, and Ken Hiltner, 1–15. New York: Routledge.
Lenton, Timothy M., et al. 2019. "Climate Tipping Points—Too Risky to Bet Against." *Nature* 575: 592–95.
Lewis, Joshua. 2019. "The Disappearing River: Infrastructural Desire in New Orleans." In *Grounding Urban Natures: Histories and Futures of Urban Ecologies*, edited by Henrik Ernstson and Sverker Sörlin, 57–82. Cambridge, MA: MIT Press.
Lewis, Tanya. 2013. "Melting Sea Ice Keeps Hungry Polar Bears on Land." *Live Science*, March 20, 2013. https://www.livescience.com/28038-sea-ice-affects-polar-bear-migration.html.
Lidström, Susanna, Simon West, Tania Katzschner, M. Isabel Pérez-Ramos, and Hedley Twidl. 2015. "Invasive Narratives and the Inverse of Slow Violence: Alien Species in Science and Society." *Environmental Humanities* 7: 1–40.
Löw, Martina, and Gunter Weidenhaus. 2017. "Borders that Relate: Conceptualizing Boundaries in Relational Space." *Current Sociology* 65, no. 4: 553–70.
Luke, Timothy W. 1997. *Ecocritique: Contesting the Politics of Nature, Economy, and Culture*. Minneapolis: University of Minnesota Press.
Lustgarten, Abram. 2020. "How Climate Migration Will Reshape America: Millions Will Be Displaced. Where Will They Go?" *New York Times Magazine*, September 15, 2020. https://www.nytimes.com/interactive/2020/09/15/magazine/climate-crisis-migration-america.html.
Macfarlane, Robert. 2016. "Generation Anthropocene: How Humans Have Altered the Planet for Ever." *The Guardian*, April 1, 2016. https://www.theguardian.com/books/2016/apr/01/generation-anthropocene-altered-planet-for-ever.
———. 2019. *Underland: A Deep Time Journey*. New York: W. W. Norton & Company.

Maran, Timo. 2017. "On the Diversity of Environmental Signs: A Typological Approach." *Biosemiotics* 10. November 9, 2017. https://doi.org/10.1007/s12304-017-9308-5.
Marchesini, Roberto. 2016. "Dialogo Ergo Sum: From a Reflexive Ontology to a Relational Ontology." *Relations: Beyond Anthropocentrism* 4, no. 2: 145–58.
———. 2021. *The Virus Paradigm: A Planetary Ecology of the Mind*. Cambridge: Cambridge University Press.
Marder, Michael. 2019. "Being Dumped." *Environmental Humanities* 11, no. 1: 180–93.
Margulis, Lynn. 1999. *The Symbiotic Planet: A New Look at Evolution*. New York: Phoenix.
Marland, Pippa, and John Parham. 2014. "Editorial: Remaindering: The Material Ecology of Junk and Composting." *Green Letters: Studies in Ecocriticism* 18, no. 1: 1–8.
Martinez, Amanda Rose. 2011. "Swirling Seas of Plastic Trash: Long-Lasting Oceanic Garbage Threatens Marine Life." *Science News for Students*, June 22, 2011. https://www.sciencenewsforstudents.org/article/swirling-seas-plastic-trash.
Mayburov, Serguey N. 2011. "Photonic Communications and Information Encoding in Biological Systems." *Journal of Samara State Technical University, Ser. Physical and Mathematical Sciences* 15, no. 2: 260–65.
Mayer, Emeran. 2016. *The Mind-Gut Connection: How the Hidden Conversation Within Our Bodies Impacts Our Mood, Our Choices, and Our Overall Health*. New York: HarperCollins.
McDermott, Amy. 2016. "Mexico's Climate Migrants Are Already Coming to the United States." *Grist*, December 29, 2016. http://grist.org/article/mexicos-climate-migrants-are-already-coming-to-the-united-states.
McKibben, Bill. 1998. "Postnatural." *Aperture* 150: 3–21.
———. (1989) 2006. *The End of Nature*. New York: Random House.
Mentz, Steve. 2017. "Enter Anthropocene, Circa 1800." In *Anthropocene Reading: Literary History in Geologic Times*, edited by Tobias Menely and Jesse Oak Taylor, 43–58. University Park: Pennsylvania State University Press.
Mesle, Robert C. 2008. *Process-Relational Philosophy: An Introduction to Alfred North Whitehead*. West Conshohocken, PA: Templeton Foundation Press.
Meysman, Filip J. R., Jack J. Middelburg, and Carlo H. R. Heip. 2006. "Bioturbation: A Fresh Look at Darwin's Last Idea." *Trends in Ecology and Evolution* 21, no. 12: 688–95.
Mezzadra, Sandro, and Bret Neilson. 2013. *Border as Method, or, The Multiplication of Labor*. Durham, NC: Duke University Press.
Midgley, Mary. 2012. "On Not Needing to Be Omnipotent." *Center for Humans and Nature*. http://www.humansandnature.org/to-be-human-mary-midgley.
Mirzoeff, Nicholas. 2014. "Visualizing the Anthropocene." *Public Culture* 26, no. 2: 213–32. http://publicculture.org/articles/view/26/2/visualizing-the-anthropocene.
Mitchell, Allan J. 2014. *Becoming Human: The Matter of Medieval Child*. Minneapolis: University of Minnesota Press.
Mitman, Gregg. 2018. "Hubris or Humility? Genealogies of the Anthropocene." In *Future Remains: A Cabinet of Curiosities for the Anthropocene*, edited by Gregg Mitman, Marco Armiero, and Robert Emmett, 59–68. Chicago: University of Chicago Press.

Moomaw, William R., Beverly Law, William Ripple, Patrick V. Verkooijen, Saleemul Huq, and Chris Gordon. 2020. "Global Scientists Call for Economic Stimulus to Address Climate Adaptation and Covid." GCA Science Statement, Global Center on Adaptation. https://gca.org/reports/global-scientists-call-for-economic-stimulus-to-address-climate-adaptation-and-covid/.

Moore, Jason W. 2016. "Introduction." In *Anthropocene or Capitalocene? Nature, History, and the Crisis of Capitalism*, edited by Jason W. Moore, 1–11. Oakland, CA: PM Press.

———. 2017. "The Capitalocene, Part I: On the Nature and Origins of Our Ecological Crisis." *Journal of Peasant Studies* 44, no. 3: 594–630.

Morrison, Susan Signe. 2015. *The Literature of Waste: Material Ecopoetics and Ethical Matter*. New York: Palgrave Macmillan

Morton, Timothy. 2010. "Guest Column: Queer Ecology." *PMLA* 125, no. 2: 273–83.

———. 2011. "The Mesh." In *Environmental Criticism for the Twenty-First Century*, edited by Stephanie LeMenager, Teresa Shewry, and Ken Hiltner, 19–30. New York: Routledge.

———. 2013a. "X-Ray." In *Prismatic Ecology: Ecotheory Beyond Green*, edited by Jeffrey Jerome Cohen, 311–27. Minneapolis: University of Minnesota Press.

———. 2013b. "At the Edge of the Smoking Pool of Death: Wolves in Throne Room." *Helvete: A Journal of Black Metal Theory* 1: 21–28.

———. 2015. "This Biosphere Which Is Not One: Toward Weird Essentialism." *Journal of the British Society for Phenomenology* 46, no. 2: 141–55.

———. 2016. *Dark Ecology: For a Logic of Future Coexistence*. New York: Columbia University Press.

National Geographic. 2019. "Symbiosis: The Art of Living Together." *National Geographic*, April 19, 2019. https://www.nationalgeographic.org/article/symbiosis-art-living-together.

Nealson, Kenneth H., Fumio Inagaki, and Ken Takai. 2005. "Hydrogen-Driven Subsurface Lithoauthotrophic Microbial Ecosystem (Slimes): Do They Exist and Why Should We Care?" *Trends in Microbiology* 13: 405–10.

Newell, Mary, Bernard Quetchenbach, and Sarah Nolan. 2020. "Introduction." In *Poetics for the More-than-Human World*, edited by Mary Newell, Bernard Quetchenbach, and Sarah Nolan, i–iii. New York: Spuyten Duyvil, Dispatches Editions.

Nixon, Rob. 2011. *Slow Violence and the Environmentalism of the Poor*. Cambridge, MA: Harvard University Press.

———. 2014. "The Anthropocene: The Promise and Pitfalls of an Epochal Idea." *Edge Effects*, November 6, 2014. http://edgeeffects.net/anthropocene-promise-and-pitfalls.

Noll, Samantha. 2017. "Climate Induced Migration: A Pragmatic Strategy for Wildlife Conservation on Farmland." *Pragmatism Today* 8, no. 2: 24–41.

———. 2018. "Nonhuman Climate Refugees: The Role that Urban Communities Should Play in Ensuring Ecological Resilience." *Environmental Ethics* 40: 23–38.

Oppermann, Serpil. 2013. "Material Ecocriticism and the Creativity of Storied Matter." *Frame* 26, no. 2: 55–70.

———. 2016a. "From Material to Posthuman Ecocriticism: Hybridity, Stories, Natures." In *Handbook of Ecocriticism and Cultural Ecology*, edited by Hubert Zapf, 273–94. Berlin: De Gruyter.

———. 2016b. "Material Ecocriticism." In *Gender/Nature*, edited by Iris van der Tuin, 89–102. San Francisco: Gale Cengage Learning.

———. 2018. "Storied Matter." In *Posthuman Glossary*, edited by Rosi Braidotti and Maria Hlavajova, 411–14. London: Bloomsbury Academic

———. 2019a. "Changing Climate and Human Bioturbation." *Bifrost Online*. https://bifrostonline.org/changing-climate-and-human-bioturbation.

———. 2019b. "How the Material World Communicates: Insights from Material Ecocriticism." In *Routledge Handbook of Ecocriticism and Environmental Communication*, edited by Scott Slovic, Swarnalatha Rangarajan, and Vidya Sarveswaran, 108–17. New York: Routledge.

Oppermann, Serpil, and Sinan Akıllı. 2021. "Introduction." In *Turkish Ecocriticism: From Neolithic to Contemporary Timescapes*, edited by Serpil Oppermann and Sinan Akıllı, 1–18. Lanham, MD: Lexington Books.

Oppermann, Serpil, and Serenella Iovino. 2017. "Introduction: The Environmental Humanities and the Challenges of the Anthropocene." In *Environmental Humanities: Voices from the Anthropocene*, edited by Serpil Oppermann and Serenella Iovino, 1–21. New York: Rowman & Littlefield.

OED (Oxford English Dictionary). https://www.oed.com.

Ozguc, Umut. 2020. "Borders, Detention, and the Disruptive Power of the Noisy-Subject." *International Political Sociology* 14, no. 1: 77–93.

Palmer, Clare, and Brendon H. M. Larson. 2014. "Should We Move the Whitebark Pine? Assisted Migration, Ethics and Global Environmental Change." *Environmental Values* 23, no. 6: 641–62.

Parisi, Luciana. 2008. "The Neoengineering of Desire." In *Queering the Non/Human*, edited by Noreen Giffney and Myra J. Hird, 283–309. Burlington, VT: Ashgate Press.

Parsons, Allan. 2009. "Narrative Environments: How Do They Matter?" *Rhizomes: Cultural Studies in Emerging Knowledge* 19. http://www.rhizomes.net/issue19/parsons/index.html.

Pell, Richard W., and Lauren P. Allen. 2015a. "Preface to a Genealogy of the Postnatural." In *Land & Animal & Nonanimal*, edited by Anna-Sophie Springer and Etienne Turpin in association with Kirsten Einfeldt and Daniela Wolf, vii-viii. Berlin: K. Verlag and Haus der Kulturen der Welt.

———. 2015b. "Bringing Postnatural History into View." *American Scientist* 103, no. 3: 224–27.

Perry, Leonard. n.d. "The How and Why of Plant Color." Summer news article. *The Green Mountain Gardener.* University of Vermont Department of Plant and Soil Science. https://pss.uvm.edu/ppp/articles/colorwhy.html.

Pettis, Jeffery S., Elinor M. Lichtenberg, Michael Andree, Jennie Stitzinger, Robyn Rose, and Dennis van Engelsdorp. 2013. "Crop Pollination Exposes Honey Bees to Pesticides Which Alters Their Susceptibility to the Gut Pathogen *Nosema ceranae*." *PLoS ONE* 8, no. 7. https://journals.plos.org/plosone/article?id=10.1371/journal.pone.0070182.

Pickering, Andrew. 1995. *The Mangle of Practice: Time, Agency, and Science*. Chicago: Chicago University Press.

Pinto, Carlos F., D. Torrico-Bazoberry, M, Penna, R. Cossio-Rodríguez, R. Cocroft, H. Appel, and H. M. Niemeyer. 2019. "Chemical Responses of Nicotiana tabacum (Solanaceae) Induced by Vibrational Signals of a Generalist Herbivore." *Journal of Chemical Ecology* 45, no. 8: 708–14. https://doi.org/10.1007/s10886-019-01089-x.

Pollan, Michael. 2001. *The Botany of Desire: A Plant's-Eye View of the World.* New York: Random House.
Porcar, Manuel, and Andrés Moya. 2010. "Craig Venter's Synthetic Bacteria: The Dawn of a New Era?" *Journal of Cosmology* 8. http://cosmology.com/ArtificialLife100.html#4.
Post, Eric, and Mads C. Forchhammer. 2002. "Synchronization of Animal Population Dynamics by Large-Scale Climate." *Nature* 420: 168–71.
Powell, Kristin, Jonathan M. Chase, and Tiffany M. Knight. 2013. "Invasive Plants Have Scale-Dependent Effects on Diversity by Altering Species-Area Relationships." *Science* 339: 316–18.
Prigogine, Ilya. 2003. *Is Future Given?* London: World Scientific Press.
Pulido, Laura. 2018. "Racism and the Anthropocene." In *Future Remains: A Cabinet of Curiosities for the Anthropocene*, edited by Gregg Mitman, Marco Armiero, and Robert S. Emmett, 116–28. Chicago: University of Chicago Press.
Purdy, Jedediah. 2015. *After Nature: A Politics for the Anthropocene.* Cambridge, MA: Harvard University Press.
Pyne, Stephen J. 2004. *Tending Fire: Coping with America's Wildland Fires.* Washington, DC: Island Press.
Quammen, David. 2020. "We Made the Coronavirus Epidemic." *New York Times*, January 28, 2020. https:// www.nytimes.com/2020/01/28/opinion/coronavirus china.html.
Quick, Deren. 2011. "Scientists Make First Step Toward Bringing Life to Inorganic Matter." *New Atlas*, September 16. http://www.gizmag.com/bringing-life-to-inoganic-matter/19855.
Quigley, Peter. 2012. *Housing the Environmental Imagination: Politics, Beauty, and Refuge in American Nature Writing.* Newcastle upon Tyne: Cambridge Scholars.
Raglon, Rebecca. 2009. "The Post Natural Wilderness and Its Writers." *Journal of Eco-Criticism.* 1, no. 1: 60–66.
Rainforest Concern. n.d. "Why Are Rainforests Are Being Destroyed?" Accessed December 20, 2021. https://www.rainforestconcern.org/forest-facts/why-are-rainforests-being-destroyed.
Reid, Julian. 2020. "Constructing Human Versus Non-Human Climate Migration in the Anthropocene: The Case of Migrating Polar Bears in Nunavut, Canada." *Anthropocenes—Human, Inhuman, Posthuman* 1, no. 1: 1–12.
Reith, Frank. 2011. "Life in the Deep Surface." *Geological Society of America* 39, no. 3: 287–88.
Revkin, Andrew. 2011. "Confronting the Anthropocene." *New York Times* (Dot Earth blog), May 11, 2011. https://dotearth.blogs.nytimes.com/2011/05/11/confronting-the-anthropocene.
Rigby, Kate. 2014. "Confronting Catastrophe: Ecocriticism in a Warming World." In *The Cambridge Companion to Literature and the Environment*, edited by Louise Westling, 212–25. New York: Cambridge University Press.
Ripple, William J., Christopher Wolf, Thomas M. Newsome, Phoebe Bernard, and William R. Moomaw. 2020. "World Scientists' Warning of a Climate Emergency." *BioScience* 70, no. 1: 8–12. https://doi.org/10.1093/biosci/biz088.
Ripple, William J., Christopher Wolf, Thomas M. Newsome, Mauro Galetti, Mohammed Alamgir, Eileen Crist, Mahmoud I. Mahmoud, and William F. Laurance. 2017. "World Scientists' Warning to Humanity: A Second Notice." *BioScience* 67, no. 12: 1026–28. https://doi.org/10.1093/biosci/bix125.

Robinson, Kim Stanley. 2020. "The Coronavirus Is Rewriting Our Imaginations." *The New Yorker*, May 1, 2020. https://www.newyorker.com/culture/annals-of-inquiry/the-coronavirus-and-our future.

Rose, Deborah Bird. 2017. "Shimmer: When All You Love Is Being Thrashed." In *Arts of Living on a Damaged Planet: Ghosts of the Anthropocene*, edited by Anna Tsing, Heather Swanson, Elaine Gan, and Nils Bubandt, G51–63. Minneapolis: University of Minnesota Press.

———. 2018. "Gifts of Life in the Shadow of Death." *HumanNature* Series, Sydney Environment Institute and the Australian Museum. Lecture. March 2018.

Rosler, Martha, Caroline Walker Bynum, Natasha Eaton, Michael Ann Holly, Amelia Jones, Michael Kelly, Robin Kelsey, Alisa LaGamma, Monika Wagner, Oliver Watson, and Tristan Weddigen. 2013. "Notes from the Field: Materiality." *The Art Bulletin* 95, no. 1: 10–37.

Ruiz, Nicholas, III. 2008. *America in Absentia*. United States: Intertheory Press.

Sagan, Carl. 1994. *Pale Blue Dot: A Vision of the Human Future in Space*. New York: Ballantine Books.

Samaddar, Ranabir. 2017. "The Ecological Migrant in Postcolonial Time." *In Life Adrift: Climate Change, Migration, Critique,* edited by Andrew Baldwin and Giovanni Bettini, 177–93. London: Rowman & Littlefield.

Sample, Ian. 2010. "Craig Venter Creates Synthetic Life Form." *The Guardian*, May 20, 2010. http://www.guardian.co.uk/science/2010/may/20/craig-venter-synthetic-life-form.

Satterfield, Terre, and Scott Slovic, eds. 2004. *What's Nature Worth? Narrative Expressions of Environmental Values*. Salt Lake City: University of Utah Press.

Schauder, Stephen, and Bonnie L. Bassler. 2001. "The Languages of Bacteria." *Genes and Development* 15: 1468–80.

Scheffers, Brett R., et al. 2016. "The Broad Footprint of Climate Change from Genes to Biomes to People" (Editor's Summary: Accumulating Impacts). *Science* 354, no. 6313: 716–32.

Schmidt, Jeremy J., Peter G. Brown, and Christopher J. Orr. 2016. "Ethics in the Anthropocene: A Research Agenda." *The Anthropocene Review* 3, no. 3: 188–200.

Schwartz, Jill. 2015. "11 of the World's Most Threatened Forests." *World Wildlife Fund*, April 17, 2015. https://www.worldwildlife.org/stories/11-of-the-world-s-most-threatened-forests.

Serres, Michel. 2012. *Biogea*. Translated by Randolph Burks. Minneapolis: Univocal Publishing.

Settele, Josef, Sandra Díaz, Eduardo Brondizio, and Dr. Peter Daszak. 2020. "COVID-19 Stimulus Measures Must Save Lives, Protect Livelihoods, and Safeguard Nature to Reduce the Risk of Future Pandemics." *IPBES*, April 27, 2020. https://ipbes.net/covid19stimulus.

Sharrock, Robert A. 1992. "Plant Photoperception: The Phytochrome System." In *Development: The Molecular Genetic Approach*, edited by Vincenzo E. A. Russo, Stuart Brody, David Cove, and Sergio Ottolenghi, 194–205. Berlin: Springer-Verlag.

Sheldrake, Merlin. 2020. *Entangled Life: How Fungi Make Our Worlds, Change Our Minds and Shape Our Future*. New York: Random House.

Slovic, Paul, and Scott Slovic. 2004/2005. "Numbers and Nerves: Toward an Effective Apprehension of Environmental Risk." *Whole Terrain: A Journal Reflective Environmental Practice* 13: 14–18.

Slovic, Scott. 2001. "Introduction." In *Getting over the Color Green: Contemporary Environmental Literature of the Southwest*, edited by Scott Slovic, xv–xxviii. Tucson: University of Arizona Press.

———. 2017. "Seasick Among the Waves of Ecocriticism: An Inquiry into Alternative Historiographic Metaphors." In *Environmental Humanities: Voices from the Anthropocene*, edited by Serpil Oppermann and Serenella Iovino, 99–111. London: Rowman & Littlefield.

Smith, David Thomas. n.d. Anthropocene Photographs. *LensCulture*. Accessed April 25, 2021. https://www.lensculture.com/articles/david-thomas-smith-anthropocene.

Smith, Keith, and David N. Petley. (1991) 2007. *Environmental Hazards: Assessing Risk and Reducing Disaster*. 5th ed. New York: Routledge.

Solnit, Rebecca. 2007. *Storming the Gates of Paradise: Landscapes for Politics*. Berkeley: University of California Press.

———. 2020. "'The Impossible Has Already Happened': What Coronavirus Can Teach Us About Hope." *The Guardian*, April 11, 2020. https://www.theguardian.com/world/2020/apr/07/what-coronavirus-can-teach-us-about-hope-rebecca-solnit.

Sönmez, Yücel. 2016."Dağ ceylanları: Yaşamak için sınırları kaldırdılar" [Mountain gazelles have overthrown borders to survive]. *Hürriyet*, November 26, 2016. http://www.hurriyet.com.tr/dag-ceylanlari-yasamak-icin-sinirlari-kaldirdilar-40288943.

Steffen, Will, Paul Crutzen, and John R. McNeill. 2007. "The Anthropocene: Are Humans Now Overwhelming the Great Forces of Nature?" *Ambio* 36, no. 8: 614–21.

Steffen, Will, Jacques Grinevald, Paul Crutzen, and John McNeill. 2011. "The Anthropocene: Conceptual and Historical Perspectives." *Philosophical Transactions of the Royal Society: Mathematical, Physical and Engineering Sciences* 36, no. 1938: 842–67.

Steffen, Will, et al. 2015. "Planetary Boundaries: Guiding Human Development on a Changing Planet." *Science* 347, no. 6223: 736–46. https://science.sciencemag.org/content/347/6223/1259855/tab-figures-data.

Steffen, Will, et al. 2018. "Trajectories of the Earth System in the Anthropocene." *PNAS: Proceedings of the National Academy of Sciences of the United States of America* 115, no. 33: 8252–59.

Stengers, Isabelle. 2015. *In Catastrophic Times: Resisting the Coming Barbarism*. Translated by Andrew Goffey. London: Open Humanities Press.

Sterling, Colin, and Rodney Harrison. 2020. "Introduction: Of Territories and Temporalities." In *Deterritorializing the Future: Heritage in, of and after the Anthropocene*, edited by Rodney Harrison and Colin Sterling, 19–54. London: Open Humanities Press.

Stirling, Ian. 2002. "Polar Bears and Seals in the Eastern Beaufort Sea and Amundsen Gulf: A Synthesis of Population Trends and Ecological Relationships over Three Decades." *Arctic* 55: 59–76.

Stirling, Ian, N. J. Lunn, and J. Iacozza. 1999. "Long-Term Trends in the Population Ecology of Polar Bears in Western Hudson Bay in Relation to Climate Change." *Arctic* 52: 294–306.

Stohlgren, Thomas J., and Marcel Rejmánek. 2014. "No Universal Scale-Dependent Impacts of Invasive Species on Native Plant Species Richness." *Biology Letters* 10, no. 1: 2–5.

Struzik, Edward. 2017. *Firestorm: How Wildfire Will Shape Our Future*. Washington, DC: Island Press.

Subramanian, Meera. 2019."Anthropocene Now: Influential Panel Votes to Recognize Earth's New Epoch." *Nature,* May 21, 2019. https://www.nature.com/articles/d41586-019-01641-5.

Sullivan, Heather I. 2012. "Dirt Theory and Material Ecocriticism." Special Collection: "Material Ecocriticism," edited by Dana Phillips and Heather I. Sullivan. *ISLE: Interdisciplinary Studies in Literature and Environment* 19, no. 3: 476–93.

Sullivan, Robert. 2006. *The Meadowlands: Wilderness Adventures on the Edge of New York City.* London: Granta Books.

Swanson, Heather, Anna Tsing, Nils Bubandt, and Elaine Gan. 2017. "Introduction: Bodies Tumbled into Bodies." In *Arts of Living on a Damaged Planet: Monsters of the Anthropocene,* edited by Anna Tsing, Heather Swanson, Elaine Gan, and Nils Bubandt, M1–12. Minneapolis: University of Minnesota Press.

Swimme, Brian. 1988. "The Cosmic Creation Story." In *The Reenchantment of Science: Postmodern Proposals,* edited by David Ray Griffin, 47–56. Albany: State University of New York Press.

———. 1998. "The Cultural Significance of the Story of the Universe." *The Epic of Evolution Quarterly* 2: 1–5. http://thegreatstory.org/Epic-Evol-Journal.html.

Swimme, Brian T., and Mary E. Tucker. 2011. *Journey of the Universe.* New Haven, CT: Yale University Press.

Switzer, David, and Nicole Frances Angeli. 2016. "Human and Non-Human Migration: Understanding Species Introduction and Translocation through Migration Ethics." *Environmental Values* 25: 443–63.

Syvitski, Jaia, et al. 2020. "Extraordinary Human Energy Consumption and Resultant Geological Impacts Beginning Around 1950 CE Initiated the proposed Anthropocene Epoch." *Communications: Earth & Environment* 1, no. 32. https://www.nature.com/articles/s43247-020-00029-y.pdf.

Szeman, Imre. 2020. "Ends." In *Anthropocene Unseen: A Lexicon,* edited by Cymene Howe and Anand Pandian, 145–48. New York: Punctum Books.

Thill, Brian. 2017. *Waste.* New York: Bloomsbury Academic.

Thomashow, Mitchell. 2002. *Bringing the Biosphere Home: Learning to Perceive Global Environmental Change.* Cambridge, MA: MIT Press.

Tölgyessy, Juraj. 1993. "Water, Air and Soil—Fundamental Sources of the Biosphere." In *Chemistry and Biology of Water, Air and Soil: Environmental Aspects,* edited by Juraj Tölgyessy, 3–13. Vol. 53. London: Elsevier.

Tsing, Anna Lowenhaupt. 2005. *An Ethnography of Global Connection.* Princeton, NJ: Princeton University Press.

———. 2015. *The Mushroom at the End of the World: On the Possibility of Life in Capitalist Ruins.* Princeton, NJ: Princeton University Press.

———. 2018. "The New Wild." *The Clearing* (online journal of Little Toller Books), December 6, 2018. https://www.littletoller.co.uk/the-clearing/the-new-wild-by-anna-tsing.

Tsing, Anna, Heather Swanson, Elaine Gan, and Nils Bubandt. 2017. "Inhabiting Multispecies Bodies." In *Arts of Living on a Damaged Planet: Monsters of the Anthropocene,* edited by Anna Tsing, Heather Swanson, Elaine Gan, and Nils Bubandt, M23. Minneapolis: University of Minnesota Press.

Tsuchida, Tsutomu, et al. 2010. "Symbiotic Bacterium Modifies Aphid Body Color." *Science* 330: 1102–4.

Tuana, Nancy. 2008. "Viscous Porosity: Witnessing Katrina." In *Material Feminisms*, edited by Stacy Alaimo and Susan Hekman, 188–213. Bloomington: Indiana University Press.

Turpin, Tom. 2012. "Insects See the Light." *On Six Legs (Purdue Extension)*, June 2012. https://www.asec.purdue.edu/natural_resources/4-H,NR,Projects/Projects /entomology/ TurpinArticles/Insects%20See%20the%20Light.pdf.

Ussery, David W. 2010."One Small Step for Bacteria, or One Giant Leap for Mankind?" *Journal of Cosmology*, June 8, 2010. http://cosmology.com/ArtificialLife100 .html#3.

Uzuner, Buket. 2008. *Istanbullu*. Translated by Kenneth J. Dakan. Istanbul: Everest Press.

van der Tuin, Iris. 2011. "The New Materialist 'Always Already': On an A-Human Humanities." *NORA: Nordic Journal of Feminist and Gender Research* 19, no. 4: 285–90.

van Dooren, Thom. 2014. *Flight Ways: Life and Loss at the Edge of Extinction*. New York: Columbia University Press.

———. 2020. [Memorial] "Story(telling)." *Swamphen: A Journal of Cultural Ecology* 7: 1–2.

van Dooren, Thom, and Deborah Bird Rose. 2012. "Storied-Places in a Multispecies City." *Humanimalia: A Journal of Human/Animal Interface Studies* 3, no. 2: 1–27.

———. 2017. "Lively Ethography: Storying Animist Worlds." In *Environmental Humanities: Voices from the Anthropocene*, edited by Serpil Oppermann and Serenella Iovino, 255–71. New York: Rowman & Littlefield.

Vermeulen, Pieter. 2020. *Literature and the Anthropocene*. London: Routledge.

Vidal, John. 2011. "UN Environment Programme: 200 Species Extinct Every Day, Unlike Anything Since Dinosaurs Disappeared 65 Million Years Ago." *Huffpost*, August 17, 2010. Updated May 26, 2011. https://www.huffingtonpost.com.au /2010/08/17/un-environment-programme-_n_684562.html.

Vigil, Sara. 2015. "Displacement as a Consequence of Climate Change Mitigation Policies." *Forced Migration Review* 49: 43–45.

Vogel, Steven. 2015. *Thinking like a Mall: Environmental Philosophy after the End of Nature*. Cambridge, MA: MIT Press.

Walia, Arjun. 2014. "New Harvard Study Proves Why the Bees Are All Disappearing." *Collective Evolution*, May 15, 2014. https://www.collective-evolution.com/2014/05 /15/new-harvard-study-proves-why-the-bees-are-all-disappearing.

Wapner, Paul. 2014. "The Changing Nature of Nature: Environmental Politics in the Anthropocene." *Global Environmental Politics* 14, no. 4: 36–54.

Wassen, Trudy M. 2012. *Bacteria: The Benign, the Bad, and the Beautiful*. Hoboken, NJ: Wiley-Blackwell.

Waters, Colin N., et al. 2016. "The Anthropocene Is Functionally and Stratigraphically Distinct from the Holocene." *Science* 351, no. 6269: 137; aad2622-1–10.

"'We Declare Our Support for Extinction Rebellion': An Open Letter from Australia's Academics." 2019. *The Guardian*, September 19, 2019. https://www.theguardian .com/science/2019/sep/20/we-declare-our-support-for-extinction-rebellion-an -open-letter-from-australias-academics.

Weir, Jessica K. 2009. *Murray River Country: An Ecological Dialogue with Traditional Owners*. Canberra: Aboriginal Studies Press.

Wendle, John. 2015. "The Ominous Story of Syria's Climate Refugees." *Scientific American*, December 17, 2015. https://www.scientificamerican.com/article/ominous-story-of-syria-climate-refugees.

Wheeler, John Archibald. 1978. "The 'Past' and the 'Delayed-Choice' Double-Slit Experiment." In *Mathematical Foundations of Quantum Theory*, edited by A. R. Marlow, 9–48. New York: Academic Press.

Wheeler, Wendy. 2011. "The Biosemiotic Turn: Abduction, or, The Nature of Creative Reason in Nature and Culture." In *Ecocritical Theory: New European Approaches*, edited by Axel Goodbody and Kate Rigby, 270–82. Charlottesville: University of Virginia Press.

———. 2014. "Natural Play, Natural Metaphor, and Natural Stories: Biosemiotic Realism." In *Material Ecocriticism*, edited by Serenella Iovino and Serpil Oppermann, 67–79. Bloomington: Indiana University Press.

White, Hayden. 1980. "The Value of Narrativity in the Representation of Reality." *Critical Inquiry* 7, no. 1: 5–27.

Whitehead, Alfred North. (1925) 1948. *Science and the Modern World*. New York: Pelican Mentor Book.

———. (1929) 1978. *Process and Reality: An Essay in Cosmology* (Corrected edition). New York: The Free Press.

Whitehead, Mark. 2014. *Environmental Transformations: A Geography of the Anthropocene*. London: Routledge.

Williams, Roger. 2013. *The Fisherman of Halicarnassus: The Man Who Made Bodrum Famous*. London: Bristol Book Press.

Willmer, Pat, Dara A. Stanley, Karin Steijven, Iain M. Matthews, and Clive V. Nuttman. 2009. "Bidirectional Flower Color and Shape Changes Allow a Second Opportunity for Pollination." *Current Biology* 19, no. 11: 919–23.

Wilson, Edward O. 2002. *The Future of Life*. New York: Vintage Books.

———. 2017. "Afterword." In *Living in the Anthropocene: Earth in the Age of Humans*, edited by W. John Kress and Jeffrey K. Stine, 161–64. Washington, DC: Smithsonian Books.

———. 2019. "Foreword." In *Biodiversity and Climate Change: Transforming the Biosphere*, edited by Thomas E. Lovejoy and Lee Hannah, xi–xii. New Haven, CT: Yale University Press.

Wince, Gaia. 2014. *Adventures in the Anthropocene: A Journey into the Heart of the Planet We Made*. Minneapolis: Milkweed Editions.

Winterson, Jeanette. 1997. *Gut Symmetries*. London: Granta Books.

Wisner, Ben, Piers Blaikie, Terry Cannon, and Ian Davis. 2004. *At Risk: Natural Hazards, People's Vulnerability and Disasters*. 2nd ed. New York: Routledge.

Wood, David. 2005. *The Step Back: Ethics and Politics After Deconstruction*. Albany: State University of New York Press.

Woods, Derek. 2014. "Scale Critique of the Anthropocene." *Minnesota Review* 83: 133–42.

World Bank. 2016. *The World Bank Annual Report*. Washington, DC: World Bank. https://openknowledge.worldbank.org/handle/10986/24985.

Wright, Angus. 2017."Environmental Degradation As a Cause of Migration: Cautionary Tales from Brazil." In *Environmental History of Modern Migrations*, edited by Marco Armiero and Richard Tucker, 159–76. London: Routledge.

Xu, Chi, Timothy A. Kohler, Timothy M. Lenton, Jens-Christian Svenning, and Marten Scheffer. 2020. "Future of the Human Climate Niche." *PNAS* 117, no. 21: 11350–55.

Yaeger, Patricia. 2008. "Editor's Column: The Death of Nature and the Apotheosis of Trash; or, Rubbish Ecology." *PMLA* 123: 321–39.

Yazgünoğlu, Kerim Can. 2019. "The Postecological World of John Burnside: Dark Green Nature, Pollution, and Eco-Grief in *Glister*." *DTCF Dergisi* 59, no. 1: 41–69.

Yong, Ed. 2016. *I Contain Multitudes: The Microbes Within Us and a Grander View of Life*. London: Vintage.

Yusoff, Kathryn. 2013. "Geologic Life: Prehistory, Climate, Futures in the Anthropocene." *Environment and Planning D: Society and Space* 31: 779–95.

Zalasiewicz, Jan. 2008. *The Earth After Us: What Legacy Will Humans Leave in the Rocks?* New York: Oxford University Press.

———. 2017. "The Extraordinary Strata of the Anthropocene." In *Environmental Humanities: Voices from the Anthropocene*, edited by Serpil Oppermann and Serenella Iovino, 115–31. New York: Rowman & Littlefield.

Zalasiewicz, Jan, Colin N. Waters, and Mark Williams. 2014. "Human Bioturbation, and the Subterranean Landscape of the Anthropocene." *Anthropocene* 6: 1–23.

Zalasiewicz, Jan, Colin N. Waters, Mark Williams, and Anthony D. Barnosky. 2019. "Technofossil Stratigraphy." In *The Anthropocene as a Geological Time Unit: A Guide to the Scientific Evidence and Current Debate*, edited by Jan Zalasiewicz, Colin N. Waters, Mark Williams, and Colin P. Summerhayes, 144–47. Cambridge: Cambridge University Press.

Zalasiewicz, Jan, Mark Williams, Will Steffen, and Paul Crutzen. 2010. "The New World of the Anthropocene." *Environmental Science and Technology* 44: 2228–31.

Zalasiewicz, Jan, Mark Williams, Colin N. Waters, Anthony D. Barnosky, and Peter Haff. 2014. "The Technofossil Record of Humans." *The Anthropocene Review* 1, no. 1: 34–43.

Zapf, Hubert. 2016. *Literature as Cultural Ecology: Sustainable Texts*. London: Bloomsbury.

Zhou, Xiaojing. 2017. "'Slow Violence' in Migrant Landscapes: 'Hollow Villages' and Tourist River Towns in China." Special Cluster: Migrant Ecologies in an (Un)-bordered World, coordinated by Serpil Oppermann, Serenella Iovino, and Zhou Xiaojing. *ISLE: Interdisciplinary Studies in Literature and Environment* 24, no. 2: 274–91.

Zylinska, Joanna. 2014. *Minimal Ethics for the Anthropocene*. Ann Arbor, MI: Open Humanities Press.

Index

A Natural Theology for Our Time
  (Hartshorne), 25
abiotic
  actors, 52
  agencies, 163
  agents, 34
  co-emergence, 8
  environment, 54, 112
  flows, 13
  material entities, 150
  material forces, 6, 58
  matter, 35
  as matter's components, 20
  objects, 2
Abram, David, 1, 2, 6, 13, 19, 23, 24, 37,
  39–41, 65, 66, 141, 142, 146, 159,
  163, 168
actants, 3, 37, 41
  See also Bennett, Jane; Latour, Bruno
actual entities, 26, 31, 172n8, 172n9
  See Whitehead, Alfred North
After Nature (Purdy), 112
agency, 5–6, 20–21, 23–24, 27, 34–37, 46,
  64, 65, 76, 117, 143, 147, 163–64
  alien, 24
  anthropocene, 2, 9, 48, 61, 65
  autonomous, 29, 163–64, 165, 171n1
  creative, 23
  distributive (distributed), 6, 26, 27
  expressive, 3, 146
  human, 16, 18–19, 23, 57–58, 61, 74,
    150, 154
  material, 3, 19–20, 27, 36, 38
  nonhuman, 19, 22–23, 37, 52, 61, 64,
    67, 72, 141, 152
  polychromatic, 150
  vibrant, 7
  See also narrative agency

agential realism, 37
  performances, 38
  See also Barad, Karen
Akaş, Cem, 76
  See also E-Motions
Akdeniz, 147
"Akdeniz Balıklarının Marifetleri"
  (Fisherman), 150–51
Alaimo, Stacy, 16, 19, 51, 56, 57, 58, 60,
  66–67, 79, 168, 171n1
Albrect, Glenn A., 106, 122, 125
algae blooms, 119
Alliance of World Scientists, 172n2
  See also Ripple, William J., et al.
America in Absentia (Ruiz), 110
Anatolia, 101, 146, 151–52, 176n7
Anatolian cultures, 152, 176n7
Anderson, Kayla, 74
"An Environmental Humanities Response
  to the COVID-19 Pandemic," 92,
  174n8
animal migration, 90
  See also nonhuman: immigrants,
    migrants, refugees
Anthropocene Working Group (AWG),
  173n5
Anthropocene Working Group of the
  International Commission on
  Stratigraphy, 52
Anthropocene Working Group of the
  International Union of Geologic
  Sciences (IUGS), 8, 50
anthropocentric, 14, 91, 131
  arrogance, 51
  "copyright control" (Morton), 64
  discourses, 25
  discursive formations, 106
  ideological codes, 162

anthropocentric (*continued*)
  ideologies, 68
  imaginary, 5
  knowledge, 124
  paradigm, 14
  perspective, 157
  reasons, 86
  values, and thought, 23, 73
anthropocentrism, 16, 44, 58, 63, 109, 157, 162
anthropogenic
  changes, 8, 61, 79
  climate change, 47
  contamination, 115
  crises, 68
  global heating, 53
  landscapes, 78, 113
  planetary change, 59
  processes, 156
  signature, 10, 115
  threats, 171n1
  transformations, 53, 103, 125
anthropomorphism, 41, 63, 65
anthropos (*anthropoi*), 8–9, 48, 50–51, 54, 57–60, 62, 63, 68–70, 73–74, 76, 78, 100, 173n10
anthroturbation, 55–56, 65
  lithic index of, 56
  technostratigraphic effects, 115
  See also bioturbation
Appel H. M, and R. B. Cocroft, 34
aquatic (domains, environments, habitats), 4, 149
  stories, 29
Armiero, Marco, 116–17, 168
  See also wasteocene; *Wasteocene*
Armiero, Marco, and Massimo De Angelis, 10, 116
Armiero, Marco, and Richard Tucker, 83
Art in the Anthropocene (Davis and Turpin), 73
Arts of Living on a Damaged Planet (Tsing, Swanson, Gan, and Bubandt), 171n2
Åsberg, Cecilia, 119, 168
  See also feminist posthumanities
Åsberg, Cecilia, and Rosi Braidotti, 161
Åsberg, Cecilia, Redi Kooback, and Ericka Johnson, 5
Askin, Ridvan, 40

Atwood, Margaret, 18
Australian academics. *See* "We Declare Our Support for Extinction Rebellion"

Bachelard, Gaston, 136
bacteria, 18–21, 28–29, 30, 33, 68, 70, 71, 72, 91
Balcı, Adem, 125, 168
Baldwin, Andrew, 82
Baldwin, Andrew, and Giovanni Bettini, 88, 90–91, 97–98
Barad, Karen, 1, 13, 14, 16–17, 19, 23, 24, 37–38, 43, 61, 158, 161, 169
Bardini, Thierry, 117
Barthes, Roland, 173n10
Bateson, Gregory, 41, 124, 130
becoming(s), 14, 17, 35, 37, 45, 59, 63, 69, 73, 78, 107, 117, 130, 141, 164, 172nn8–9
  agentic, 6
  creative, 14, 22, 25–27, 29, 30, 36–37, 39, 41–43, 64, 138
  dynamic, 20–21
  earthly, 78, 105
  expressive, 14, 27, 29, 137
  generative, 61
  intra-active, 17, 24
  multispecies, 143
  See also agency; Hartshorne, Charles; matter
Becoming Animal (Abram), 66
becoming with, 72, 105
bees, 30, 140, 143, 157, 158, 163
Beirne, Piers, and Caitlin Kelty-Huber, 86
Bennett, Jane, 18, 20, 21, 22, 23, 36, 39, 41, 67, 88, 152, 161, 163, 168
Betts, Alexander, Evan Easton-Calabria, and Kate Pincock, 93
biochromes, 137, 145, 176n6
Biodiversity and Climate Change (Lovejoy and Lee), 45
Biogea (Serres), 2, 162
biomes, 4, 60, 65, 66, 72, 132
biosphere, 8, 10, 11, 12, 18, 49, 56, 59, 106, 111, 116, 118, 119–20, 134, 136, 138, 142, 156, 159, 171n3
biospheric life, 108, 120
bioturbation, 53–55, 61, 62, 64–65, 68
  See also anthroturbation

Birch, Charles, 34
  See also Hartshorne, Charles; relationality; Whitehead, Alfred North
Blanchard, Jacob, 88
Bleicher, Steven, 139, 140, 144
Bodrum (Halicarnassus), 146, 148–50, 152, 159, 176nn3–7, 177n9
  See also Fisherman of Halicarnassus
Bohm, David, 23, 24, 35, 140
Bohm, David, and B. J. Hiley, 32
Bohm, David, and David F. Peat, 12, 161
Bosphorus, 67, 101
Botany of Desire, The (Pollan), 6
Boyd, Roger, 133
Bradley, James, 121, 130
Braidotti, Rosi, 37, 67, 91, 168
Brown, Frank A., 145
Brown, Frank A., et al., 137
Brown, Lester R., 103
Bryant, Levi R., 4, 14, 157, 171n1
Bubandt, Nils, 143
Buell, Lawrence, 102
Burnside, John, 126, 129
  See also *Glister*

Callaway, Ewen, 21
  See also iCHELLS
Carranza, Nancy, 40
Carroll, Bruce, 74
Cartesian
  dreams of control, 68
  dualism, 33
  view of life, 35
Castree, Noel, 111
Center for PostNatural History, 111, 175n6
Chaisson, Eric, 40–41, 42
Chakrabarty, Dipesh, 57, 89
Chiacu, Doina, and Valerie Volcovici, 173n7
Chroma (Jarman), 136
chromoscapes, 139
chromospheres, 146
Clare, Eli, 132–33
Clark, Nigel, 53, 97, 115
Clark, Timoty, 57, 60, 118
cli-fi (climate change fiction), 107, 121, 125
climate change, 8, 24, 45, 47–48, 52, 53–54, 58, 59, 72, 79–85, 88–90, 92, 98, 100, 107, 109, 113, 119, 123, 125, 155, 156, 164, 172n1, 173nn6–7 (ch. 2), 173n12 (ch. 2), 173n1 (ch. 3), 175n8
climate refugees, 81–83, 85, 87–88, 93, 97
Cobb John B., Jr., 35
coexistence, 5, 14, 21, 28, 30, 49, 72, 112, 115, 129, 145, 152, 156, 161
Cohen, Jeffrey, J., 3, 11, 16, 37, 39, 41, 42, 48, 52, 59, 60, 64, 65, 66, 70, 72, 114, 135–36, 138, 150, 151, 154–56, 158, 176n7
Cohen, Jeffrey J., and Lowell Duckert, 66
Colebrook, Claire, 4, 14, 51, 104, 168
coloration, 141, 145, 150
Companion Species Manifesto, The (Haraway), 17, 171n2
compound individuals, 15, 25–31, 33, 36–39, 43, 169, 172n8
  See also Hartshorne, Charles
Constantine, Kate, 94
Contemporary Color (Bleicher), 139, 140, 144
Coole, Diana, 37
Coole, Diana, and Samantha Frost, 21, 26, 30, 36
Cooper, Geoffrey J. T., et al., 20–21
  See also iCHELLs
Couldrey, Marion, and Jenny Peebles, 85
COVID-19 (coronavirus), 11, 22, 45–46, 67, 92–93, 109, 174n8
Cox, Kieran D., et al., 155
Crawford, Ian, 149
  See also Fisherman of Halicarnassus
creative experience(s), 15, 16, 20, 26, 28–29, 31, 36, 40, 43, 142
Creative Synthesis and Philosophic Method (Hartshorne), 25
creativity, 5, 7, 11, 13, 14–15, 16, 17, 21, 24–30, 33, 36–37, 39, 43, 66, 97, 108, 149, 150, 151, 162, 172n8
Crist, Eileen, 51
"Crochet Coral Reef" project, 173n12
Cronon, William, 158
Crutzen, Paul J., and Eugene Stoermer, 49, 50–52
Cubitt, Sean, 132
cultural ecology, 136

cultural imaginary(ies), 62, 64, 74, 95, 136, 151, 164, 165
Cyclades Islands, 148
See also Bodrum

Dannenberg, Astrid, and Sonja Zitzelsberger, 173n6
Davis, Heather, and Etienne Turpin, 73
Davis, Mike, 113
Decision IPCC/XLV-2, Sixth Assessment Report (AR6), 172n1
de-doxify, 58, 173n10
Degeorges, Patrick, 158
Degeorges, Patrick, and Serpil Opperman, 48, 138, 139, 140
DeLanda, Manuel, 4–5, 22, 37, 71
DeLoughrey, Elizabeth, 108
Demirsoy, Ali, 141, 143–44, 176n4
Democracy of Objects, The (Bryant), 171n1
Denizen, Seth, 69
Derocher, Andrew E., Nicholas J. Lunn, and Ian Sterling, 89
Derrida, Jacques, 2
Devlin, Hannah, 176n2
Dibley, Ben, 52, 72
Di Chiro, Giovanna, 118, 175n10
Dickinson, Adam, 53, 168
diffractive thinking, 17
See also Barad, Karen
Dillard, Annie, 16
disanthropocentric, 57, 78, 89, 131
See also nonanthropocentric
disenchantment (disenchanted), 43–44, 68, 75, 115, 122, 131, 156
Doerr, Anthony, 18
doxa, 173n10
Duckert, Lowell, 168
Dunn, Oliva, and Francois Gemenne, 86
Düren, Rahşan (installation artist), 10, 73–78

Earth After Us, The (Zalasiewicz), 51
Earth Charter, 161, 177n1
ecology(ies)
anthropocene, 112
Bodrum, 176n7
colors, 11, 162, 137, 139, 147, 152, 154, 156–60, 162
cultural, 17, 136

dark, 11, 115, 152, 155–56, 165
forests, 107
green, 141–42, 147
migrant, 11, 79–105
nonanthropocentric, 158
plant, 94
political, 100
postgreen, 156
postnatural, 10, 106–132
prismatic, 10, 139
rubbish, 117
ecological imaginary(ies), 62–63, 74, 95, 136, 151, 164–65
ecological intelligence, 143, 176n5
ecophobia, 4, 46
ecosystem engineering, 54–55
Ege'den Denize Bırakılmış Bir Çiçek (Fisherman), 146, 152
Elementals, The (Llywelyn, novel), 5
Ellsworth, Elizabeth, and Jamie Kruse, 56
E-Motions (Düren, art installation), 10, 73–78
Endangered Species Act (US), 88
End of Nature, The (McKibben) 113–14, 155
endosymbiosis, 28
Enroth, Henrik, 106
environmental ethics, 100, 155
Environmental History of Modern Migrations (Armiero and Tucker), 83
entanglement(s), 7, 9, 17, 18, 28, 37, 49, 52, 62, 72, 73, 74, 92, 96, 103, 105, 107, 114, 115, 135–36, 143, 147, 148, 151, 155, 158, 159, 161–63
epipelagic zone, 108, 175n4
epistemology, 1, 152
Ergin, Meliz, 81–82
Estok, Simon C., 4, 46, 57, 111, 154, 157, 168
ethics
of responsibility, 48
of scale, 57, 59–60
expressive creativity, 8, 15, 36, 38, 162
See also compound individuals; Hartshorne, Charles; Whitehead, Alfred North

Farrier, David, 122
Fedrizzi, Alessandro et al., 33

feminist posthumanities, 5
Fernández, María José, 81
Fishel, Stefanie R., 29
Fisher, Malcolm, 96
Fisherman of Halicarnassus, 146–52, 158, 159, 176n3, 176nn7–8
Flight Ways (van Dooren), 87
Foote, Stephanie, 119
forced migration, 86, 88
Forced Migration Review (academic journal), 174n6
Frank, Priscilla, 174n9
Frank, Reith, 56

Gaard, Greta, 58, 99–100, 109
Gabbott, Sarah, Sarah Key, Catherine Russell, Yasmin Yohan, and Jan Zalasiewicz, 108
Gabet, Emmanuel J., O. J. Reichman, and Eric W. Seabloom, 54
Gadd, Jeremy, 95
Gagliano, Monica, 35, 70, 145, 162
Gan, Elaine, 35, 71, 99, 135, 162
Gan, Elaine, Anna Tsing, Heather Swanson, and Nils Bubandt, 162–63, 165
Gane, Nicholas (interview with Donna Haraway), 164
gazella gazella (mountain gazelles), 85
gedankenexperiment, 32
Geiger, Laura, 90
geobiochemical
  forces, 48, 52
  entities, 56
  human activities, 8–9, 57
geological epochality, 52, 60, 68
Geological Society Stratigraphy Commission, 8, 50
geomorphism, 56
geomorphology, 173n8
geomorphological processes, 49, 56, 109, 164, 174n8
geosphere, 8, 10, 49, 116, 173n8
GEOSS Platform (Global Earth Observation System of Systems' Platform), 173n1
geostory, 18, 28, 29, 52, 61, 107, 131
  See also Latour, Bruno
Getting over the Color Green (Slovic), 153

Geymen, Abdurrahman, and Ibrahim Baz, 101
Gibson, Daniel G. et al., 21, 171n5
Gienger, Michael, 145–46
Glick, Daniel, 46
Glister (Burnside, novel), 107, 121–31
Goldman Sachs Report (Khan), 53
Goleman, Daniel, 176n5
Great Pacific Garbage Patch, 111, 172n6
Grebenstein, Emily, 94, 174n10
Greiner, Clemens, and Patrick Sakdapolrak, 49
Griffin, David Ray, 27, 31, 33, 39–40, 156, 172n8, 175n8
  See also disenchantment; individuals (high-grade, low-grade); reenchantment; relationality
Griffiths, Matthew, 121
Grosz, Elizabeth, 37
  See also agency; matter
Gulf of Mexico, 156
Gunderson, Lance H., and Donald Ludwig, 132
  See also Holling, C. S., Lance H. Gunderson, and Donald Ludwig; panarchy
Grusin, Richard, 12
Gupta, V. P., 176n1

Hagopian, Joachim, 157
Hamilton, Clive, Christophe Bonneuil, and François Gemenne, 69
Hamilton, Stephen G., and Andrew E. Derocher, 89
Haraway, Donna, 4, 8, 13, 17–18, 26, 27, 49, 52–53, 58, 63, 68, 70, 72, 74, 86, 105, 109, 122, 126, 130, 131, 141, 143, 150, 164, 165, 168, 171n2, 173n12
Harrison, Summer, 70
Hartman, Steven, et al., 92
Hartman, Steven, and Serpil Oppermann, 46, 104, 172n2
Hartshorne, Charles, 15, 25–40, 42–43
  See also becoming(s): creative; compound individuals
Hassan, Nora, et al., 15
Haydarpaşa (train station in Istanbul), 74–76, 78
Hayles, N. Katherine, 14, 22, 46

Haynes, Patrice, 41, 172n7
Head, Lesley, 9, 48
Heise, Ursula K., 7, 110, 158, 168
Hekman, Susan, 22
Helmreich, Stefan, 157, 165
Heringman, Noah, 10–11, 49
Herman, David, 49, 172n3
Hill, Jessica, 174n11
Hird, Myra J., 117
Ho, Mae-Wan, and Fritz-Abert Popp, 140, 142
Holdren, John, 175n8
Holling, Crawford Buzz (also Holling, C. S.), 107–8, 132
See also panarchy
Holling, C. S., Lance H. Gunderson, and Donald Ludwig, 132, 134
See also panarchy
Holly, Michael Ann, 6
Holocene, 8, 50, 106
Holten, Katie, 63–64
Homer, 148–49, 152, 177n9
Homer-Dixon, Thomas, 107–8
Hong Kong Geological Survey, 173n8
Hulme, Mike, 97–98
Hunter, Lawrence E., 3–4
Huntingford, Chris, and Lina M. Mercado, 53, 80
hydraulic fracking, 62, 69
hydrocarbons, 56, 118
hydrosphere, 8, 10, 49, 116, 173n8
hypercapitalism, 121

iCHELLs, 20–21, 23
İmbat Serinliği, 159
Ingold, Tim, 42, 61
individuals (high grade, low-grade), 28–31, 33–35, 39, 172n9
See also compound individual; Hartshorne, Charles
Intergovernmental Panel on Climate Change (IPCC)'s Sixth Assessment Cycle, 47
Intergovernmental Science-Policy Platform on Biodiversity and Ecosystem Services, 92
International Union of Geologic Sciences (IUGS), 8, 50

intra-action, 19, 37, 52, 73
See also Barad, Karen
invasive species, 67, 72, 94–96, 132
Iovino, Serenella, and Serpil Oppermann, 16, 41, 61, 63
IPCC (Intergovernmental Panel on Climate Change, 2018), 46–48, 80, 172n1, 174n4
Istanbullu (Uzuner, novel), 101–2, 151

Jacques, Vincent, et al., 32
Jambeck, Jenna R. et al., 175n5
Jarman, Derek, 136
Jordan, Chris, 153, 172n10
Joseph, Jonathan, 122–23
Journey of the Universe (Swimme and Tucker), 165–66
Joy, Eileen, 5

kakosmos. *See* Latour, Bruno
Kamilo Beach, 152–53
Kapitza, Katharina, Heike Zimmermann, Berta Martin-Lopez, and Henrik von Wehrden, 95
Kaplan, Sarah, 45–46
Kauffman, Stuart A., 6, 29, 163–64
Kerry, John (US secretary of state), 53
Khan, Yusuf, 53
Kingsnorth, Paul, 112
Kirby, Vicki, 37, 71
Kitab-ı Bahriye (Reis), 177n9
Kleinman, Adam, 37
See also Barad, Karen
Kohn, Eduardo, 71, 124, 162–63
Kolbert, Elizabeth, 53, 118
Kolinjivadi, Vijay, 67
Konner, Jeremy, 171n6, 175n9
Krauss, Werner, 114
Kristensen, Erik, et al., 54

LaCugna, Catherine M., 25
Langston, Nancy, 110–11
Larson, Brendon M. H., 95, 96
Latour, Bruno, 2, 15, 42, 52, 107, 131, 132, 158, 171n2
Laysan Albatross, 43, 67, 153
Leakey, Richard, and Roger Lewin, 45
Lekan, Thomas M., 121

Llywelyn, Morgan, 5
LeMenager, Stephanie, 107, 120–21
LeMenager, Stephanie, and Stephanie Foot, 122
LeMenager, Teresa Shewry, and Ken Hiltner, 58
Lenton, Timothy M., et al., 172n2
Lewis, Joshua, 109
Lewis, Tanya, 88
Lidström, Susanna, Simon West, Tania Katzschner, M. Isabel Perez-Ramos, and Hedley Twidl, 59
Lovejoy, Thomas E., and Lee Hannah, 45
Löw, Martina, and Gunter Weidenhaus, 99
Luke, Timothy W, 111
Lustgarten, Abram, 83–84, 175n7

Macfarlane, Robert, 27, 42, 75
Majestic Plastic Bag, The (Konner, documentary), 171n6, 175n9
mangle, 19, 37
Maran, Timo, 66
Marchesini, Roberto, 12, 25, 40, 93
Marder, Michael, 93, 120
Margulis, Lynn, 28
 See also symbiogenesis
Marland, Pippa, and John Parham (2014), 117
Martinez, Amanda Rose, 177n10
material-discursive, 1, 16, 22, 63, 97, 98, 114, 152, 161
 See also Barad, Karen
material ecocriticism, 5, 7, 10, 13, 15–17, 23–25, 27, 36, 38, 44, 48, 61–64, 67, 136, 164
material-semiotic, 36, 64, 65, 141
 See also Haraway, Donna
matter (materiality)
 agentic, 7, 36
 expressive, 15, 22
 expressive dynamics, 44, 63
 semiotic, 15, 17
 storied, 136, 137, 162–63
 vibrant, 23, 36–38
 See also agency
Mavi Sürgün (Fisherman), 147
Mayburov, Serguey N., 15
Mayer, Emeran, 70

McDermott, Amy, 82
McKibben, Bill, 113–14, 155
Meadowlands, The (R. Sullivan), 23–24
Mediterranean, 81, 86, 97, 99, 108, 139, 146–51, 156, 158, 176nn3–7, 177n9
Meeting the Universe Halfway (Barad), 1
Mentz, Steve, 68–69
Mesle, Robert C., 32–33, 36
Meysman, Filip J. R., Jack J. Middelburg, and Carlo H. R. Heip, 54–55
Mezzadra, Sandro, and Brett Neilson, 99
microbial, 18, 28, 56, 62, 69, 91
 see also COVID-19
microclimate, 173n11
microplastics, 10, 93, 108, 115–16, 153, 155, 176n5
Midgley, Mary, 60
Midway Island, 153
Midway (Jordan, documentary), 153, 172n10
Mind-Gut Connection, The (Mayer), 70
Mirzoeff, Nicholas, 112, 124
Mitchell, Allan J., 58–59
Mitman, Gregg, 91
monochromatic, 135, 139, 141–42
Moomaw, William R., et al., 123
Moore, Jason W., 107, 119
Morrison, Susan Signe, 117
Morton, Timothy, 64, 65, 68, 115, 117, 153, 156, 157
mountain gazelles (*Gazella gazella*), 85–87
Mount Ida (Kaz Dağları), 119, 175–76n12
Mousse (Kleinman), 37
multispecies
 becoming(s), 131, 143
 coexistence, 71–72
 entanglements, 17, 92
 habitats, 8, 48
 life, 108, 110, 159, 162
 relations, relationalities, 9, 135, 159
 stories, storytelling, 49, 70–72
Mushroom at the End of the World, The (Tsing), 93

narrative agency, 7, 15, 23, 36, 38–43, 65–67, 71, 140–41, 149, 165, 169
NASA Earth Observatory, 174n3
naturalcultural, 17–18, 111, 115, 125,

naturalcultural (*continued*)
    136, 137, 150–51, 161
naturecultures, 17, 72, 83, 137, 139
    See also Haraway, Donna
Nealson, Kenneth H., Fumio Inagaki, and Ken Takai, 56
New Materialisms (Coole and Frost), 36
Newell, Mary, Bernard Quetchenbach, and Sarah Nolan, 107
New Shoots Poetry Anthology (Skilbeck-Porter), 95
Newsletter of the Anthropocene Working Group, 173n5
Nixon, Rob, 48, 97
Noll, Samantha, 88, 90
nonanthropocentric, 5, 11, 23, 44, 107, 124, 158–59
    See also disanthropocentric
nonhuman, 2, 5–6, 9–15, 17, 23–29, 35, 40–44, 49, 62, 66, 69–73, 79–80, 85–93, 96–99, 104, 107, 111, 113, 115–18, 120, 124, 128, 131, 133, 135, 138–39, 142, 146–48, 153–54, 156–60, 162–64, 171n1, 172–73n3, 176n3
    agencies, 19–20, 23, 37, 40, 52, 61, 64, 67, 141, 152
    immigrants, migrants, refugees, 79, 81, 88, 90–91

onto-epistemology. *See* Barad, Karen
ontology, 1, 19, 26, 43, 61, 145, 152, 157
    dark, 7, 10
    onto-tale, 88–89, 91
    relational, 15, 25–26, 104, 161–62, 172n7
    See also Bennett, Jane
Oppermann, Serpil, 2, 4, 5, 13, 17, 20, 38, 40, 53, 66, 67, 161, 162
Oppermann, Serpil, and Serenella Iovino, 127, 162, 164
Oppermann, Serpil, and Sinan Akilli, 175–76n12
organic realism, 26, 172n8
    See also Whitehead, Alfred North
Ozguc, Umut, 97, 109

Palmer, Clare, and Brendon H. M. Larson, 88

Pan, 108, 132
panarchy, 107, 108, 132–33
Parisi, Luciana, 20
Parsons, Allan, 14
Pell, Richard W., and Lauren P. Allen, 111
Perry, Leonard, 138
Pettis, Jeffery S., et al., 177n11
phenology, 106, 174n1
photoperception. *See* Demirsoy, Ali
Pickering, Andrew, 19, 37
Pinto, Carlos F., et al., 34
Piri Reis, 177n9
plastic(s), 18, 22, 41–42, 43, 61, 70, 72, 80, 108, 111, 115, 116, 119, 139, 151, 152–53, 155, 156, 171n6, 175n5, 177n10
polar bears, 80, 88–89, 90
Pollan, Michael, 6, 22
pollution, 18, 23, 44, 55, 58, 67, 80, 87, 100, 101, 108, 110, 112, 114, 116, 118–19, 131, 132, 152, 155, 156, 158, 175n10
polychromatic, 10, 137, 140–41, 146–48, 150, 156, 176n7
Porcar, Manuel, and Andres Moya, 21
postgreen, 154–57
Post, Eric, and Mads C. Forchhammer, 89
posthumanism, 14, 58
    See also feminist posthumanities
postnaturalization processes, 109, 125
postnatures, 10, 106, 120, 124–25, 131–32
Powell, Kristin, Jonathan M. Chase, and Tiffany M. Knight, 94
prehension, 33, 172n9
    See also Whitehead, Alfred North
Prigogine, Ilya, 41
prismatic, 135–36, 138–39, 141–43, 145–51, 155–56, 158–59
Prismatic Ecology (Cohen), 138
Process and Reality (A. N. Whitehead), 26, 172n8, 172n9
Processes of Life, The (Hunter), 3–4
Process-Relational Philosophy (Mesle), 32
Pruitt, Scott, 173n7
Pulido, Laura, 80
Purdy, Jedediah, 112
Pyne, Stephen J., 112

Quammen, David, 92
quantum physics, 6, 23, 32–33, 140, 161
　See also Bohm, David
Quick, Deren, 171n4
Quigley, Peter, 158
quorum sensing, 29
　See also bacteria

Raglon, Rebecca, 118
reenchantment, 156
Reid, Julian, 89
Reith, Frank, 56
relationality, 4, 11, 14, 25, 26, 42, 63, 81, 89, 91, 99, 119, 132, 135, 159, 161–62, 164
resilience, 107, 108, 121–25, 128, 132–34, 139
Revkin, Andrew, 51
Rigby, Kate, Rigby, 113
Ripple, William J., et al., 47, 110, 123, 172n2
Robinson, Kim Stanley, 11, 93, 106, 134
Rose, Deborah Bird, 135, 137, 138, 160
Rosler, Martha et al., 6
Ruiz, Nicholas, III, 8, 110

Sagan, Carl, 45
Samaddar, Ranabir, 82
Sample, Ian, 21
　See also iCHELLS
Satterfield, Terre, and Scott Slovic, 158
Schauder, Stephen, and Bonnie L. Bassler, 29
Scheffers, Brett R., et al., 105
Schmidt, Jeremy J., Peter G. Brown, and Christopher J. Orr, 72
Schwartz, Jill, 175n2
Science and the Modern World (A. N. Whitehead), 172n9
Serres, Michel, 2, 3, 162
Settele, Joseph, et al., 92
shale gas, 61, 64–65
　See also bioturbation
Sharrock, Robert A., 144
Sheldrake, Merlin, 91, 96
sites of narrativity, 71, 124, 130, 131, 138
　See also narrative agency
Skilbeck-Porter, Ella. See *New Shoots Poetry Anthology*

Slovic, Paul, and Scott Slovic, 49
Slovic, Scott, 104, 153, 158
Smith, David Thomas, 75, 173n13
Smith, Keith, and David N. Petley, 123, 125
Solnit, Rebecca, 46, 91
Sönmez, Yücel, 86
Staying with the Trouble (Haraway), 122
Steffen, Will, Paul Crutzen, and John R. McNeill, 50
Steffen, Will, Jacques Grinevald, Paul Crutzen, and John McNeill, 139
Steffen, Will, et al., 54, 56, 139, 165
Stengers, Isabelle, 106
Sterling, Colin, and Rodney Harrison, 125
Stirling, Ian, 89
Stirling, Ian, N. J. Lunn, and J. Iacozza, 89
Stoermer, Eugene, 49
　See also Crutzen, Paul J.
Stohlgren, Thomas J., and Marcel Rejmánek, 94
Stone (Cohen), 39
storylines, 40
storymap, 64
storyworld, 49, 172n3
Struzik, Edward, 113
Subramanian, Meera, 50
Sullivan, Heather I., 154
Sullivan, Robert, 23–24
Swanson, Heather, Anna Tsing, and Nils Bubandt, 14, 42, 142, 143, 163
Swimme, Brian, 40, 42
Swimme, Brian T., and Mary Evelyn Tucker, 24, 25, 165–66
Switzer, David, and Nicole Frances Angeli, 90
symbiogenesis, 5, 71, 143
symbiosis, 29, 40
　See also endosymbiosis
symbiotic, 28, 141, 142–43, 159
Symbiotic Planet (Margulis), 28
Syvitski, Jaia, et al., 175nn3–5
Szeman, Imre, 130

technofossils, 10, 115–16
　See also anthroturbation; bioturbation
terra ignota, 165
Thill, Brian, 116–17
Thomashow, Mitchell, 149

"Toughest Brief, The" (Fisher), 96
Toxic Bodies (Langston), 110–11
Tölgyessy, Juraj, 119, 171n3
transcorporeality, 18–19
    See also Alaimo, Stacy
Tsing, Anna (Lowenhaupt), 64
    See also *Mushroom at the End of the World, The*
Tsing, Anna, et al., 69, 73, 93–94, 112–13, 121, 163
Tsuchida, Tsutomu, 142
Tuana, Nancy, 62
Turpin, Tom, 144–45

Underland (Macfarlane), 27, 42
Ussery, David W., 21
    See also iCHELLS
Uzuner, Buket, 101, 151

van der Tuin, Iris, 22
van Dooren, Thom, 87, 89, 96, 164
van Dooren, Thom, and Deborah Bird Rose, 14, 130, 164
Venter, Craig, 21
    See also iCHELLS
Vermeulen, Pieter, 125, 129
Vibrant Matter (Bennett), 18
Vidal, John, 45
Vigil, Sarah, 81
Vogel, Steven, 114

Walia, Arjun, 177n11
WALL-E (Stanton, film), 117–18
Wapner, Paul, 114
Wassen, Trudy M., 28
Waste (Thill), 116–17
wasteocene, 10, 115, 116–17, 120, 127
Wasteocene (Armiero), 117
Waters, Colin N., et al., 9, 111
Weber, Max, 156
"We Declare Our Support for Extinction Rebellion," 47
We Have Never Been Modern (Latour), 171n2
Wheeler, John Archibald, 32
Wheeler, Wendy, 40, 66
White, Hayden, 124
Whitehead, Alfred North, 26, 31–32, 172n8, 172n9

prehension, 172n9
Whitehead, Mark, 58–59, 62, 87, 119
Weir, Jessica, 126, 164
Wendle, John, 81
"What is commonly called a weed" (Gadd, poem), 95
wildfires, 45, 82, 109, 112, 114
wildlife, 79, 86, 109
Williams, Roger, 148–49, 176n3
    See also Fisherman of Halicarnassus
Willmer, Pat, et al., 143, 145
Wilson, Edward O., 45, 136
Wince, Gaia, 50
Winterson, Jeanette, 12
Wisner, et al., 121
Wolfe, Cary, 4
Wood, David, 119, 121
Woods, Derek, 52, 57, 58
worlding(s), 4, 7, 16, 57, 154, 163, 173n9
world-making, 17, 27, 122
World on the Edge (Brown), 103
"World Scientists' Warning to Humanity," 47, 110, 172n2
"World Scientists' Warning of a Climate Emergency," 47, 172n2
"World Wildlife Fund," 175n2
Wright, Angus, 83

xenobiotic
    chemicals, 111
    substances, 67, 110
Xu, Chi, et al., 85

Yaeger, Patricia, 117, 154
Yazgünoğlu, Kerim Can, 125
Yong, Ed, 177n2
Yusoff, Kathryn, 60

Zalasiewicz, Jan, 51, 177n3
    See also "Anthropocene Working Group"
Zalasiewicz, Jan, Colin N. Waters, and Mark Williams, 54–55
Zalasiewicz, Jan, Colin N. Waters, Mark Williams, and Anthony D. Barnosky, 115–16
Zalasiewicz, Jan, et al., 8, 10, 50
Zalasiewicz, Jan, Mark Williams, Will Steffen, and Paul Crutzen, 56, 131

Zalasiewicz, Jan, Mark Williams, Colin N. Waters, Anthony D. Barnosky, and Peter Haff, 115–16

Zapf, Hubert, 136
Zhou, Xiaojing, 82
Zylinska, Joanna, 57